Efficient Logistics

DIRECTIONS IN DEVELOPMENT
Countries and Regions

Efficient Logistics

A Key to Vietnam's Competitiveness

Luis C. Blancas, John Isbell, Monica Isbell, Hua Joo Tan, Wendy Tao

THE WORLD BANK
Washington, D.C.

Library of Congress Cataloging-in-Publication Data

Blancas, Luis C. Efficient logistics : a key to Vietnam's competitiveness / Luis C. Blancas, John Isbell, Monica Isbell, Hua Joo Tan, Wendy Ta.
   1 online resource. — (Directions in development)
   Includes bibliographical references. Description based on print version record and CIP data provided by publisher; resource not viewed.
ISBN 978-1-4648-0104-4 (epub) — ISBN 978-1-4648-0103-7 (alk. paper)
   1. Freight and freightage—Vietnam. 2. Business logistics—Vietnam. 3. Industrial policy—Vietnam. 4. Economic development—Vietnam. 5. Vietnam—Economic policy. I. World Bank. II. Title.
   HE199.V5
   388'.04409597—dc23   2013041631

Contents

Boxes

Figures

Maps

Tables

Foreword

The old economic structure is no longer relevant: Vietnam needs to improve its competitiveness, facilitate stronger levels of creativity in economic production, and recognize that in a Vietnamese economy that is increasingly open and integrated to the global economy the low-hanging fruits have nearly been harvested.
—H.E. Bùi Quang Vinh, Minister of Planning and Investment, Socialist Republic of Vietnam, July 15, 2013

Over the past 20 years Vietnam has achieved sustained economic growth primarily driven by a rapidly expanding labor force and a shift in economic activity away from low-productivity subsistence agriculture toward the higher-productivity manufacturing and services sectors. Crucially, supported by pro-poor social policies, strong growth was accompanied by remarkable poverty reduction outcomes. Vietnam's continued macroeconomic stability, increasing economic liberalization, and young, vast labor pool have increased the country's attractiveness as a destination for foreign direct investment—particularly as labor costs have increased in key competing markets, most notably China.

Vietnam's socioeconomic success story, however, now faces both short- and long-term challenges. Since the onset of the global economic crisis of 2008–2009, the Vietnamese economy has undergone a particularly challenging period of declining foreign capital inflows and subdued, as well as more contested, export markets. Recent reductions in economic growth, seen for the first time since the Asian economic crisis of 1999, highlight the importance of strengthening economic resiliency.

Over the longer term, Vietnam is faced with the challenge that both its main drivers of past growth—labor force growth and intersectoral shifts in economic activity—are being depleted and need to be replaced by intrasectoral productivity improvements.

More efficient transport and logistics can play a significant role in increasing productivity going forward. By making supply chains more predictable, better transport and logistics allow manufacturers, transportation carriers, logistics service providers, and trade regulators to minimize avoidable delays, thereby increasing output per unit of time while reducing the cost of doing business. Such competitiveness enhancements can better position Vietnam to benefit from global demand, to better serve domestic markets, to attract investment, and to generate quality jobs.

This report makes the case that improvements in export, import, and domestic logistics operations as a driver of future growth for Vietnam are fully within grasp. The report highlights opportunities to make freight itineraries more reliable, to make roads safer and more conducive to high-volume commercial use, to increase port sector efficiencies, and to better integrate barges, trucks, warehouses, and gateways. It also proposes interventions and policies that can address these challenges over the short term and following years.

I hope this report will contribute to a dialogue that can bring together public and private sector stakeholders, including the World Bank, as we continue to explore and support ways to make Vietnam's economy more competitive and dynamic going forward.

John A. Roome
Director
Sustainable Development
East Asia and the Pacific
World Bank

Acknowledgements

This diagnostic report was prepared by the East Asia and Pacific Region of the World Bank. The work was led by Luis C. Blancas (Transport Specialist, EASIN), under the overall guidance of John Roome (Sector Director, EASSD), Victoria Kwakwa (Country Director, EACVF), Jennifer Sara (Sector Manager, EASVS), Abhas Jha (Sector Manager, EASIN), and Paul Vallely (Senior Transport Specialist and Transport Cluster Leader, EASVS). The report's co-authors are Luis C. Blancas of the World Bank; John Isbell, Monica Isbell, and Wendy Tao of Cambridge Systematics, Inc.; and Hua Joo Tan, Consultant.

The team is grateful for detailed comments provided by World Bank peer reviewers Arturo Ardila Gomez (Senior Urban Transport Specialist, LCSTR), James Anderson (Senior Governance Specialist, EASPV), Monica Alina Mustra (Trade Specialist, PRMTR), Jordan Schwartz (Manager, TWISI), Deepak Mishra (Lead Economist, EASPR), and Myla Taylor Williams (Country Program Coordinator, EACVQ). Comments on earlier drafts were received from M. Baher El-Hifnawi (Lead Transport Economist, ECSTR), Simon David Ellis (Senior Transport Economist, SASDT), Duc Minh Pham (Senior Economist, EASPV), Reynaldo Bench (Senior Port Specialist, TWITR), Dung Anh Hoang (Senior Transport Specialist, EASVS), and Christopher De Serio (Operations Analyst, EASIN). Thao Phuong Tuong (Team Assistant, EACVF), Carla Teresa Sarmiento (Resource Management Assistant, EAPCA), Iris David (Program Assistant, EASIN), Teresita Ortega (Program Assistant, EASWE), and Cristina Hernandez (Program Assistant, EASWE) provided excellent production support throughout.

The information and insight obtained from numerous private companies, transport carriers, logistics service providers, trade groups, and government officials in Vietnam and elsewhere are gratefully recognized.

Finally, the team acknowledges the generous support from the Australian Agency for International Development (AusAID) provided through the World Bank East Asia and Pacific Infrastructure for Growth Trust Fund (EAAIG).

About the Authors

Luis C. Blancas is a Transport Specialist with the Sustainable Development Department in the East Asia and the Pacific region of the World Bank. Since 2010 he has led and participated in the preparation and supervision of several World Bank-financed transport infrastructure projects in Vietnam, including interventions to expand capacity and increase efficiency in the country's Red River Delta and Mekong River Delta inland waterway networks and projects to develop Vietnam's expressway sector. He has also conducted public sector technical assistance and analytical work in transport and logistics in China, Malaysia, and Vietnam. Prior to joining the World Bank he was an Associate with MergeGlobal, a financial and strategic advisor to firms in the global transport and logistics industry; a Research Analyst at the Fiscal Affairs Department of the International Monetary Fund; and a management consultant with Deloitte Consulting's Mexico and Central America practice. Mr. Blancas holds a Master's degree in Management Science and Engineering from Stanford University and a B.A. in Economics from Mexico's Monterrey Institute of Technology.

John Isbell is a Freight and Logistics Specialist with Cambridge Systematics, Inc. He has more than 34 years of experience in the areas of global supply chain management, performance-based contracts, and value creation in transportation service provision and management. Prior to becoming a consultant to public and private sector entities in the broad areas of transport and logistics he was Director of Corporate Delivery Logistics for Nike, Inc. During the last 10 of his 31 years with Nike, he directed the activities of the Corporate Delivery Logistics group, which was responsible for the strategic direction and global management of Nike's logistics service providers delivering origin consolidation, ocean freight, and air freight of both in-line and product samples, supply chain security, and claims management. Mr. Isbell holds an M.B.A. from Portland State University.

Monica Isbell is Practice Leader for Supply Chain and Logistics at Cambridge Systematics, Inc. She has more than 32 years of experience as an international logistician, focused on helping private sector companies streamline their supply chains and optimize their processes. She also has helped ports, departments of transportation, metropolitan planning organizations, and others to develop strategies to better meet the needs of shippers and logistics service providers. Prior to joining Cambridge Systematics, she was founder and President of Starboard Alliance Company LLC, an international trade, transportation, and supply chain consulting practice. Ms. Isbell also has held executive positions with Columbia Sportswear Company, Asics Tiger Corp, Direct Line Cargo Management Services/DHL Global Forwarding, and Sea-Land Service. Ms. Isbell holds a B.A. from Princeton University.

Hua Joo Tan is an Independent Maritime Consultant with more than 15 years of experience. As a Managing Director of American President Lines (APL) Vietnam, he managed the ocean shipping and supply chain management services of APL and APL Logistics with more than 150 staff in four locations across Vietnam. He also served as member of the Board of Directors of the second largest container port in Vietnam and as chairman of a container shipping company operating in the Vietnam-Singapore feeder trade. He led the Ports Subgroup of the Infrastructure Working Group of the Vietnam Business Forum. As leader of the ports group, Mr. Tan led the efforts to spearhead the industry's concerns on ports and related infrastructure issues in Vietnam, including the preparation of position papers and conduction of discussions with government ministries, including the biannual Forum discussions and the introduction of Terminal Handling Charges at Vietnamese ports. Mr. Tan holds an M.B.A. from Stanford University and a B.A. in Economics from the University of Oxford.

Wendy Tao is an Associate Consultant with Cambridge Systematics, Inc. She has eight years of experience in transport economics and has assisted the Southern California Association of Governments (SCAG) in assessing the supply adequacy of industrial/warehouse and intermodal facilities relative to future growth. Prior to joining Cambridge Systematics, Ms. Tao was the Hanoi coordinator of the Partnership for Sustainable Urban Transport in Asia, for which she collected and evaluated greenhouse gas data along with information to evaluate air quality, traffic, and safety for the Hanoi government. As part of a U.S. Strategic Highway Research Program project focused on the interactions between transportation capacity, economic systems, and land use, Ms. Tao conducted a targeted case study on Global III Intermodal Terminal in Rochelle, Illinois, as well as highway facilities in California, including the Sonora bypasses, SR 99, and Hollister SR 156. Ms. Tao holds an M.S. in Transportation Engineering and City Planning from the University of California, Berkeley, and a B.S. in Economics and Environmental Policy from the University of Pennsylvania Wharton School.

Abbreviations

AEC	ASEAN Economic Community
AMS	Automated Manifest Service
ASEAN	Association of Southeast Asian Nations
BCO	beneficial cargo owner
BOT	Build-Operate-Transfer
CFS	Container Freight Station
CIC	Container Imbalance Charge
CICT	Cai Lan International Container Terminal
CMICT	Cai Mep–Thi Vai International Terminal
CMIT	Cai Mep International Terminal
CM-TV	Cai Mep–Thi Vai
C-TPAT	Customs-Trade Partnership Against Terrorism
CY	container yard
DWT	deadweight tons
EDI	electronic data interchange
EU	European Union
FDI	foreign direct investment
FEU	40-foot equivalent unit container
FTP	File Transfer Protocol
GoV	Government of Vietnam
GPS	Global Positioning System
GDP	gross domestic product
HCMC	Ho Chi Minh City
ICD	inland container depot
ISF	International Security Filing
IT	information technology
IWT	Inland Waterway Transport
JETRO	Japan External Trade Organization
JIT	just-in-time

LNG	liquid natural gas
LO/LO	lift on/lift off
LPI	Logistics Performance Index
LPR	License Plate Reader
LSP	logistics service provider
MCIP	Multimodal Corridor Investment Plan
MoT	Ministry of Transport of Vietnam
MTO	marine terminal operator
NBA	Noi Bai Airport
NH	National Highway
OECD	Organization for Economic Co-operation and Development
PPP	public-private partnership
SAR	special administrative region
SCSC	Saigon Cargo Service Corporation
SITC	Standard International Trade Classification
SITV	Saigon International Terminals Vietnam
SOE	state-owned enterprise
SNP	Saigon New Port
SP	Saigon Port
SPCT	Saigon Premier Container Terminal
SP-PSA	Saigon Port–Port of Singapore Authority International Port
SSIT	SP–SSA International Terminal
STS	ship-to-shore
TCCT	Tan Cang–Cai Mep Container Terminal
TCIT	Tan Cang–Cai Mep International Terminal
TCS	Tan Son Nhat Cargo Services
TEU	20-foot equivalent unit container
THC	terminal handling charge
TPP	Trans-Pacific Partnership
TSNA	Tan Son Nhat Airport
VCIS	Vietnam Customs Information System
VICT	Vietnam International Container Terminals
VNACCS	Vietnam Automated Cargo and Port Consolidated System
VND	Vietnamese dong
VOC	vehicle operating costs
VPA	Vietnam Port Association
WTO	World Trade Organization

Overview

The Government of Vietnam (GoV) has articulated the goal for Vietnam to become an industrialized country by 2020. Vietnam has attained sustained economic growth and widespread poverty reduction over the past 20 years. This impressive growth performance—largely based on the promotion of exports and investment—placed Vietnam among the world's five fastest-growing economies of the 1990–2010 period and has benefited, particularly over the past 10 years, from attractive labor cost rates relative to key Asian peers, like China. Yet as labor supply growth decelerates over the next couple of decades, achieving the country's vision to 2020 and beyond will require a much greater focus on productivity improvements as a source of growth. In this respect, competitiveness, and in particular higher transport and logistics efficiency, is increasingly becoming a critical growth sustainability driver for Vietnam.

The performance of Vietnam's trade logistics *system* (defined as infrastructure provision, facilities and equipment, service delivery, and the institutional and regulatory environment supporting logistics operations), while stronger than that of some regional peers, trails some of the more globally integrated developing Asian nations. As a rapidly growing economy in transition (e.g., it has recently joined the ranks of middle income countries), Vietnam has provided basic infrastructure access to an industrial and manufacturing base that is increasingly interconnected with the rest of the world. This, coupled with a history of social and political stability following the economic reforms of the late 1980s and a favorable geographic position relative to the world's busiest maritime trade lanes and container hubs, has facilitated a strong trade sector performance over the past 20 years. Yet improving logistics efficiency remains a development challenge. While no single, definitive measure of logistics performance exists, several indicators suggest that Vietnam's logistics (along such dimensions as inventory carrying costs in supply chains, the incidence of transport and handling delays, the availability of talent in logistics management, and the processing of permits and clearances in international trade) underperforms that of China, Malaysia, and Thailand among developing countries in Asia. Because Vietnam's logistics costs are perceived to be high relative to these key peers, reducing logistics costs can be a major component of the broader GoV agenda towards solidifying the country's long-term economic development trajectory.

The purpose of this report is to identify the most pressing challenges driving transportation and logistics costs in Vietnam and to recommend policies and interventions that could strengthen competitiveness. The methodology used in the report was multifaceted. Numerous freight stakeholders, trade associations, and government ministries were interviewed face to face in August 2012 through tailored questionnaires. The study assessed the existing conditions of key ports, highways, and airports with site visits and first-hand observations. The analysis also benefited from a thorough review of the literature, including past World Bank studies, to better integrate this available body of knowledge into a cohesive analytical framework.

The report finds that, to the extent that logistics operations in Vietnam are costlier than similar operations in other countries in the region, this is due to a persistent lack of reliability throughout the supply chain. When logistics costs are broken down by their component parts, it is apparent that Vietnam's relative logistics underperformance does not originate from the transport costs side of the equation—particularly given the present overcapacity in many transport sectors, which tends to drive down transportation rates—but primarily from the warehousing and inventory carrying costs side of the equation. The latter are directly dependent on supply chain reliability and predictability. As Vietnam seeks to compete in the world economy and trade in higher-value added goods under just-in-time production and time-definite local, regional, and intercontinental itineraries, improving reliability will become critical. This challenge can and should be seen as a key catalyst for reform.

The primary sources of unreliability in supply chains linking Vietnam with the rest of the world are the following:

1. Government regulations are cumbersome and not easily understood. As a result, there is inconsistent interpretation, implementation, and enforcement of government regulations across provinces and among government officials. This leads to import and export clearance processing that takes longer and is less predictable than in peer countries, redundant inventory in beneficial cargo owner (BCO) supply chains, and higher administrative costs for BCOs and logistics service providers (LSPs).

2. There is a widespread belief among the BCO and LSP community that facilitation payments ("tea money") to officials from the General Department of Vietnam Customs (Vietnam Customs, for short) and the highway police are needed to keep imported and exported components, raw materials, and finished goods moving through supply chains with minimal delays. This belief leads to a high incidence of such payments in practice, artificially inflating logistics costs for customs clearance, customs brokerage, cargo inspections, and trucking. Moreover, this adds a nontransparent, uneven layer to international (and to a lesser extent domestic) trade activity.

Efficient Logistics • http://dx.doi.org/10.1596/978-1-4648-0103-7

3. Transportation infrastructure projects are planned and executed largely in isolation, without employing a strategic, multimodal corridor approach and with little regard to supply-demand considerations. This has created, or contributed to, among other issues, the following reliability bottlenecks:
   a. The port and marine terminal system is highly fragmented, as planners have emphasized quantity over quality, leading to overcapacity (most notably in the southern port range);
   b. Highway projects to enable adequate access to inland container depots, marine ports, and airports are seldom planned and implemented as integrated facilities (and often plagued by delays), contributing to highway congestion and undermining the port system's cargo catchment potential;
   c. The financing of many port and road infrastructure projects has weak foundations due to (a) faulty assessments of future demand, which undermines private sector interest, (b) the prevalence of high construction costs relative to peer countries, and (c) the persistent participation of state-owned enterprises, many of which are highly indebted and often venture well outside their core business (Vinalines is a case in point);
   d. Logistics parks—the clustering of handling, light manufacturing, transportation, and logistics activities in proximity to gateways, major arteries, and demand centers—remain a nascent sector with little in the way of strategic plans for development over the medium term; and
   e. Rail is not a meaningful mode of transport for freight.
4. A fragmented trucking industry delivers substandard service to BCOs relative to peer countries.
5. The new deep-water marine terminals at Cai Mep-Thi Vai are severely underutilized and lack critical mass to serve as transshipment centers, and the container shipping carriers serving them are finding it increasingly less attractive to call at these locations with the very large vessels that are now the backbone of their intercontinental operations.

Five initiatives, able of being implemented within the next 5–10 years, are recommended to improve predictability in supply chains and boost competitiveness:

1. *Modernize the customs clearance system.* The current customs clearance process is a hybrid of two methods: electronic (completing documentation and applying for a Vietnam Customs entry number via the Vietnam Customs portal) and manual (physical documents hand-delivered to Vietnam Customs officials for signature). It is subject to unpredictable interpretation of regulations by Vietnam Customs officials, resulting in (1) extended delays in clearing customs, especially for imports and (2) the incidence of facilitation payments to prevent more lengthy delays. Currently, only one multinational BCO in Vietnam enjoys the "gold standard" of having a completely paperless operation with Vietnam Customs, granted to it as a means to attract significant foreign direct investment to Southern Vietnam.

Vietnam Customs should redouble its efforts to fully automate the clearance process by 2014 as planned. This will significantly reduce human intervention and paper work and provide a consistent, predictable, and transparent clearance process. This system will enable products to be cleared in a timely manner since all interactions with Vietnam Customs officials regarding establishing tariff classifications, product valuation, proper licenses, and other customs formalities will be settled in advance of the actual importation and exportation of cargo.

Vietnam Customs should also adopt the World Customs Organization standards for product classification and other customs clearance filing practices. This would relieve customs brokers and BCOs from having to customize their internal systems to exchange information with Vietnam Customs.

2. *Ensure transparent and consistently interpreted, applied, and enforced government regulations and operations related to international trade.* Beyond customs, freight stakeholders encounter unnecessary operating costs due to the inconsistent implementation and interpretation of nonintegrated government regulations. For example, securing import and export clearance when not only customs but other technical requirements are taken into account takes longer in Vietnam than in Malaysia, a key regional benchmark. This report projects that the extra time involved in clearing international shipments in Vietnam will cost BCOs an estimated $96 million in 2012 and $182 million in 2020 in avoidable logistics costs.

Similar to the case of Vietnam Customs, facilitation payments to the police greatly reduce transparency in the importation and exportation of products. In all, this study estimates that facilitation payments add approximately 15 percent to the cost of an imported 40-foot container and about 13 percent to the cost of an exported container of general merchandise cargo.

To facilitate international trade while reducing costs to freight stakeholders, the GoV should (1) establish more readily applicable circulars and decrees to promote consistent interpretation, application and enforcement of regulations; (2) audit the performance of individual Vietnam Customs and other officials across provinces; (3) review the regulations governing international trade in effect in Vietnam to determine room for simplification, ideally in consultation with the freight stakeholder community; (4) reduce the number of documents and certificates required to import and export; and (5) embark on a communications campaign that promotes transparency in supply chain transactions and engages the BCO and LSP community, whose members in many instances assume that facilitation payments are necessary as a matter of course.

3. *Plan multimodal transportation infrastructure projects using an integrated corridor approach.* The execution of transportation infrastructure planning in Vietnam reflects a monomodal approach in which the various departments (ports, inland waterways, highways, rail, and air) within the Ministry of Transport (MoT) appear to function as distinct entities. Limited interaction between departments and with provincial governments has resulted in inconsistent or disjointed planning and mismatched timing in the implementation of transportation

projects, as well as minimal involvement of key freight stakeholders. This environment results in infrastructure projects being executed in a piecemeal manner rather than on the basis of multimodal coordination. The MoT should move toward adopting a holistic, multimodal, multisectoral approach to planning and executing freight infrastructure projects.

Of particular priority is the Lach Huyen deep-water port facility planned for the Haiphong area. The GoV should strengthen the planning and executing oversight of this project to ensure that (1) implementation slippages (e.g., funding bottlenecks and technical delays) are avoided, (2) land-side and inland waterway connectivity improvements are aligned with port construction schedules, and (3) local congestion impacts within Haiphong city are mitigated.

Highway congestion has a cost to both freight and nonfreight system users. It is estimated that congestion will cost BCOs $152 million in 2012 and $274 million in 2020. The economic impact of congestion to all system users is estimated to be $1.7 billion annually.

4. *Promote a more professional trucking industry.* Vietnam's trucking industry is fragmented, with less than 10 large trucking companies and about 100 small to midsized firms; the majority of the remaining carriers are single-truck operations with limited barriers to entry. The market is still splintered with many trucking companies competing on low rates rather than quality service. Noncompensatory rates contribute to Vietnam's high incidence of traffic fatalities, highway congestion, damage to roadbeds, and air pollution. Root causes of this include the fact that (1) not all truck drivers are properly licensed, (2) the national fleet is old and many operators cannot afford to properly maintain their equipment, (3) trucks and containers are often overloaded, and (4) truck breakdowns on highways are frequent.

   Trucking regulations overseeing the above issues should be overhauled and their enforcement strengthened. In particular, safeguards should be in place such that regulations cannot easily be circumvented by facilitation payments to government officials and the police. Revised regulations should focus on rigorous truck driver license testing and semiannual vehicle and chassis roadability inspections. Axle loads can be better enforced through more extensive use of modern (e.g., weigh-in-motion- and systems-enabled, adequately staffed) permanent weigh stations and the automated monitoring of marine terminal scales, complemented by regular unscheduled inspections through mobile scales. Consolidation of the trucking industry can be further encouraged by promoting access to more affordable credit for truck carriers. Options can be explored to reduce the incidence of empty backhauls, promote joint-venture investments by foreign trucking companies, and develop stronger emissions control standards.

5. *Foster expanded business opportunities at Cai Mep-Thi Vai.* The seaport master plan has not fostered a balance between supply and demand in container handling at marine terminals. The problem is more serious in the South than in the North as a result of a proliferation of new terminal construction that

started after 2006 on the basis of haphazard granting of new port operating licenses. As of September 2012, utilization was 18 percent at Cai Mep-Thi Vai, and it is expected to barely reach 40 percent by 2020. This suggests the GoV should take what action it can to minimize further capacity additions unless demand prospects were to significantly improve.

In the short run, to encourage more linehaul services to call Cai Mep-Thi Vai, the GoV could (1) further reduce tonnage dues on a temporary basis and (2) promote the role of Cai Mep-Thi Vai as a transshipment hub for other Vietnamese and international (e.g., Cambodian) ports. Over the medium term, the provision of integrated multimodal access to this critical port range will be needed.

While the above priority recommendations (and those of the report at large) accurately reflect the sentiment of major freight stakeholders, key further avenues for research and engagement are suggested. These include (1) a better understanding of Vietnam's opaque trucking industry (asset and nonasset based) and the root causes that impede its modernization at a faster pace; (2) detailed return-on-investment analyses for on-dock rail and similar investments that may contribute to a larger role of rail intermodal in the country's freight mix; (3) an analysis of the nature of the ideal role the GoV should play, if any, in elevating the logistics management capacity of small and medium-sized shippers (particularly domestic); and (4) the drivers, market sizing, bottlenecks, and policies for development of the warehousing/integrated logistics (e.g., logistics parks) sector. Although this list is far from exhaustive, its components reflect another logistics bottleneck in Vietnam: the lack of detailed data gathering and research that can shed light on key issues and submarkets in logistics, and the lack of formal avenues of engagement between public and private sector actors. Improvements on this front, through, for example, the introduction of a National Logistics Committee (which can be modeled in those established by regional peers Malaysia and Thailand) and/or a National Logistics Observatory (particularly for data gathering at the corridor level) can contribute to competitiveness by facilitating public and public-private decision making.

CHAPTER 1

Introduction

The Government of Vietnam (GoV) seeks to promote economic growth, attract foreign direct investment (FDI), increase employment opportunities, and raise prosperity. It has increasingly embarked on efforts to attract multinational companies and enable domestic companies to achieve international standards, and it has set an ambitious goal for Vietnam to become an industrialized country by 2020. It is believed that trade competitiveness, primarily driven by productivity-enhancing freight logistics, can play a major role in this multi-pronged effort. This is the context that motivated this report.

Objective and Scope

The report has three objectives: (1) to define and describe the drivers shaping logistics costs in Vietnam, (2) to select the challenges and opportunities for reducing logistics costs and increasing competitiveness that the GoV should tackle with the highest level of priority within the next 5–10 years, and (3) to propose infrastructure and policy-based interventions to address the selected priority bottlenecks.

To achieve the above goals, this report set out to

- Characterize and identify key performance gaps in *infrastructure provision*, particularly with regard to Vietnam's main freight corridors for domestic and international freight flows.
- Assess *institutional, regulatory, and procedural bottlenecks* that may create supply chain unpredictability and increase logistics costs.
- Review access to quality *for-hire transportation and third-party logistics services*, including the status of facilities and equipment.
- Highlight areas where *information technology (IT) and automation* can stream-line processes in international trade and reduce costs.
- Analyze the main challenges facing the *deep-water port sector*.

Although domestic logistics issues are addressed by the report to some extent and the views of domestic beneficial cargo owners (BCOs) were taken into consideration through face-to-face interviews, the main focus of the report regards improving competitiveness in international supply chains.[1] This is consistent with Vietnam's model of economic growth, which is highly reliant on not only exports but also imports of raw materials, machinery, and components necessary to produce export commodities. Further, emphasis is largely placed on containerized trade—the portion of freight flows moving in domestic trailers and containers, international (i.e., maritime) containers, and air cargo unit load devices. This type of freight (mostly comprising manufactured goods and nonbulk primary products, including food) accounts for the majority of trade by value and therefore (a) represents the most time- and disruption-sensitive portion of international supply chains and (b) captures a disproportionate share of logistics costs.

Approach and Methodology

The report was conducted between August and December 2012. The analytical approach to the report, based on three main pillars representing the three objectives outlined above, is depicted in figure 1.1.

The following activities were implemented as part of the report's methodology:

1. A literature review was undertaken using a variety of sources. A key aim of this exercise was to integrate into a cohesive narrative insights from previous studies on topics relevant to Vietnam's transportation and logistics—many of which had remained largely disconnected to date. A list of sources is reflected in the references.
2. Market research was conducted to describe, quantitatively when possible, the current state of Vietnam's economy and the transport and logistics sector. Details on the calculations underlying most of the report's quantitative estimates are presented in appendix A.
3. Direct feedback was obtained from a variety of freight stakeholders. Detailed questionnaires were prepared by stakeholder sector—international and domestic BCOs, ocean carriers, logistics service providers (LSPs), marine terminal operators (MTOs), and trucking companies—to yield information about stakeholder-specific operational requirements, challenges, and major issues. The team compiled and vetted a list of potential companies to interview. Based on this list, the team scheduled and conducted in-person interviews with 73 entities in August 2012, most of them in Vietnam.
4. Concurrently, a separate list of BCOs, generally small to midsize enterprises, was prepared. These stakeholders were requested to complete an exporter-importer questionnaire using an online survey tool. Four companies completed this online questionnaire, the results of which were merged into the exporter-importer master file.
5. Interviews were also conducted with four GoV ministries and four industry and trade associations of Vietnam. A full list of the firms and entities interviewed and surveyed is provided in appendix C.

Figure 1.1 Analytical Approach

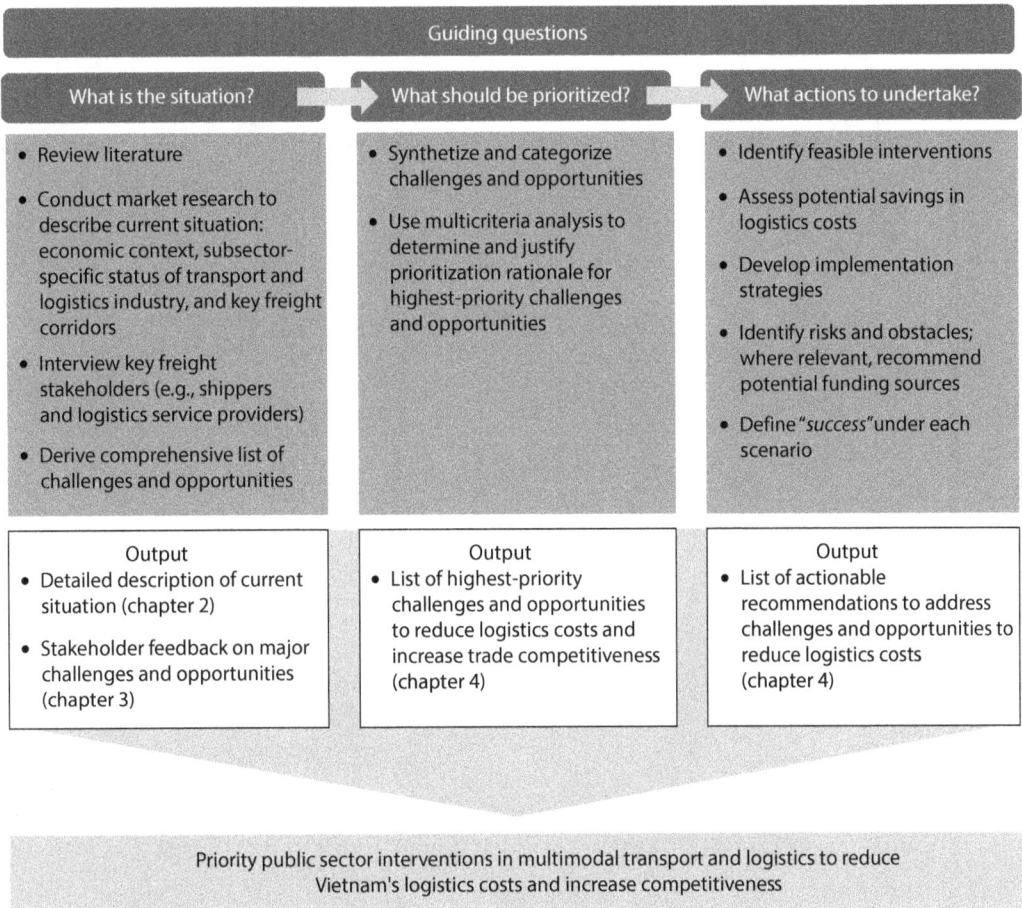

Guiding questions		
What is the situation?	What should be prioritized?	What actions to undertake?
• Review literature • Conduct market research to describe current situation: economic context, subsector-specific status of transport and logistics industry, and key freight corridors • Interview key freight stakeholders (e.g., shippers and logistics service providers) • Derive comprehensive list of challenges and opportunities	• Synthetize and categorize challenges and opportunities • Use multicriteria analysis to determine and justify prioritization rationale for highest-priority challenges and opportunities	• Identify feasible interventions • Assess potential savings in logistics costs • Develop implementation strategies • Identify risks and obstacles; where relevant, recommend potential funding sources • Define "*success*" under each scenario
Output • Detailed description of current situation (chapter 2) • Stakeholder feedback on major challenges and opportunities (chapter 3)	Output • List of highest-priority challenges and opportunities to reduce logistics costs and increase trade competitiveness (chapter 4)	Output • List of actionable recommendations to address challenges and opportunities to reduce logistics costs (chapter 4)

Priority public sector interventions in multimodal transport and logistics to reduce Vietnam's logistics costs and increase competitiveness

6. A list of key challenges was compiled based on (a) analysis of interview testimonies, (b) findings from market research and the literature review, and (c) the study team's own logistics-related professional experience in Vietnam as industry practitioners (e.g., in container shipping and manufacturing). These challenges were then ranked using multicriteria analysis, from which a list of the five highest-priority challenges in transportation and logistics facing Vietnam was obtained.

7. Last, recommendations were developed on potential public and public-private initiatives to address the chosen highest-priority challenges. Recommendations were further contextualized and fleshed out by (a) defining feasible implementation strategies, (b) highlighting implementation risks, (c) identifying roles, responsibilities, and potential funding mechanisms where relevant, and (d) defining feasible outputs and outcomes from the recommended measures as a suggested definition of implementation success.

Note

1. For the purposes of this report, a country's international competitiveness is the extent to which foreign entities (e.g., multinational firms) can source or manufacture products in the country in question and bring them to consumption markets (typically their home markets) at a lower level of total logistics costs per cubic meter (including transport, trade, and inventory carrying costs) compared to sourcing or manufacturing in other foreign countries.

CHAPTER 2

Vietnam's Current Situation

Economic Overview

Gross Domestic Product and Reliance on Export-Driven Growth

Over the past two decades,[1] Vietnam has achieved sustained, rapid economic growth, moving from a primarily agriculture-based economy to one emphasizing industry and export-oriented activity (see figure 2.1).

Vietnam's annual rate of gross domestic product (GDP) growth has been steady at 6–8 percent over the past 20 years (see table 2.1). By economic sector, some of the highest rates of growth have been registered for the industry and construction sector, particularly during the periods 1990–95 and 2001–05. Growth in primary natural resources (agriculture, forestry, and fisheries) has slowed in the period 2006–11, while growth in services has increased.

Vietnam's 2007 inclusion as a member of the World Trade Organization (WTO) has led to further changes in the country's economic position, attracting increased FDI and germinating more home-grown, privately owned enterprises. This has combined with a history of rapid growth in international trade to heighten then need for a robust transportation and logistics sector.

Despite two decades of sustained growth, solid poverty reduction and largely positive economic trends, in the last few years key macroeconomic indicators in Vietnam have foreshadowed a more tempered outlook. Real GDP growth has decelerated, going from 6.8 percent in 2010 to 5.9 percent in 2011, and further to 5.0 percent in 2012—the lowest annual expansion for Vietnam since 1999 and only the second time the country has grown at 5.0 percent or less since 1990 (Vietnam General Statistics Office 2011). Having reached double-digit rates (of near or above 20 percent) in recent years, inflation has become an everyday concern for Vietnamese citizens and investors alike. This tenuous balance between growth, inflation, and the sustenance of FDI will continue to be a challenge and only highlights the need to increase trade competitiveness, including transportation and logistics, as a means to continue to attract international businesses.

Transportation and logistics are critical to the everyday functioning of investment- and export-led economic models like Vietnam's. Main exported commodities include primary products such as agribusiness commodities

Figure 2.1 Vietnam GDP by Industry Sector, 1990–2011
Trillion Vietnamese dong

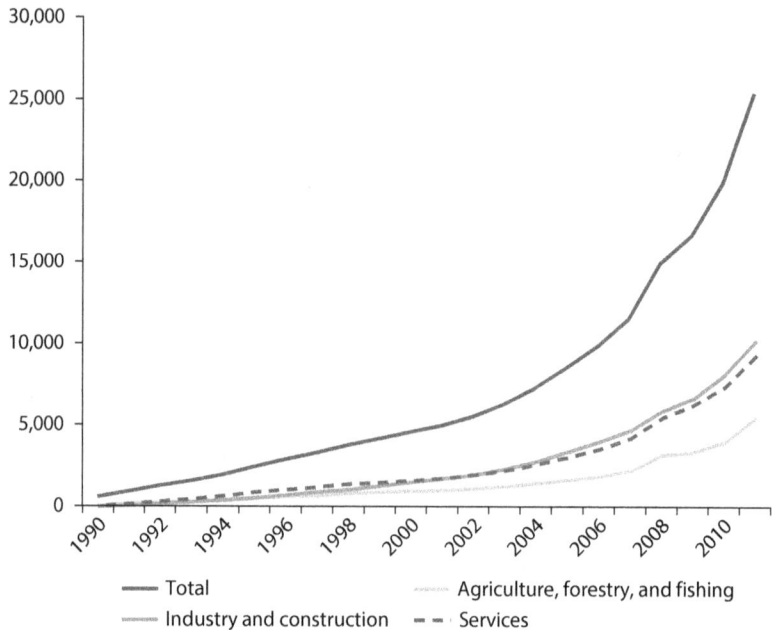

Total — Agriculture, forestry, and fishing — Industry and construction — Services

Source: Vietnam General Statistics Office 2011.
Note: GDP = gross domestic product. Data for 2011 are preliminary.

Table 2.1 Vietnam Average Annual GDP Growth by Sector

Sector	Average annual percentage growth in real terms			
	1990–95	1996–2000	2001–05	2006–11
GDP growth rate	**7.9**	**6.2**	**7.4**	**6.3**
Agriculture, forestry, and fisheries	4.0	4.3	4.0	3.3
Industry and construction	11.3	9.2	10.0	6.7
Services	8.2	4.8	6.6	7.2

Source: Vietnam General Statistics Office 2011.
Note: GDP = gross domestic product.

(e.g., seafood, rice, and coffee) and crude oil, and manufactured products like garments and textiles, footwear, wood products (e.g., furniture), and electronics. In a recent Trade and Transport Facilitation Assessment for Vietnam conducted by the World Bank (Pham *et al.* 2013), six commodities were selected as Vietnam's foremost strategic export commodities: electronic components, footwear, apparel and textiles, seafood, coffee, and rice. Figure 2.2 illustrates the production origin distribution of these key commodities, by region. The Red River Delta (home to Hanoi) and South East (home to Ho Chi Minh City [HCMC]) regions are dominant production origins for manufactured products. The broader Mekong River Delta region (including the adjacent South East region) accounts

Figure 2.2 Regional Origin of Vietnam's Six Key Export Commodities

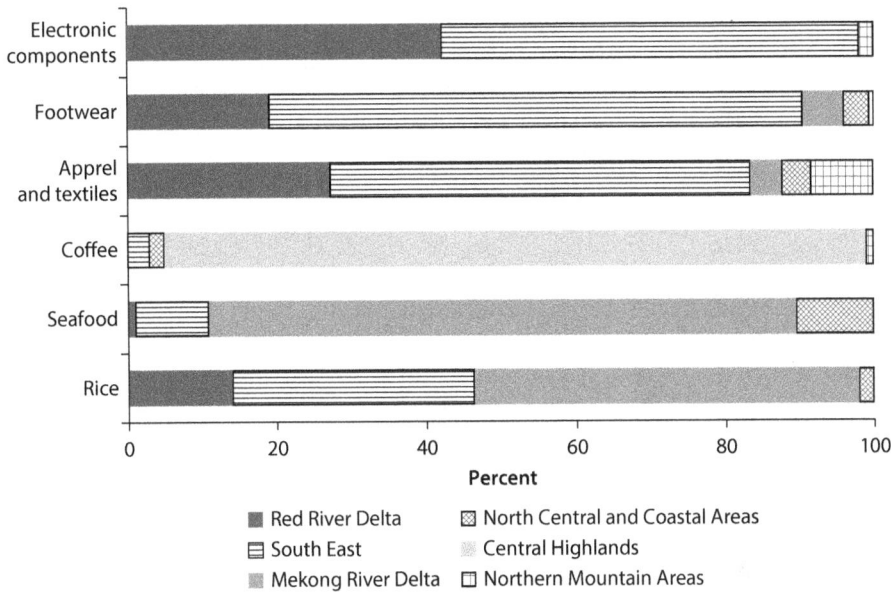

Source: TDSI 2012.

for the majority of rice and seafood exports. Coffee production is concentrated in the Central Highlands region.

Vietnam imports proportionally more manufactured products (e.g., machinery and parts, fuel [imported after processing], fabrics, steel, and electronics) than raw materials or primary products, and the import content of Vietnamese exports is substantial. Imports account for 58 percent[2] of the dollar value of manufactured products that are most likely to be used in the manufacture of exports. Take two of Vietnam's largest exports—apparel and footwear. Imported raw materials used in the manufacturing of apparel exports account for 70–80 percent of the value of the end product. The equivalent number for footwear exports stands at around 50 percent. This heavy reliance on imported inputs impacts Vietnam's trade balance and makes for a unique set of logistics challenges, where realizing efficiencies in import supply chains becomes particularly critical. From a logistics perspective, this means that Vietnam generally lacks the supplier clusters and integrated supply chains that have been so critical in the development of other export-led economies, most notably China but pioneered decades ago in Japan. Import dependence substantially increases the overall risk profile of assembly lines and supply chains and is particularly critical to certain industries, such as auto manufacturing.

Vietnam's trade patterns are concentrated (see table 2.2). The United States, the European Union (EU), China, and Japan account for more than half of the country's exports major. Similarly, China alone accounts for nearly a quarter of Vietnam's imports. Imports from China, the Republic of Korea, Japan, Taiwan, and the EU already represent 60 percent of the country's total.

Table 2.2 Vietnam's Top 12 Trading Partners, 2011

Exports			Imports		
Destination country	Value (million $)	Percent total	Origination country	Value (million $)	Percent total
United States	16,928	17	China	24,594	23
European Union	16,545	17	Korea, Rep.	13,176	12
China	11,125	11	Japan	10,400	10
Japan	10,781	11	Taiwan	8,557	8
Korea, Rep.	4,715	5	European Union	7,747	7
Malaysia	2,832	3	Singapore	6,391	6
Australia	2,519	3	Thailand	6,384	6
Cambodia	2,407	2	United States	4,529	4
Indonesia	2,359	2	Malaysia	3,920	4
Singapore	2,286	2	India	2,346	2
Hong Kong SAR, China	2,206	2	Indonesia	2,248	2
South Africa	1,864	2	Australia	2,123	2

Source: Vietnam General Statistics Office 2011.
Note: Countries in the EU refer to the EU-27 grouping.

Demographic and Socioeconomic Overview

Vietnam has been benefiting from what is sometimes referred to as a "demographic dividend"—the acceleration of economic growth derived from an increasing supply of young workers coupled with a declining dependency ratio.[3] As the populations of neighboring countries such as Japan, Korea, and China have aged, the percentage of the Vietnamese population between the ages of 15 and 64 has seen faster growth (as of 2009, 69 percent of Vietnam's population was in that age bracket; Vietnam General Statistics Office 2011). This has provided Vietnam with a competitive advantage in labor costs. While China's manufacturing labor costs are growing at double-digit rates—and have done so for several years—Vietnam's labor costs remain attractive throughout developing Asia (see figure 2.3). Yet the country's demographic shift is rapidly changing. It is projected that Vietnam's working age population will grow at a rate of 0.6 percent per year in the next decade, compared with 2.8 percent in the 10 years to 2010 (Breu and Dobbs 2012). In order for Vietnam to maintain its competitive edge, productivity gains will need to gradually replace, and in the short term more prominently complement, the growth-boosting effect of an expanding work force.

Vietnam's population distribution is largely concentrated in two regions: the Northern region (the Red River Delta and the region around Hanoi) and the Southern region (the Mekong River Delta and the region around HCMC). Each of these regions accommodates one-third (10 million) of the total national urban population (World Bank 2011). Not surprisingly, these regions account for a significant amount of the country's GDP and, by extension, its demand for logistics and transport services (see map 2.1). The municipality of HCMC alone is responsible for 23 percent of the nation's total output, followed by the HCMC-adjacent provinces of Dong Nai, Ba Ria-Vung Tau, and Binh Duong in Southern

Figure 2.3 Average Worker Monthly Base Salary in Select Cities of Developing Asian Countries, 2011

Dollars

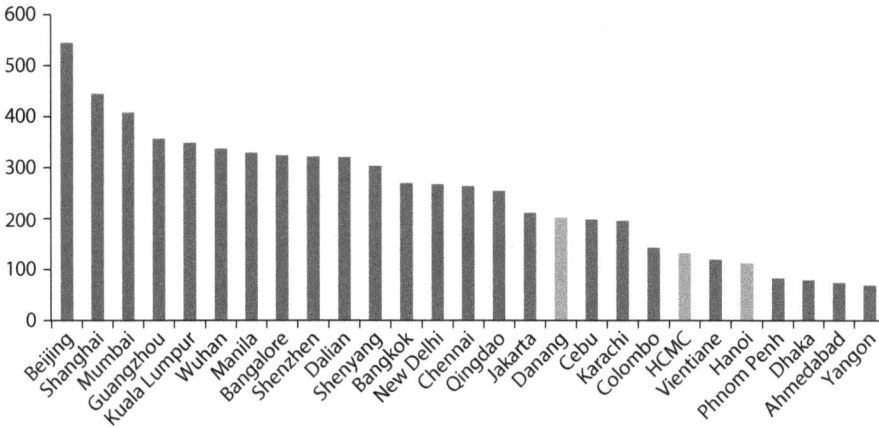

Source: JETRO 2012.
Note: Red bars represent cities in Vietnam. HCMC = Ho Chi Minh City.

Vietnam, and the municipality of Hanoi in Northern Vietnam, each comprising 10 percent of output. In other words, five municipalities/provinces (out of a total of 63 provincial-level jurisdictions) are responsible for more than half of national output. In 2011 the HCMC and Hanoi areas accounted for 62.4 percent and 34.7 percent, respectively, of Vietnam's ocean container throughput.

Business Climate

Vietnam is seen by actual and prospective international investors as an attractive yet challenging base for sourcing and manufacturing.[4] The World Bank's *Doing Business in 2013* (2012a) database ranks Vietnam 99 out of 185 economies on a set of indicators ranging from starting a business to dealing with construction permits, getting electricity, registering property, getting credit, protecting investors, paying taxes, trading across borders, enforcing contracts, and resolving insolvency (World Bank 2012a). Vietnam's ranking compares favorably with that of neighbors Cambodia, Indonesia, the Lao People's Democratic Republic, and the Philippines, but is below that of China, Malaysia, and Thailand, and the East Asia and Pacific regional average.

Since the mid-1990s, and particularly over the past 10 years, Vietnam has consistently attracted international firms looking to open factories and conduct transnational operations. However, key challenges remain to not only attract new investments but also retain those that have arrived. This section will discuss four such challenges: (1) macroeconomic stability and inflation, (2) inconsistent regulatory environment and administrative burdens, (3) facilitation payments and other forms of corruption, and (4) transparency, intellectual property, and "soft" trade barriers.

Map 2.1 Vietnam: Economic Geography

Population density
(proxy for economic activity)

Vietnam's key
logistics-intense regions

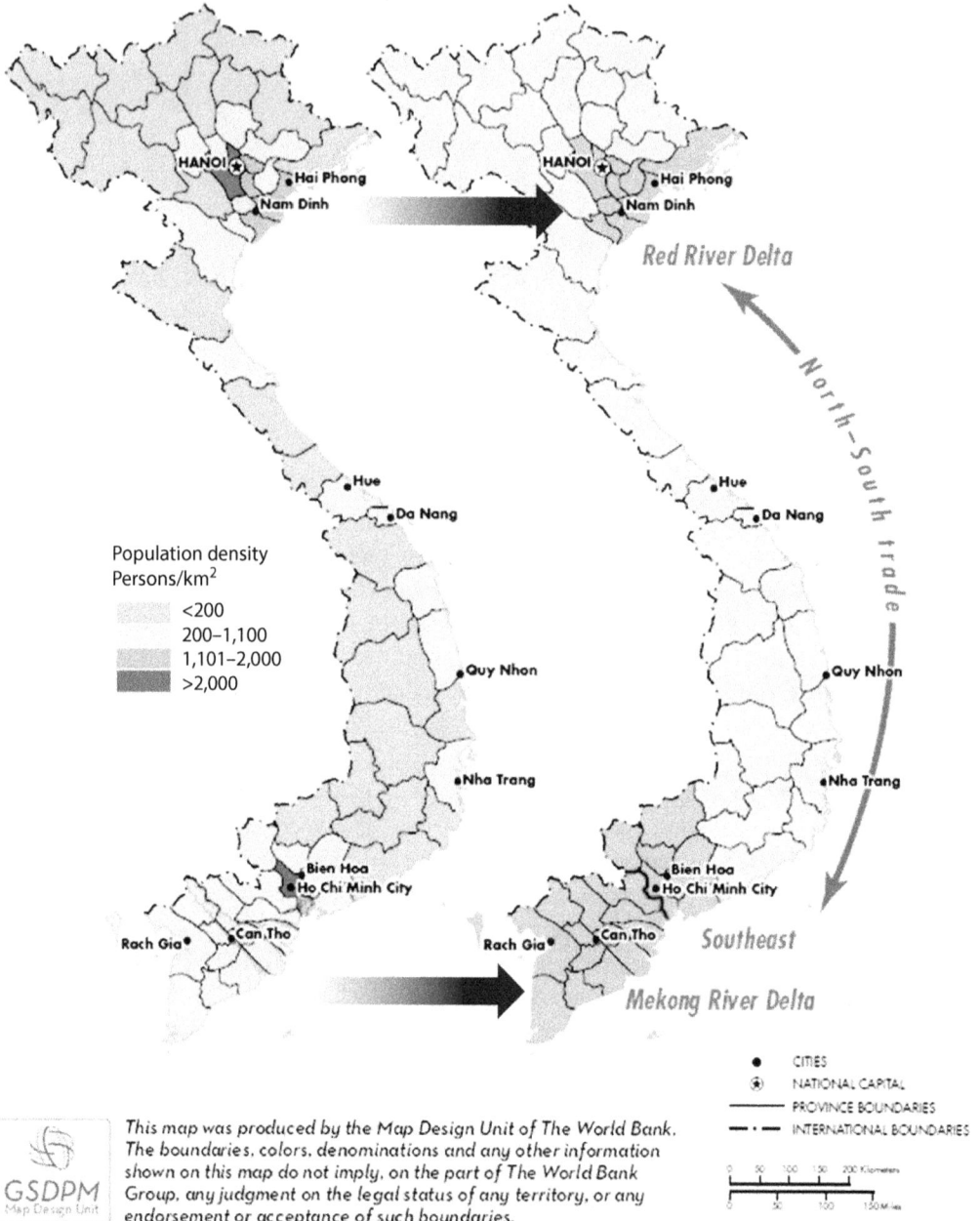

HANOI
Hai Phong
Nam Dinh

HANOI
Hai Phong
Nam Dinh

Red River Delta

North–South trade

Population density
Persons/km²

<200
200–1,100
1,101–2,000
>2,000

Hue
Da Nang

Hue
Da Nang

Quy Nhon

Quy Nhon

Nha Trang

Nha Trang

Bien Hoa
Ho Chi Minh City

Bien Hoa
Ho Chi Minh City

Rach Gia
Can Tho

Rach Gia
Can Tho

Southeast

Mekong River Delta

CITIES
NATIONAL CAPITAL
PROVINCE BOUNDARIES
INTERNATIONAL BOUNDARIES

*This map was produced by the Map Design Unit of The World Bank.
The boundaries, colors, denominations and any other information
shown on this map do not imply, on the part of The World Bank
Group, any judgment on the legal status of any territory, or any
endorsement or acceptance of such boundaries.*

GSDPM
Map Design Unit

0   50   100   150   200 Kilometers
0   50   100   150 Miles

Source: Authors with data from Vietnam General Statistics Office.

Macroeconomic Stability and Inflation

Vietnam has seen double-digit inflationary pressure in recent years. Consumer prices increased 23 percent in 2008 and 19 percent in 2011. Between 2007 and 2011, Vietnam's average annual inflation rate (14 percent) was significantly higher than that of any of its main Southeast Asian developing economy neighbors.[5] While this has reduced purchasing power for everyday goods and services, it has also driven borrowing costs out of reach for many businesses and entrepreneurs. This recent history of instability forced the State Bank of Vietnam, Vietnam's central bank, to switch its policy stance from primarily supporting growth to primarily taming inflation and bolstering market confidence. In February 2012, Vietnam passed Resolution 11, a major effort to restore macroeconomic stability and slow the growth of an "overheating" economy.[6] The resolution's goals are to address high levels of inflation, tension in the foreign exchange market, high nominal interest rates, and declining foreign exchange reserves.[7]

Beyond causing market instability, inflation jeopardizes Vietnam's ability to provide a low-cost workforce for labor-intensive industries. A recent survey of 50 U.S. importers found that Vietnam was considered the most attractive alternative to China as a sourcing location for manufactured products (Kulisch 2012). Perceptions like these, which suggest that Vietnam faces a significant opportunity to continue to gain global manufacturing share, could be reversed if the country's macroeconomic fundamentals continue to cause market anxiety.

Inconsistent Regulatory Environment and Administrative Burdens

Managing unpredictability and coping with delays are critical components of conducting business in Vietnam. According to the US-ASEAN Business Council, "Vietnam does not implement regulations consistently … the government may start down a good path, but then special interest groups pressure the government for special favors, which throws the government off-course." Regulatory uncertainty adds to the administrative burden of freight stakeholders, who are subject to monitoring over 5,700 Administrative Procedures and 9,000 legal documents (EuroCham 2012).

While much remains to be done, some efforts are under way to reduce regulatory complexity. For example, *Project 30*, an initiative sponsored by the U.S. Vietnam Trade Council and the U.S. Agency for International Development, aims to reduce compliance costs for businesses and citizens by 30 percent by documenting administrative procedures in a database and developing a plan to simplify them (Schwarz 2010). As Vietnam continues to provide basic infrastructure, regulatory reforms will become an increasingly central component of any strategy to increase competitiveness.

Facilitation Payments and Other Forms of Corruption

Facilitation payments to the General Department of Vietnam Customs (hereafter "Vietnam Customs" or simply "Customs") officials and the police are a common occurrence in Vietnam, despite this being illegal under Vietnamese anticorruption laws.[8] These payments most typically take place to expedite the customs clearance process or to mitigate traffic citations that delay the delivery of containers en route to factories or ports. Several factors contribute to this. A lack of meritocracy in both access to public sector jobs and the achievement of career progression milestones (such as salary increases and promotions) is a primary driving force behind the incidence of facilitation payments.[9] But the supply side also plays a major role, as freight stakeholders—and notably logistics service providers (LSPs)[10] on behalf of BCOs—generally perceive and/or assume these payments to be "normal" or a "standard practice" and often initiate them on that basis.

Facilitation takes place in a variety of ways, from invitations to entertainment (e.g., social events and sporting activities) to outright cash payments of "tea" money. In whatever form it takes, facilitation payments are built into the customs brokerage and trucking rates LSPs and trucking companies charge BCOs, as confirmed by firms interviewed for this study. As a result, it is estimated that facilitation payments range from 10 percent to 15 percent of the total origin cost to import a container of raw materials or to export a container of general merchandise. This is not insignificant and contrasts with the fact that facilitation payments are often considered "petty" and not a "serious" source of economic impact.

It is noted that facilitation payments are the most common but hardly the only form of corruption impacting domestic and international supply chains. Actions undertaken with the intention of using public funds for one's own benefit, falsifying the import or export value of products, deceitfully misclassifying cargo to receive more favorable duty rates, or outright bribery to reduce operating costs are additional examples of corrupt practices—and considered as such by both Vietnamese and international law. Overwhelmingly, businesses, both domestic and foreign, during interviews for this study stated the need for a more transparent supply chain where there is visibility in product flow and a clear and open customs clearance process with transparent costs.

The Government of Vietnam (GoV) implemented an Anti-Corruption Law in 2005 (since revised in 2007), that criminalizes corruption; the law focused extensively on public sector corruption. In addition, in 2009 the GoV adopted a National Anti-Corruption Strategy to 2020, which explicitly recognizes the role of openness and transparency in reducing corruption (World Bank 2009). While modest improvements have been attained, most international firms interviewed for this report still consider corruption an impediment to their operations and a source of logistics costs.

Transparency, Intellectual Property, and "Soft" Trade Barriers

International standards for many businesses relate not to the "hard" infrastructure of investments in quality roads, bridges and ports, but to "soft" infrastructure such as labor conditions, legal rights, environmental protection, and transparency. Many recent international agreements, such as the entry into the WTO and the ASEAN Economic Community (AEC), require Vietnam to bring the level of transparency and business climate up to an international standard. The most recent effort relates to compliance with the Trans-Pacific Partnership (TPP), a new regional trade agreement originally meant to be signed by the end of 2012 (Williams 2013). This is a multilateral free trade agreement aimed at expanding the flow of goods, services, and capital across borders and to encourage a free trade area between nine different nations. The TPP is one of many efforts of the last several years to bring Vietnam to the forefront in terms of international trade. However, it is still uncertain how quickly the business climate will change because of these agreements.

Freight Transport Market Structure

Vietnam's freight transport market, on a tonnage basis, is dominated by two modes: inland waterway transport (IWT) and the roads sector. When demand is measured in ton-kilometers (ton-km), coastal shipping (a mode naturally exposed to long lengths of haul), emerges as a third dominant mode. Table 2.3 shows the estimated modal share for freight volumes in Vietnam in 2008 and the projected modal share for 2030, as estimated by a recent comprehensive study of the Vietnam transport system (JICA 2009). It is noteworthy that the projected reductions in modal share captured by inland waterways are the direct result of Vietnam's economic transition to becoming a more manufacturing-intensive economy by 2030. Manufactured products are overwhelmingly containerized and have a higher value-to-weight ratio than most

Table 2.3 Vietnam's Freight Volumes by Mode, 2008 and Forecast to 2030

Year	Road	Rail	Inland waterway	Coastal shipping	Air	All modes
(millions of tons)[a]						
2008	181	8	193	17	0.1	400
2030	640	47	395	38	0.3	1,119
Tonnage share (%)						
2008	45.4	1.9	48.3	4.4	0.0	100
2030	57.2	4.2	35.3	3.4	0.0	100
Average length of haul (km)						
2008	143	400	112	1,161	1,404	178
2030	201	509	122	1,107	1,348	217
Billions of ton-km						
2008	26	3	22	20	0.1	71
2030	129	24	48	42	0.4	243
Ton-km share (%)						
2008	36.6	4.3	30.4	28.5	0.1	100
2030	53.0	9.8	19.9	17.2	0.2	100
Average annual growth rate (%) 2008–30						
Tons	5.9	8.5	3.3	3.6	6.5	4.8
Ton-km	7.5	9.7	3.7	3.4	6.3	5.7

Source: Blancas and El-Hifnawi (2013) compiled using data from JICA (2009).
a. Per-day data as reported by JICA (2009) multiplied by 300.

Efficient Logistics • http://dx.doi.org/10.1596/978-1-4648-0103-7

commodities currently moving over the waterways. Accordingly, the share of freight flows captured by the roads sector is expected to increase from 45.4 percent in 2008 to 57.2 percent in 2030. It is also worth emphasizing that rail is expected to continue to be a relatively insignificant mode of freight transport even through 2030.

Transportation Planning Structure

Transportation planning and management in Vietnam is conducted at the national, provincial, and local levels (see figure 2.4). The Ministry of Transport (MoT) has responsibility over planning, constructing, and maintaining national-level transport infrastructure and for assisting local governments in project selection. It also sets national-level policy and regulations. Every five years, in the context of the national Public Investment Program, the MoT prepares a five-year plan outlining long-term transport strategies. Every 12 months it prepares an annual plan for inclusion in the annual state budget, consistent with the priorities and directives set forth in the five-year plan. Provincial Departments of Transport are in charge of implementing provincial-level transportation projects with MoT support, under the guidance of Provincial People's Committees.

Figure 2.4 Structure of Government Institutions in the Transport Sector

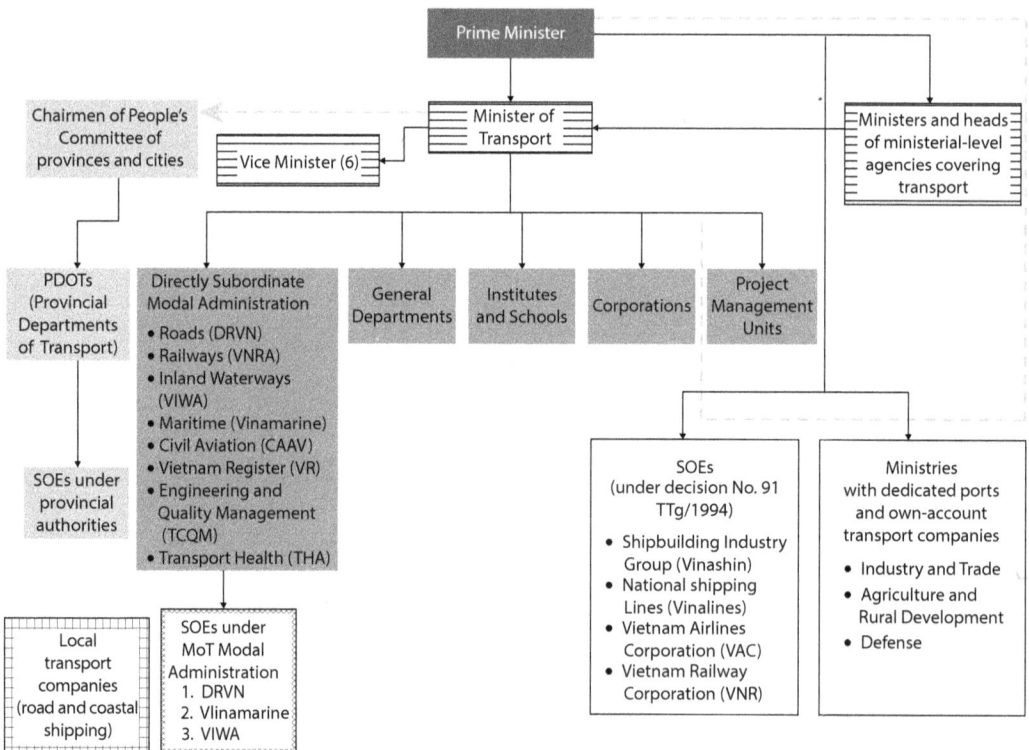

Source: Ministry of Transport of Vietnam. See appendix G for details.
Note: SOE = State-Owned Enterprise.

Under the MoT, sectoral departments responsible for ports, inland waterways, highways, rail, and airports tend to operate in silos or "stove pipes" when developing, funding, implementing, and operating transportation infrastructure projects. Projects that may require interdisciplinary planning are in practice split into subprojects assigned to different agencies. This fragmented planning process results, for example, in access roads to new ports not being completed when the ports' terminals open to handle cargo, or newly built bridges that become clearance bottlenecks for IWT.

Logistics Costs

Table 2.4 lists the cost to import[11] a single 40-foot container (FEU) of raw materials or components into Vietnam from Busan, Korea, to be used in the manufacture of export products. Estimated at $1,015, the cost is $8 per FEU higher than the equivalent cost for Yantian, China, and $280 lower than that for Jakarta, Indonesia. The $515 per FEU origin cost includes estimated facilitation payments to Customs officials and police of $78, or 15.1 percent (see appendix A) of the total origin cost.

Table 2.5 shows the cost to export[12] a single 40-foot container of general merchandise from HCMC to Los Angeles, California, that a major BCO might pay in 2012. The total landed cost, without destination duty, is $92 less expensive than a shipment from Yantian, China, to Los Angeles and $205 less than a shipment from Jakarta, Indonesia, to Los Angeles. Vietnam's $572 per FEU origin cost, which includes estimated facilitation payments to Customs officials and

Table 2.4 Import Cost Comparisons for 40-Foot Container of General Merchandise
U.S. dollars

	Import: estimated landed cost per FEU at origin from Busan, Korea, Rep.			
Country	Origin cost	Ocean freight	Total	Over/under Vietnam's landed cost per FEU
Vietnam	515	500	1,015	n.a.
China	707	300	1,007	(8)
Indonesia	595	700	1,295	280

Source: Authors. See table A.2 for further details.
Note: FEU = 40-foot equivalent unit container; n.a. = not applicable.

Table 2.5 Export Landed Cost Comparisons for 40-Foot Container of General Merchandise
U.S. dollars

	Estimated landed cost per FEU in Los Angeles, California			
Country	Origin cost	Ocean freight	Total	Over/under Vietnam's landed cost per FEU
Vietnam	572	1,960	2,532	n.a.
China	774	1,850	2,624	92
Indonesia	637	2,100	2,737	205

Source: Authors. See table A.2 for further details.
Note: FEU = 40-foot equivalent unit container; n.a. = not applicable.

Efficient Logistics • http://dx.doi.org/10.1596/978-1-4648-0103-7

police of $76.5, or 13.4 percent (see table A.5) of the total origin cost, is less than the comparable origin costs in South China and Indonesia.

The above results, which suggest that Vietnam's logistics costs are about on par with China's and below those of Indonesia, may appear contrary to oft-cited reports that Vietnam's logistics costs are 25 percent of GDP (JICA 2009; KPMG 2010; Vietnam Chamber of Commerce and Industry 2012). Such a level of costs, the reports contend, compares unfavorably with China and Indonesia, where logistics costs are estimated to be on the order of 18–20 percent of GDP. However, these ratios must be taken with great caution for at least two reasons. First, some studies have also stated that Vietnam's logistics costs as a percentage of GDP are much lower, closer to 15 percent (Meyrick and Associates Transport development and strategy institute, and BPO 2006) and, by one estimate, perhaps as low as 13 percent.[13] Thus, there appears to be a wide margin of variation around any one estimate. Second, and most importantly, substantially all of the above reports fail to publish the methodologies and data sources behind their estimates, making their accuracy and validity difficult to assess. This is in stark contrast to technical studies developed by an increasing number of countries around the world (Brazil, Finland, South Africa, and the United States are but a few examples) where nationwide logistics costs are estimated on the basis of clearly defined methodologies that are open to scientific scrutiny.[14] Since Vietnam is yet to conduct formal assessments of this kind,[15] available estimates suggesting logistics costs to be up to 25 percent of GDP can only be seen as rough indications of how high these costs truly are.

What is available for Vietnam on the basis of verifiable, analytically consistent methodologies are logistics and trade facilitation indices that (1) are summary measures of nationwide logistics efficiency, (2) are calculated primarily based on structured surveys of logistics operators and industry practitioners (these surveys are often complemented by quantitative data on logistics performance), and (3) by virtue of their methodology, are meaningfully comparable across countries (something that may not always be the case when logistics costs, in monetary terms, are expressed as a ratio to GDP). One such metric, widely used by academics, policymakers, and practitioners, is the World Bank's International Logistics Performance Index (LPI; Arvis et al. 2012). According to the 2012 International LPI rankings, Vietnam outperforms regional peers Cambodia, Indonesia, Lao PDR, and Myanmar, is about on par with the Philippines, and lags China, Malaysia, and Thailand. This finding, coupled with existing high-level estimates of logistics costs as a percentage of GDP in Vietnam, would suggest that Vietnam's logistics costs relative to its peers situate the country somewhere in the middle of the Southeast Asia region—below those of some countries but still above those of key competitors in extended supply chains. This broadly reflects Vietnam's newly earned position as a lower middle income country, where many of the lower-hanging fruits in logistics performance (e.g., access to basic road infrastructure, adequate electricity supply, and availability of basic services) have been harvested, and productivity-boosting, well-coordinated (e.g., multimodal) investments and institutional reforms have now become a priority.

The following obstacles are key contributors to logistics costs in Vietnam being higher than those of some regional peers:

1. High reliance on trucking as a mode compared with less expensive rail for shipping products over longer distances. Because of Vietnam's elongated geography, this can be a sizable cost given the distances from HCMC/Mekong Delta, where the majority of nonimported consumer goods are grown or manufactured, to distribution facilities in the central and northern regions.
2. Facilitation payments are made to Customs and police officials to keep products flowing through supply chains; this increases the cost of customs clearance and trucking and increases itinerary unpredictability.
3. Congestion related to inadequate highway infrastructure (e.g., weight limits and bridge clearances on key roads are often incompatible with container traffic) and the still poor quality of many highways reduces the speed (intercity truck speeds in Vietnam average 35 km per hour; World Bank 2011), reliability, and load capacity of truck shipments.
4. The distribution network is fragmented, forcing BCOs to contract with many companies (suppliers, LSPs, trucking companies, etc.) to get their products to market, making it difficult for long-standing relationships (e.g., core carrier programs) to be established with supply chain partners.
5. The national truck fleet is old.[16] This increases maintenance expenses for truckers, and frequent truck breakdowns further contribute to unpredictable transit times. Higher-value goods are handled by LSPs that offer international standards for road transport service at a higher delivery cost. Some value-dense electronic products are shipped from HCMC to Danang or Hanoi by air and delivered only over the last mile by truck to urban retail outlets.
6. Clearing customs is a more time-consuming and unpredictable process compared with some of Vietnam's peers, forcing just-in-time (JIT) manufacturers to carry more inventory to keep production lines operating.
7. Domestic BCOs shipping lower-value products overwhelmingly contract with domestic LSPs that focus on cost rather than service, resulting in erratic and extended transit times that have to be covered by higher inventory levels.
8. With nearly 30 reported fatal motor crashes daily, Vietnam's roads remain unsafe. In addition to the needless toll in human lives that this causes, unsafe roads contribute to unreliability in supply chains and increase logistics costs.

Status of Existing Infrastructure

Ports and Marine Terminals

Vietnam's container trade is sizable and has a strong record of sustained growth— mirroring the economy as a whole. Vietnamese container terminals handled 7.7 million TEUs in 2011 (see table 2.6). The sector generated over $300 million of revenue from handling and associated port charges that year.

In another parallel to the broader economy, container-handling activity in Vietnam is highly concentrated: It is focused on the two key shipping centers of

Table 2.6 Vietnam: Container Ports, Handling Volumes, 2007–11

Port throughput (TEUs)	2011	2010	2009	2008	2007
Southern region	4,801,324	4,509,312	3,821,471	3,736,663	3,502,900
Saigon New Port (Cat Lai)	2,597,684	2,559,305	2,460,000	2,017,863	1,849,746
VICT	374,248	297,561	306,834	540,122	572,045
Saigon Port	308,937	401,982	378,226	510,496	350,418
ICD Phuoc Long (Midstream)	168,714	145,252	224,757	303,688	370,379
Ben Nghe	154,573	210,549	140,922	188,815	218,004
Bong Sen	56,543	4,498	23,896	24,252	24,000
Binh Duong	62,182	97,782	60,000	109,943	72,033
SPCT	139,772	95,934	8,000	0	0
Dong Nai	3,191	0	0	0	0
Cai Mep-Thi Vai terminals	893,150	657,335	191,929	0	0
Others	42,330	39,114	26,907	41,484	46,275
Central region	219,365	202,983	142,229	154,594	128,954
Danang	114,373	89,199	69,720	61,881	53,372
Qui Nhon	62,549	72,224	54,649	72,276	61,826
Nha Trang	727	2,573	3,942	4,322	4,556
Others	41,716	38,987	13,918	16,115	9,200
Northern region	2,662,605	2,442,541	2,159,941	1,569,485	1,238,453
Haiphong Port (Hoang Dieu/Chua Ve)	727,000	795,000	715,831	790,000	683,689
Other Haiphong Terminals	884,500	864,555	874,171	526,503	402,864
Dinh Vu Terminals	907,124	664,647	459,000	232,982	131,200
Cai Lan (excluding barge moves)	143,981	118,839	110,939	20,000	20,700
Total	7,683,294	7,154,836	6,123,641	5,460,742	4,870,307
Growth % year over year	7.4	16.8	12.1	12.1	29.5
Compound annual growth rate (%) 2000–11	16.8				
HCMC/Cai Mep region as % of total	62.4	63.0	62.4	68.4	71.9
Haiphong/Cai Lan region as % of total	34.7	34.1	35.3	28.7	25.4

Source: Authors, Vietnam Port Association, interviews with port operators, and Liner Research Services.
Note: ICD = Inland Container Depot; TEU = 20-foot equivalent unit container.

HCMC and Haiphong, including their respective satellite ports of Cai Mep-Thi Vai and Cai Lan. Put together, these locations account for 97 percent of the country's total container-handling volumes.[17]

Vietnam's container flows grew at an impressive average annual rate of 16.8 percent between 2000 and 2011 (see figure 2.5). However, after an initial period of rapid growth (from a low base) between 2000 and 2007, when annual growth averaged 19.7 percent, growth rates since have tempered to about 12 percent per annum. Going forward, it is estimated[18] that Vietnam's nationwide container volumes will grow at an average annual rate of 8–9 percent through 2020.

Regional volume breakdowns reveal differentiated growth rates over the past 10 years. The northern region recorded the highest average growth in container volumes over the 2000–11 period (24.5 percent), while the relatively more mature southern region recorded an annual growth rate of 14.3 percent. In addition to rapid development of manufacturing activity in the Hanoi area

Figure 2.5 Vietnam: Container Handling Volume by Region, 2000–11

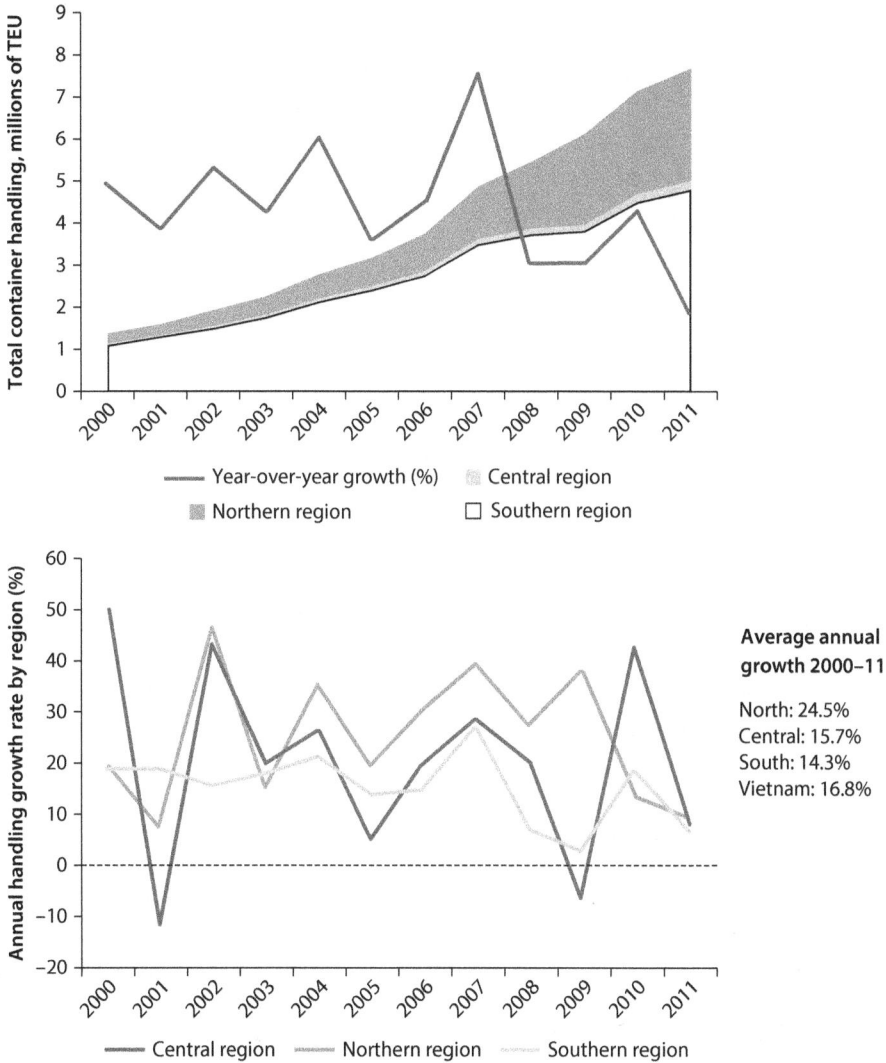

Year-over-year growth (%)   Central region
Northern region   Southern region

Average annual growth 2000–11

North: 24.5%
Central: 15.7%
South: 14.3%
Vietnam: 16.8%

Central region   Northern region   Southern region

Source: Liner Research Services and Vietnam Port Authority.
Note: TEU = 20-foot equivalent unit container.

(e.g., electronics), growth at the northern ports has been supported by the grow-ing cross-border transit trade with southern China, through the border gates at Mong Cai, Lang Son, and Lao Cai. Although official statistics on container move-ment at the border gates are lacking, this cargo is estimated to account for approximately 400,000 TEUs, or 15 percent of the throughput passing through the Haiphong and Cai Lan terminals in 2011. It is expected that container flows at Northern Vietnam ports will continue to grow slightly faster than those of Southern Vietnam through 2020, at annual rates of approximately 8.5–9.0 percent and 8.0–8.5 percent, respectively.

Port Planning Process

Vietnam has adopted a centralized port planning process. A seaport system development master plan is issued every 10 years. The most recent seaport master plans were approved in October 1999 (Decision No. 202/1999/QD-TTg), for the Master Plan to 2010, and in December 2009 (Decision No. 2190/QD-TTg) for the Master Plan to 2020.

The current master plan separates the Vietnam seaport system under six groups, with national ports separated into three categories (see map 2.2):

• An international transit port: Van Phong (planned)
• International gateway ports: Haiphong and Ba Ria-Vung Tau and
• Various regional major ports, including HCMC.

Despite the periodic formulation of seaport master plans, Vietnam's port planning process has tended to emphasize quantity over quality. Far from responding to an overarching national strategy on ports and multimodal transport, local governments continue to exert significant influence on the issuance of new port development licenses, elevating the risk of approving wasteful investment projects and fostering demand-supply mismatches.

Nowhere is this truer than in HCMC and the Cai Mep-Thi Vai port range. Just as cargo volumes began decelerating in 2007–08, several licenses were granted in quick succession (and contrary to what initial plans suggested—the very plans upon which the financial viability of many such investments was determined) in a rush to develop Vietnam's nascent deep-water port sector at Cai Mep-Thi Vai, about 80 kilometers outside HCMC. By mid-2009, as the new terminals became operational, slower-growing volumes began to be dispersed over a growing number of terminals, both in HCMC proper and at Cai Mep-Thi Vai.

The resulting overcapacity led to severe price competition among marine terminal operators (MTOs), which still continues and undermines the financial sustainability of both new and existing facilities. As volume growth has remained subdued in the wake of the global financial and economic crises and the continued economic challenges outlined earlier, many of the new deep-water ports are becoming increasingly less attractive to global container shipping carriers, whose profitability is largely determined by economies of scale. Meanwhile, policies that could bring more volumes to starved facilities, such as better and more rapid development of land-side infrastructure in the hinterland of Cai Mep-Thi Vai, relocation or closure of HCMC inner-city ports, and financial incentives to container shipping carriers (through lower fees, for example), are yet to materialize.

But planning and execution challenges in the ports sector are not limited to Southern Vietnam. The GoV continues to promote the building of a major transshipment port at Van Phong despite the lack of cargo demand and investor interest. A similar problem with overbuilding and lack of coordinated policy solutions as in Cai Mep-Thi Vai may be developing in the northern region, with the simultaneous construction of new terminal facilities at Haiphong, Dinh Vu, Cai Lan, Lach Huyen, and potentially South Do Son.

Map 2.2 Vietnam: Six Port Groups and Main Container Ports (above 10,000 TEUs per annum)

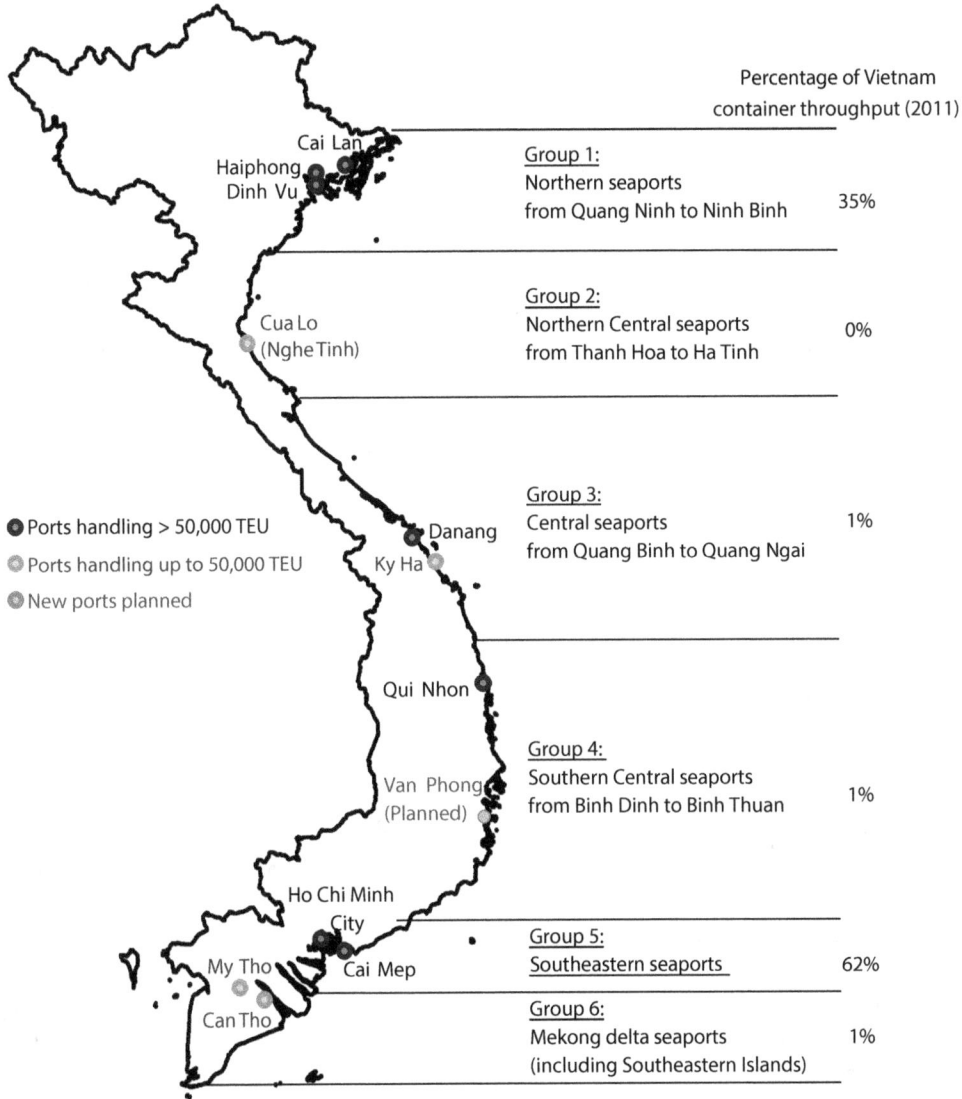

Percentage of Vietnam
container throughput (2011)

Cai Lan
Haiphong
Dinh Vu

Group 1:
Northern seaports
from Quang Ninh to Ninh Binh   35%

Cua Lo
(Nghe Tinh)

Group 2:
Northern Central seaports   0%
from Thanh Hoa to Ha Tinh

● Ports handling > 50,000 TEU
○ Ports handling up to 50,000 TEU
◐ New ports planned

Danang
Ky Ha

Group 3:
Central seaports   1%
from Quang Binh to Quang Ngai

Qui Nhon

Van Phong
(Planned)

Group 4:
Southern Central seaports   1%
from Binh Dinh to Binh Thuan

Ho Chi Minh
City
My Tho   Cai Mep
Can Tho

Group 5:
Southeastern seaports   62%

Group 6:
Mekong delta seaports   1%
(including Southeastern Islands)

Source: Liner Research Services.
Note: TEU = 20-foot equivalent unit container.

The following sections will take a closer look at the imbalances plaguing Vietnam's ports sector. Given the prominence of this sector in logistics operations, these imbalances have inevitably impacted the country's overall international competitiveness.

Demand and Supply Mismatch at Southern Ports

The 2000–10 Master Plan did not anticipate the significant growth in container volumes registered in Vietnam during 2000–08. Given the concentration of international trade volumes in the broader HCMC region, this resulted in severe congestion at HCMC inner-city ports, particularly during 2006–08. The pressure of congestion, coupled with concerted private sector calls for expanded, more capable (e.g., deep-water, more automated) handling facilities, created sufficient momentum for the opening up of investment opportunities in maritime ports in Southern Vietnam through public-private partnerships. However, since the Master Plan lacked appropriate means to regulate new container-handling capacity in light of growing demand, the ensuing construction of new port terminals at Cai Mep-Thi Vai did not respond to integrated long-term planning and was exacerbated by lax controls over the concession granting process at a time when global MTOs were eager to enter an underserved Vietnam market. This led to oversupply of container terminal capacity in the HCMC region, which began to be felt as early as 2010 but had continued to worsen through 2012 (with additional terminals still planned as of year-end 2012).

To be sure, the Cai Mep-Thi Vai marine terminals (first opened in May 2009) marked a watershed in Vietnam's connectivity and held the promise of significant benefits to BCOs. For the first time, ocean carriers were able to offer direct services from Vietnam to North America and Europe without the need to use feeder vessels for connections at regional transshipment hubs like Singapore or Hong Kong SAR, China. The elimination of feeder and transshipment costs is estimated to save about $150–300/TEU[19] for containers shipped to and from Vietnam.

The overcapacity problem caused by the rapid expansion of terminal capacity since 2009 remains a serious concern. As of September 2012, the utilization rate of existing container terminals in Cai Mep-Thi Vai was only 18 percent of their current capacity of 5.2 million TEUs (see table 2.7 and figure 2.6). Three of the five existing terminals at Cai Mep-Thi Vai (SITV, SP-PSA, and TCCT) currently have no regular container vessel calls. In what will almost certainly contribute to furthering the existing imbalance, two more terminals (SSIT and CMICT-ODA) are due to open in 2013, which will bring a further 2.2 million TEUs of capacity to Cai Mep-Thi Vai in the very short term. Construction of an eighth terminal, Gemalink, is currently suspended but could add a further 1.2 million TEUs of capacity as early as 2013. A second phase of the existing SP-PSA facility, representing an additional 1.1 million TEUs, is also in the planning stage. In all, approved and planned projects could double current Cai Mep-Thi Vai capacity (bringing it to 10.3 million TEUs) in a matter of a few years.

Given its physical proximity to HCMC, Cai Mep-Thi Vai's capacity expansion cannot be seen in isolation but in the context of HCMC's inner-city ports. The latter ports also face oversupply: Apart from Cat Lai, which is close to full capacity, all the other terminals are currently underutilized (table 2.7). Similar to Cai Mep-Thi Vai, five more terminals with container-handling capabilities (and a combined capacity of 1.75 million TEUs) are scheduled to be launched in the HCMC area, in Hiep Phuoc and Phu Huu districts (table 2.8).

Based on projected demand growth of 8–9 percent per annum over the 2011–20 period, the capacity utilization at HCMC and Cai Mep-Thi Vai ports

Table 2.7 Vietnam: Current Terminals at Ho Chi Minh City and Cai Mep-Thi Vai

Ho Chi Minh City	Cat Lai	VICT	SPCT	Saigon Port		Ben Nghe	Gemadept	Total
Operator:	SNP	FLDC	DP World	Tan Thuan	Khanh Hoi	SAMCO	Gemadept	HCMC
Number of berths	7	4	3	4	4	4	Midstream	26
Berth length (m)	1,200	678	500	713	873	816	Buoys	4,780
Terminal area (ha)	100	20	23	—	7	32	—	182
Maximum depth alongside (m)	12	11	11	12	10	11	10	12
STS gantry cranes	17	7	5	2	0	2	0	33
Other cranes	3	0	0	5	4	3	16	31
Handling capacity (m TEU)	3.00	0.80	0.75	0.60		0.30	0.25	5.70
2011 volumes (m TEU)	2.60	0.37	0.14	0.31		0.15	0.17	3.74
Terminal utilization (%)	87	47	19	51		51	67	66

Cai Mep-Thi Vai	SITV	SP-PSA	TCCT	TCIT	CMIT	Total
Operator:	HPH	PSA	SNP	HJS/MOL/ WH/SNP	APMT	CM-TV
Number of berths	3	2	1	2	2	10
Berth length (m)	730	600	300	590	600	2,820
Terminal area (ha)	34	27	20	40	48	169
Maximum depth alongside (m)	14	14	15.8	15.8	16.5	16.5
STS gantry cranes	6	6	3	6	5	26
Other cranes	1	0	0	0	0	1
Handling capacity (m TEU)	1.20	1.10	0.60	1.20	1.10	5.20
2011 volumes (m TEU)	0.10	0.26	0.19	0.28	0.09	0.92
Terminal utilization (%)	8	23	32	23	9	18

Source: Authors based on Vietnam Port Association and interviews with port operators.
Note: — = not available. STS = ship-to-shore; TEU = 20-foot equivalent unit container.

will reach only 63 percent in 2020, even without adding the potential capacity from the Gemalink or SP-PSA Phase 2 projects (see figure 2.7).

On the demand side, weaker than expected cargo volumes, the consolidation of ocean carrier services due to the formation of new alliances, and the withdrawal of a number of strings (notably by global container shipping carriers CSAV and Zim) due to carrier downsizing have resulted in a reduction in the number of linehaul services calling at Cai Mep-Thi Vai from a peak of 15 services in June 2011 to only eight services as of September 2012 (see figure 2.8 and table 2.9).

The vast majority (an estimated 95 percent) of containers currently handled at Cai Mep-Thi Vai are barged to or from HCMC, a factor that should be taken into consideration when planning and implementing land-side infrastructure for the new ports. Besides cost alone (barging costs are one-third of the cost of trucking containers to or from Cai Mep-Thi Vai), the existing poor condition of the road infrastructure in the corridor and general BCO preference to receive and

Figure 2.6 Estimated Terminal Utilization Levels at HCMC and Cai Mep-Thi Vai Ports

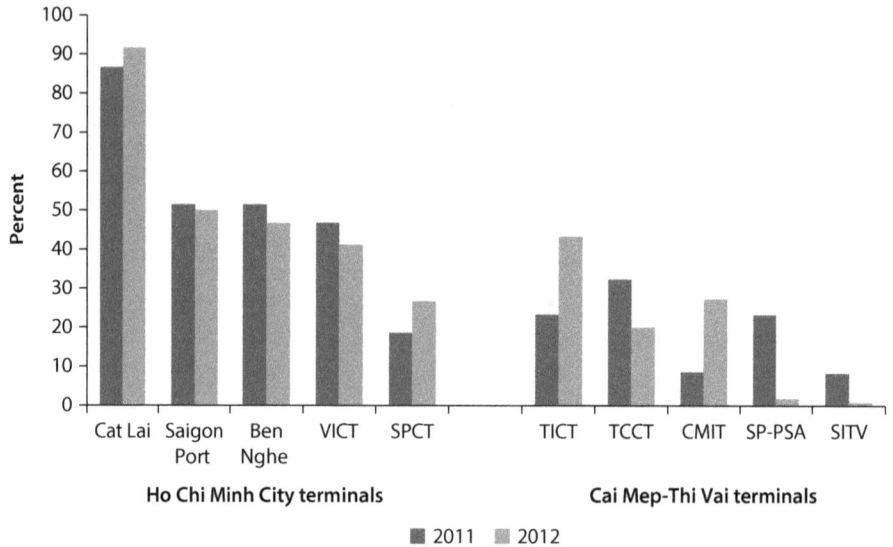

Source: Vietnam Port Association, interviews with port operators, and Liner Research Services.

Table 2.8 Vietnam: New Terminals Planned at Ho Chi Minh City and Cai Mep-Thi Vai

Ho Chi Minh City	Cat Lai Petec site	Ben Nghe Phu Huu	ITC Phu Huu	SP Hiep Phuoc	SNP Hiep Phuoc	Total new
Operator:	SNP	SAMCO	ITC	Saigon Port	SNP	HCMC
Number of berths	1	2	3	5	2	11
Berth length (m)	214	320	600	800	444	1,934
Terminal area (ha)	12	24	41	54	15	131
Maximum depth alongside (m)	12	12	11	11	11	12
STS gantry cranes	3	3	4	—	4	10
Other cranes	0	0	0	—	2	0
Handling capacity (m TEU)	0.30	0.35	0.60	0.50	0.45	1.75
Due to open	2013	2013	2013	2013	2014	

Cai Mep-Thi Vai	SSIT	CMICT	Gemalink Phase 1/Phase 2		SP-PSA Phase 2	Total new
Operator:	SSA	PMU-85	GMD/CMA CGM		PSA	
Number of berths	2	2	3	1	2	10
Berth length (m)	600	600	800	359	600	2,959
Terminal area (ha)	48	48	33	39	27	195
Maximum depth alongside (m)	16	16	16	16	14	16
STS gantry cranes	4	4	8	—	—	16
Other cranes	0	0	0	—	—	0
Handling capacity (m TEU)	0.80	0.80	1.20	1.20	1.10	5.10
Due to open	2013	2013	Likely 2013	—	—	

Source: Authors based on Vietnam Port Association and interviews with port operators.
Note: — = not available. STS = ship-to-shore; TEU = 20-foot equivalent unit container.

Figure 2.7 Vietnam: Demand and Supply at Southern Region Ports, 2000–20

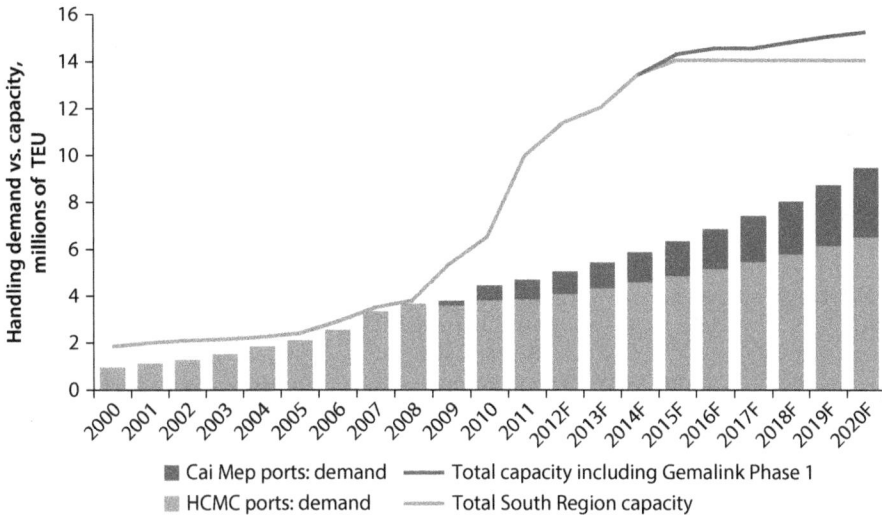

Cai Mep ports: demand ▪ — Total capacity including Gemalink Phase 1
HCMC ports: demand ▪ — Total South Region capacity

Source: Vietnam Port Association, interviews with port operators, and Liner Research Services.
Note: TEU = 20-foot equivalent unit container; F = forecast.

Figure 2.8 Number of Weekly Linehaul Services Calling at Cai Mep-Thi Vai, 2009–12

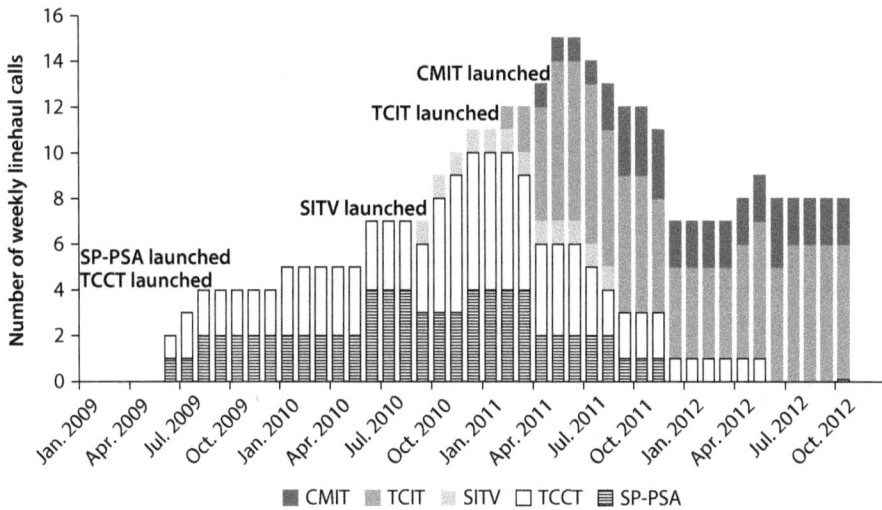

■ CMIT   ▪ TCIT   ▪ SITV   □ TCCT   ▦ SP-PSA

Source: Vietnam Port Association, interviews with port operators, and Liner Research Services.

deliver cargo closer to HCMC have contributed to a high incidence of barging in Cai Mep-Thi Vai supply chains. Although barging provides a cost effective and environmentally more sustainable mode of transport compared with trucking, barging costs (of about $30 per TEU, including lift on/lift off) are borne by ocean carriers (rather than BCOs), and it is uncertain whether ocean carriers are recovering that cost in the rates they charge BCOs. Given the competitive nature of

Efficient Logistics • http://dx.doi.org/10.1596/978-1-4648-0103-7

Table 2.9 Linehaul Services[20] Calling at Cai Mep-Thi Vai as of September 2012

Operator	Service	Vessels used	Port rotation
MOL	CHS 3 Intra-Asia	4 × 4,200–4,400 TEUs	Cai Mep, Hong Kong SAR, China, Osaka, Kobe, Yokkaichi, Yokohama, Tokyo, Hong Kong, Singapore, Port Klang, Jakarta, Port Kelang, Singapore, Cai Mep
MOL/ Evergreen	SVS/AUE 3 FE-USEC	10 × 4,700–6,300 TEUs	Cai Mep, Hong Kong SAR, China, Yantian, Singapore, (Suez), Algeciras, Norfolk, Savannah, Jacksonville, Charleston, Algeciras, (Suez), Singapore, Cai Mep
Grand Alliance	AEX FE-USEC	10 × 5,300–5,900 TEUs	Cai Mep, Laem Chabang, Singapore, Colombo, Cagliari, Halifax, New York, Savannah, Norfolk, New York, Halifax, Cagliari, Jeddah, Colombo, Singapore, Cai Mep
New World Alliance	PSX FE-USEC	8 × 6,300–6,700 TEUs	Cai Mep, Hong Kong SAR, China, Yantian, Los Angeles, Oakland, Seattle, Vancouver, Tokyo, Yantian, Hong Kong, Laem Chabang, Cai Mep
G 6	Loop 1 FE-N Eur	11 × 8,100–9,000 TEUs	Cai Mep, Singapore, Jeddah, Rotterdam, Hamburg, Southampton, Le Havre, Singapore, Hong Kong, Kobe, Nagoya, Shimizu, Tokyo, Hong Kong SAR, China, Cai Mep
CKYH	AWE4 FE-USEC	9 × 5,600–6,600 TEUs	Cai Mep, Shekou, Hong Kong SAR, China, Yantian, Singapore, (Suez), New York, Norfolk, Savannah, (Suez), Singapore, Cai Mep
CKYH	PSI FE-USWC	13 × 5,300–5,700 TEUs	Cai Mep, Hong Kong SAR, China, Yantian, Ningbo, Long Beach, Oakland, Busan, Shanghai, Ningbo, Hong Kong, Yantian, Singapore, Port Said, Naples, La Spezia, Livorno, Port Said, Singapore, Cai Mep
Maersk	TP-6 FE-USWC	15 × 9,500–9,700 TEUs	Cai Mep, Nansha, Yantian, Hong Kong SAR, China, Los Angeles, Vostochny, Ningbo, Shanghai, Xiamen, Yantian, Tanjung Pelepas, Algeciras, Bremerhaven, Bremerhaven, Hamburg, Felixstowe, Le Havre, Tangier, Salalah, Tanjung Pelepas, Cai Mep

Source: Liner Research Services.
Note: TEU = 20-foot equivalent unit container.

ocean rate negotiations, ocean carriers are not always fully compensated for their operating costs. On the other hand, ocean carriers incur lower slot costs on mother vessels (such as those calling Cai Mep-Thi Vai) compared with feeder vessels, and this lower slot cost may cover the barge expense.

Aligning Demand and Supply at Northern Ports

Demand-supply mismatches in container port handling capacity could also arise in the northern region (both over- and undersupply), with the concurrent development of new port projects at Dinh Vu, Cai Lan and Lach Huyen (see table 2.10). To properly mitigate this risk, the GoV will need to regulate development of new capacity in Northern Vietnam to ensure that demand and supply are reasonably matched.

Assuming that container volumes grow at the projected 8.5–9.0 percent in the 2011–20 period, existing terminal capacity in the northern region will be insufficient to meet market demand by 2018 (see figure 2.9). Specifically, demand at the northern region ports is expected to reach 5–6 million TEUs by 2020, up from about 2.7 million TEUs in 2011. Existing capacity of 4.8 million TEUs would be reached by 2018. Even with additional capacity from two new

Table 2.10 Current and Expected Terminals in Northern Vietnam: Haiphong, Dinh Vu, Cai Lan, and Lach Huyen

Haiphong terminals	Hoang Dieu	Nam Hai	Doanxa	Transvina	Green Port	Chua Ve
Operator	Haiphong Port	Gemadept	Doanxa Port	Transvina	Viconship	Haiphong Port
Length (m)	413	144	220	169	320	895
Number of berths	3	1	1	1	2	5
CY yard (ha)	14	7	8	5	10	20
Draft (m)	8.4	8.4	8.4	7.8	7.8	8.5
Shore cranes	3	2	3	2	5	5
Gantry cranes	0	0	0	0	0	6
TEU (2011)	176,000	200,000	227,439	127,061	330,000	551,003
Capacity (TEU)	200,000	200,000	250,000	200,000	400,000	800,000
Utilization %	88	100	91	64	83	69

Dinh Vu terminals	SNP 189	Hai An	PTSC	Dinh Vu	Tan Cang	Nam Hai Dinh Vu	Vinashin DV
Operator	SNP	Marina Hanoi	PTSC	Dinh Vu Port JSC	Haiphong Port	Gemadept/ VIPCO	Vinalines
Length (m)	230	150	250	425	980	450	630
Number of berths	1	1	1	3	5	3	4
CY Yard (ha)	11.7	15	13	24	30	15	21
Draft (m)	8.5	8.5	8.5	8.7	9	9	9
Shore cranes	1	2	2	5	6	4	—
Gantry cranes	2	0	0	2	2	0	—
TEU (2011)	From August 12	100,000	76,475	439,649	291,000	From 2013	From 2014
Capacity(TEU)	200,000	200,000	200,000	500,000	800,000	300,000	500,000
Utilization %		50	38	88	36		

Cai Lan terminals	CICT	Quang Ninh
Operator	SSA	Vinalines
Length (m)	594	680
Number of berths	3	3
CY yard (ha)	18	14
Draft (m)	13	13
Shore cranes	0	0
Gantry cranes	4	2
TEU (2011)	From September 2012	143,981
Capacity (TEU)	500,000	250,000
Utilization %		58

table continues next page

Efficient Logistics • http://dx.doi.org/10.1596/978-1-4648-0103-7

Table 2.10 Current and Expected Terminals in Northern Vietnam: Haiphong, Dinh Vu, Cai Lan, and Lach Huyen *(continued)*

Lach Huyen terminals	Lach Huyen Phase 1	Lach Huyen Phase 2
Operator	MOLNYKIT/ Vinalines	TBD
Length (m)	750	Up to 2,100
No. of berths	2	Up to 9
CY yard (ha)	45	Up to 200
Draft (m)	14	14
Shore cranes	0	—
Gantry cranes	—	—
TEU (2011)	From 2016	—
Capacity	1,000,000	—

Source: Authors based on Vietnam Port Association and interviews with port operators.
Note: — = not available. TEU = 20-foot equivalent unit container.

Figure 2.9 Vietnam: Demand-Supply at Northern Ports without Lach Huyen

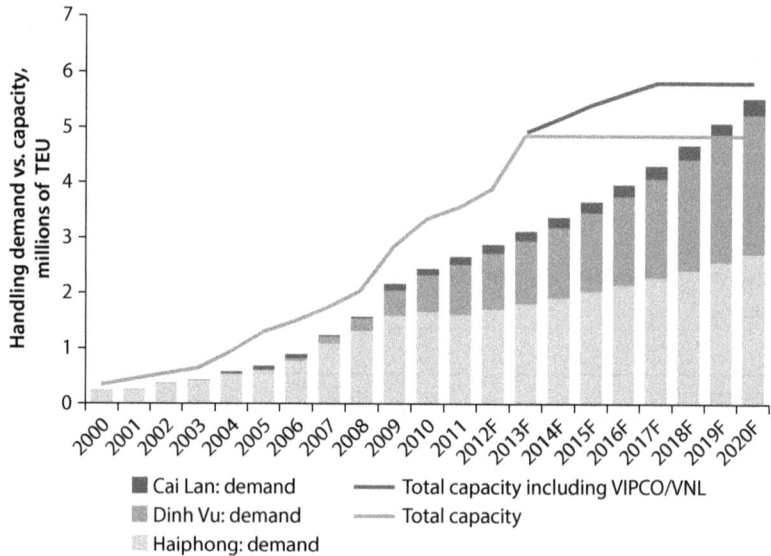

Source: Vietnam Port Association, interviews with port operators, and Liner Research Services.
Note: TEU = 20-foot equivalent unit container; F = forecast.

terminals planned in Dinh Vu, which would raise total capacity to 5.8 million TEUs, the terminals are still expected to reach full capacity by 2020.

In addition to potentially running out of capacity in the medium term, there is a strong case to be made that the northern region is already underserved with regard to container port handling services. Haiphong is the only port in the world today that combines annual handling volumes of over 2.5 million TEUs with draft limits of less than 9 meters. There is a need for a deep-water port in

Northern Vietnam to cater to the growth in market volumes as well as the global trend toward the use of larger containerships.

The 2016 planned opening of Lach Huyen, a deep-water port facility to be located in the Haiphong area, could bring about immediate benefits by allowing vessels of between 2,000 and 8,000 TEUs to call at Northern Vietnam for the first time. Unit costs per TEU for such ships are significantly lower than those for existing ships, which could result in savings of up to 60 percent for ocean carriers. The expected cost savings from the elimination of feeder and transshipment costs for Haiphong cargo is estimated at an additional $100–200 per TEU, with much of the cost savings expected to be passed on to BCOs.

A recent JETRO (2012) survey of transport costs in Asian countries between 2006 and 2011 showed that the cost of shipping a container from Vietnam to Yokohama was between $50 and $485 per FEU higher when originated at Haiphong compared with HCMC (see figure 2.10). Similarly, a shipment from Vietnam to Los Angeles was between $400 and 1,500 per FEU higher when Haiphong rather than HCMC was the origin. Although freight differentials are due to numerous factors, including container imbalance, frequency of sailings, competition among carriers, and seasonal fluctuations, part of the reason for the higher rates out of Haiphong was the higher costs of transshipment and the use of less efficient vessels of below 1,200 TEUs.

Figure 2.10 Comparison of Ocean Freight Rates to Japan and the United States, 2006–11

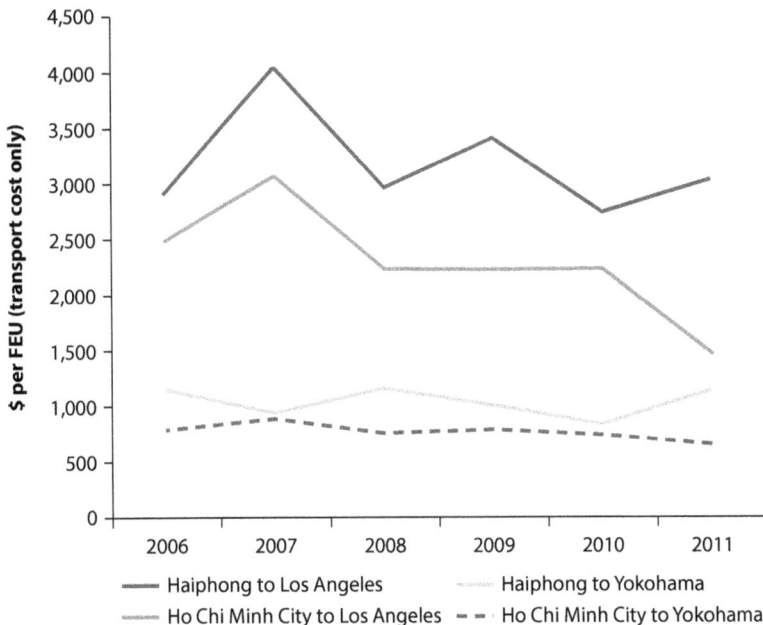

Source: JETRO 2012.
Note: FEU = 40-foot equivalent unit container.

Figure 2.11 Haiphong/Cai Lan Port Utilization Rates by Terminal, 2010–20

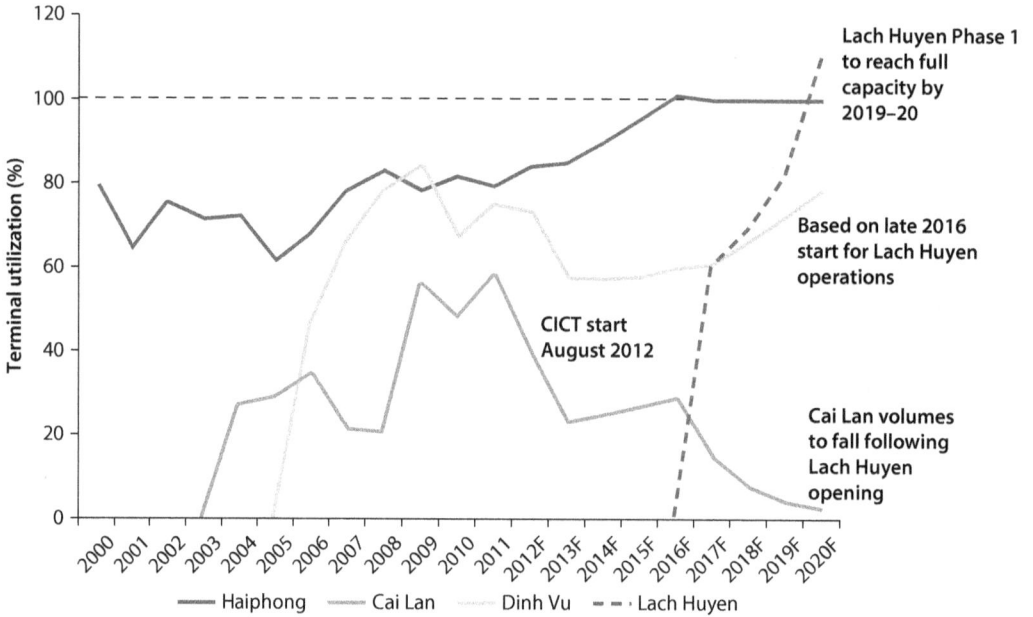

Source: Authors based on input from Vietnam Port Association, interviews with port operators, and Liner Research Services.
Note: F = forecast.

Due to the benefits of deploying larger vessels in Northern Vietnam, the utilization of Lach Huyen is expected to be high (see figure 2.11), with all vessels of above 1,200 TEUs expected to call at Lach Huyen. Even though there are vessels of between 1,200 and 1,500 TEUs currently calling at Dinh Vu, these vessels are generally not fully laden because of channel draft restrictions.

Based on the planned launch of Lach Huyen in 2016, volumes at the port are expected to reach full capacity (of about one million TEUs) within four years (see figure 2.12). This would require the early planning for the development of Lach Huyen Phase 2 to meet the potential demand after 2020 in conjunction with plans to manage overall regional capacity.

What is more, managing overall regional capacity will also be necessary in the context of Lach Huyen's Phase 1. As shown in figure 2.11, the launch of Lach Huyen would have an adverse impact on other terminals, particularly those at Dinh Vu and Cai Lan. Portions of the capacity at the latter terminals (and in the case of Cai Lan, likely most of it) will be rendered redundant.

That the oversupply threat is most apparent in Cai Lan can be seen in the port's operating history to date. Opened in 2004, Cai Lan port has so far failed to capture significant container volumes. After eight years of operations, Cai Lan has been able only to attract two weekly calls, and the volumes handled are only 6 percent of total volumes at Haiphong and Dinh Vu. About 80 percent of the containers handled at Cai Lan are barged to Haiphong, because of BCOs' preference to receive and deliver containers at Haiphong terminals—despite Cai Lan's

Figure 2.12 Vietnam: Demand and Supply at Northern Region Ports, 2000–20

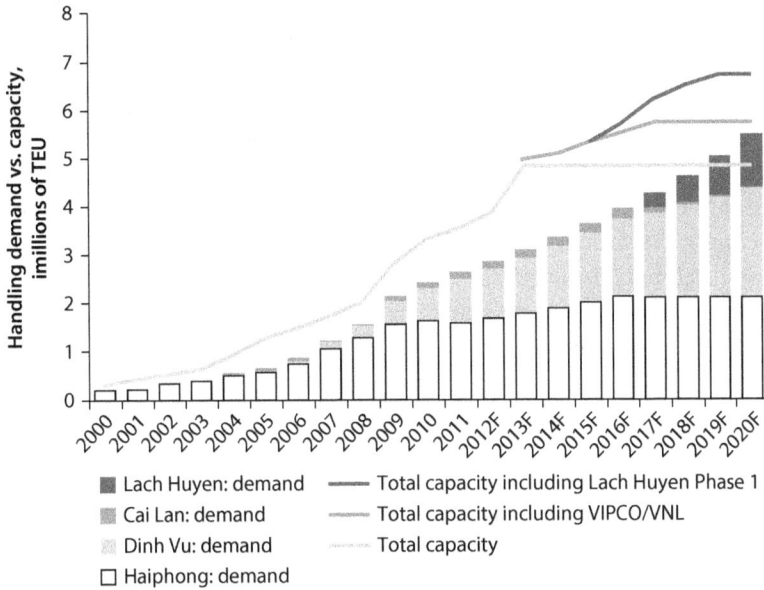

Legend:
- ■ Lach Huyen: demand — Total capacity including Lach Huyen Phase 1
- ▨ Cai Lan: demand — Total capacity including VIPCO/VNL
- ▨ Dinh Vu: demand — Total capacity
- ☐ Haiphong: demand

Source: Authors based on input from Vietnam Port Association, interviews with port operators, and Liner Research Services.
Note: TEU = 20-foot equivalent unit container. F = forecast.

Figure 2.13 Average Container Vessel Sizes Calling Haiphong and Cai Lan, September 2012

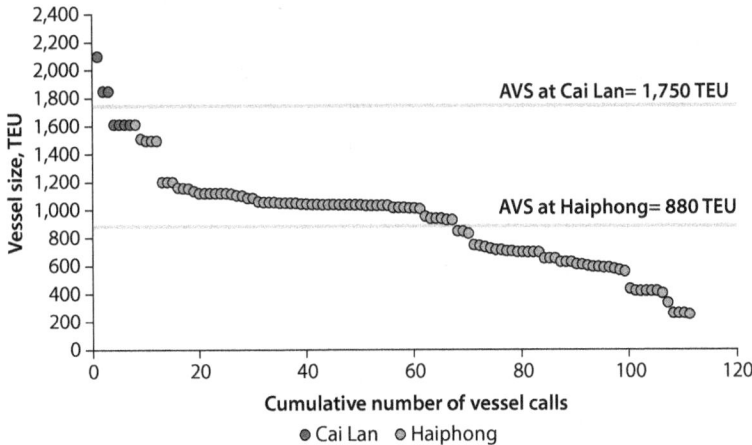

AVS at Cai Lan= 1,750 TEU

AVS at Haiphong= 880 TEU

Cumulative number of vessel calls

● Cai Lan   ○ Haiphong

Source: Vietnam Port Authority and Linear Research Services.
Note: TEU = 20-foot equivalent unit container; AVS = Average vessel size.

current ability to receive ships of up to 3,000 TEUs, modest by global standards but still significantly higher than what Haiphong is able to accommodate at present (see figure 2.13). BCOs' preference for Haiphong stems from the latter port's perceived infrastructure advantage (not only in terms of physical infrastructure, but also with respect to Haiphong's ready availability of shipping agents, customs clearance facilities, warehouses, Inland Container Depots [ICDs], and trucking companies), as well as the existence of truck weight limits on the Cai Lan-Hanoi National Highway 18.

Despite weak demand at Cai Lan, a second terminal—CICT, a joint venture between Vinalines and SSA—was launched in August 2012. This added a further 500,000 TEUs of annual handling capacity to the existing 250,000 TEUs at Quang Ninh port. The total volume at Cai Lan was only 143,981 TEUs in 2011 (based on vessel moves only, excluding barge moves to avoid double counting), with expected terminal utilization at only about 20 percent.

The development of gateways at Cai Lan, Dinh Vu, and Lach Huyen in close succession and the excess capacity risk this generates is another example of resource waste in the country's port planning system, and one that closely resembles the case of Southern Vietnamese ports.

Ignoring the Potential for Transshipment at Cai Mep-Thi Vai

The GoV has not provided incentives to the MTOs at Cai Mep-Thi Vai to cater to both domestic transshipment cargo (from Northern and Central Vietnam) and international transshipment cargo (mainly from Cambodia), despite a clear demand for such moves.

In particular, specific calls have been made to address the following issues by ocean carriers and terminal operators:

• Cabotage rules limit the ability of foreign flag carriers to carry containers between Vietnamese ports, including international cargo bound for other countries. The removal of this rule would promote the use of Cai Mep-Thi Vai as a transshipment hub for cargo to and from Central and Northern Vietnam. Current Vietnamese flag carriers operating on the domestic sector are not able to handle such volumes, while existing Central and Northern Vietnam cargo bound for Europe and the United States is currently transshipped in third-country hubs.

• The fragmentation of, and lack of interterminal connectivity between, the various terminals at Cai Mep-Thi Vai inhibit the growth of transshipment volumes, as terminals lack sufficient scale and volume, while feeders would have to call at multiple terminals to cater to multiple linehaul services.

• Circular 164/2010/TT-BTC and Circular 41/2012/TT-BTC provide for a 40 percent discount on tonnage dues and 50 percent discount on pilotage for vessels above 50,000 GT (about 4,000 TEUs) calling at the port of Cai Mep-Thi Vai. There are calls for the GoV to provide additional incentives for vessels to service Cai Mep-Thi Vai, including for vessels between 25,000 and 50,000 GT (2,000–4,000 TEUs), which are currently unable to call at HCMC ports, and vessels above 90,000 GT (above 8,000 TEUs), which are now the primary vessels used in the Far East–Europe trade (and increasingly in the Transpacific).

• Navigation of containerships of above 80,000 deadweight tons (DWT) (about 7,000 TEUs) to ports in the Cai Mep-Thi Vai area continue to require ad hoc berthing approvals from local authorities each time they berth, despite the fact that ships of up to 160,000 DWT (14,000 TEUs) have already berthed at the port.

• GoV-imposed restrictions on Cambodian-bound containers for the imports of used machinery and automobiles have limited the use of Vietnamese ports for Cambodian cargo.

Insufficient Landside and Other Supporting Infrastructure

The development of new port facilities in Vietnam has not been accompanied by the concurrent and timely development of appropriate land-side infrastructure to support the movement of container volumes at the ports. This is partly a result of the fragmented state of the current port network, which places a significant strain on local and national infrastructure development resources. Problems relating to land clearance, disbursement of funds, and investment procurement are the most commonly cited reasons for the slow development of many key road subsector infrastructure projects.

Among the most urgent road infrastructure bottlenecks relating to the current port network are the following:

• Northern and Central Regions
  – Dinh Vu road connections to Haiphong City and NH 5, with part of the road currently still unpaved and highly congested. In particular, heavy congestion is reported at the intersection of Nguyen Binh Khiem-Le Thanh Tong-Dinh Vu.
  – NH 18 connecting Cai Lan port to Hanoi. Although improvements to the highway have been made, truck weight limits have continued to divert a significant part of Cai Lan's container traffic to Haiphong via barges.
  – Hinterland connections to Tien Sa Port in Danang.
• Southern Region
  – Congestion on the HCMC-Hanoi NH 1 to the NH 51 junction. Although NH 51 is being widened, there are inadequate intersections and too many pedestrians and motorbikes crossing the highway at random locations due to the lack of proper intersections. Several sections remain incomplete, with damage already starting to show.
  – Interprovincial road 25B to Cat Lai port in HCMC.
  – Lack of road connections to the new Phu Huu port complex, where the construction of the first terminal was completed in July 2010. The port requires a connecting road between Phu Huu Port and Nguyen Duy Trinh Road and expansion of Nguyen Duy Trinh Road to accommodate container truck traffic.
  – The road to the new Phu My Bridge[21] in HCMC is a combination of dirt and substandard paving and has not been upgraded to be consistent with the bridge construction.
  – Construction of Road D3 linking the Saigon Port–Hiep Phuoc terminal new port to Hiep Phuoc Industrial Park. Roads to the Hiep Phuoc industrial

zone, including Saigon Premier Container Terminal (SPCT), remain unfinished despite the launch of the terminal in 2009.

- Road 965 linking National Road 51 to Cai Mep-Thi Vai port and the Cai Mep-Thi Vai interterminal. Although the first terminal at Cai Mep-Thi Vai began operations in 2009, the road connections to the terminals are still incomplete.

In addition, the Vietnam Port Authority (VPA) has also highlighted the need to ensure the timely completion of the channel components for the ports under construction or investment, specifically the following issues.

Channel Access

There is a general need to dredge the channels leading to Haiphong Port; ports in the central area including the ports of Cua Lo, Quang Binh, Thuan An, Danang, and Quinhon; and to Cat Lai, Hiep Phuoc, and Can Tho Port in the south of the country, all of which remain inadequate.

For the channel to the Cai Mep-Thi Vai area in particular, the VPA has called for its timely upgrading to accommodate the use of larger vessels of above 80,000 DWT. There have been repeated calls for the GoV to consider the revision of the master plan to have the channel dredged deeper for large container vessels of more than 100,000 DWT to call the ports in this area, in order to develop Cai Mep-Thi Vai into an internationally competitive port.

In addition, the VPA has drawn attention to two more channel access issues in the southern region:

- For the channel on the Hau River, there is a need to continue dredging the existing channel to maintain the navigability at least as before while waiting for the implementation of the new channel via the Quan Chanh Bo Canal.
- For the Soai Rap channel to the Hiep Phuoc area, the VPA has also called for a solution to dredge up to the master plan and as committed with the investors in port and port urban projects in this area.

Facilitation of Night Navigation

The VPA has called for the addition of safety measures such as navigational aids, lighting, and dredging to ease current restrictions on night time navigation and improve navigation flow, in particular to the ports in the Haiphong and HCMC areas.

Unsustainable Financing Framework for Port Infrastructure

The GoV has relied primarily on the state-owned Vinalines as the main domestic investor for the country's main port projects (see table 2.11).

Vinalines's involvement in numerous port projects has resulted in several challenges. For example:

- It has strained Vinalines's limited financial resources, with losses at several of the new terminal projects, imposing a significant financial burden on

Table 2.11 Vinalines' Shareholdings of Main Vietnamese Ports and Planned Projects

Port	Location	Vinalines share (%)
Quang Ninh Port	Cai Lan	100
Cai Lan International Container Terminal (CICT)	Cai Lan	51
Doan Xa Port	Haiphong	51
Haiphong Port	Haiphong	100
Vinalines Dinh Vu Port	Dinh Vu	60.3
Lach Huyen (HPCT)	Lach Huyen	51
Danang Port	Danang	100
Nha Trang Port	Nha Trang	100
Van Phong (project suspended)	Van Phong	100
Saigon Port	HCMC	100
Saigon Port-PSA International Port (SP-SSA)	Cai Mep	51
Cai Mep International Terminal (CMIT)	Cai Mep	51
Saigon Port-SSA International Terminal (SSIT)	Cai Mep	51

Source: Authors based on interview with Vinalines.
Note: Vinalines operates other facilities, including Can Tho, Cam Ranh, Cau Cui, Nghe Tinh, and Vat Cach.

the company. According to the State Inspectorate of Vietnam, Vinalines incurred a total loss of VND 252 billion from its joint-venture ports in Cai Mep-Thi Vai in 2007–10. Losses at these ports increased to a reported VND 460 billion in 2011 and are expected to continue to escalate with the current oversupply situation.

• Vinalines's weak financial position has also resulted in delays in the implementation of the Lach Huyen project, where it acts as the project's largest private investor. Vinalines is reported to have defaulted on five loans worth over VND 23.06 trillion and does not have the capacity to raise additional funds to finance the large-scale (and highly strategic) Lach Huyen port project.

• Weak project management and alleged corruption by Vinalines officials (Brummit 2012) have resulted in unnecessary waste of resources, including at the planned Van Phong International Transshipment Port project.

• Vinalines's participation in competing port projects within the same locations (with separate groups of local and foreign partners) raises issues of potential conflicts of interest. For example, Saigon Port competes with the three Vinalines/Saigon Port–invested terminals at Cai Mep (SP-PSA, CMIT, and SSIT), which are direct competitors themselves. Similar governance weaknesses exist in northern ports, where the Haiphong port is in direct competition with the two Vinalines ports at Cai Lan, as well as the planned Vinalines Dinh Vu and Lach Huyen projects.[22]

The current financing framework, substantially centered on a state-owned company that is under significant financial stress with weak governance, does not appear sustainable. Vinalines reported a net loss of VND 1,439 billion in the first half of 2012, in which two notable subsidiaries (Vinashin Lines and Bien Dong, transferred from Vinashin in 2010) incurred a loss of VND 700 billion, while another Vinalines subsidiary, Falcon, recorded a loss of VND 267 billion. Vinalines's balance sheet was not available, but it would likely be difficult for the company to raise significant new capital without government support.

A more sustainable financing framework to support Vietnam's port infrastructure investment requirements needs to be found. This would likely involve greater private sector participation and the lifting of the 49 percent capital investment limit on foreign investors.

Key Impacts of Port Planning Challenges on Logistics Efficiency

The promotion of multiple small ports in both the HCMC-Cai Mep and Haiphong-Cai Lan corridors has made Vietnam the most fragmented container terminal market in the world. It is the only market where each of the top four global port operators—PSA, Hutchison Port Holdings, DP World, and APM Terminals—are engaged in direct competition.

As depicted in map 2.3, there are currently 11 container terminals with annual handling capacity of over 100,000 TEUs in the HCMC-Cai Mep area

Map 2.3 Vietnam: Greater HCMC Main Container Terminals

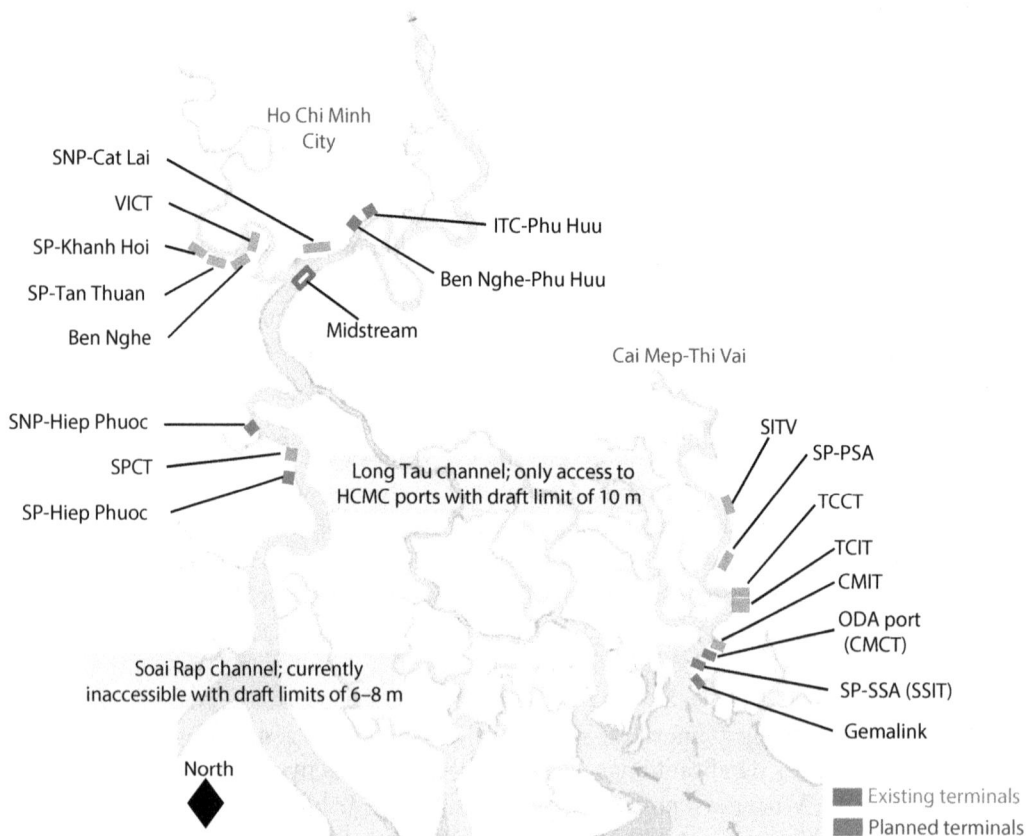

Source: Liner Research Services.

alone, with no fewer than seven more new facilities to be added and whose construction has already started. This does not include various other projects planned at Hiep Phuoc, Cat Lai, Nhon Trach, Nha Be, Long An, Dong Nai, Phuoc An, My Xuan, Lower Cai Mep, and Ben Dinh-Sao Mai. Some of these projects have been stalled with foreign interests, including China Merchants pulling out from its planned investments. Despite this, both the local and central governments continue to promote additional port projects in the face of a chronic oversupply problem.

The majority of the terminals at Cai Mep have average berth lengths of only 300 meters per berth when the ideal length would be 350–400 meters. For a two-berth terminal, this would mean a total berth length of 700–800 meters instead of the current 600 meters. The problem this creates is that if two 350-meter ships arrive at the same time to berth at one terminal, one ship would have to wait away from the dock at anchor even if neighboring terminals are empty. This is the inefficiency created by the fragmented system now in place. The existing terminals are also not connected either by contiguous wharf or direct road links, which hinders the development of these ports as transshipment hubs. The current berth designs could limit transshipment cargo operations, where containers delivered by a feeder vessel cannot be efficiently transferred to a mother vessel due to limited berthing space for both vessels, or with feeder and mother vessels located in different, nonconnected terminals.

A similar fragmentation problem is apparent in the Northern region. There are 12 operational container terminals in Northern Vietnam, including two terminals that were launched in 2012 alone (see map 2.4). Two more terminals are planned in the Dinh Vu area, in addition to the major new port complex planned at Lach Huyen.

The fragmented port system results in significant inefficiencies and wasteful investments, arising primarily from the following:

- Additional land-side infrastructure investments required to connect multiple marine terminals
- Additional dredging and channel maintenance expenses required to facilitate vessel navigation to the various port locations
- Inability to leverage economies of scale at individual terminals, with significant duplication of costs due to congestion at certain terminals and under-utilization of assets in other terminals
- Difficulties in facilitating transshipment volumes, with a lack of interterminal connections
- Dispersion of cargo volumes, prohibiting the development of hub terminals with centralized logistics infrastructure: The system results in the fragmentation of downstream services, including ICDs, empty container depots, bonded and nonbonded warehouses, trucking companies, and customs clearance facilities
- Additional costs to BCOs and ocean carriers arising from the need to maintain multiple cargo drop-off and pick-up points or vessels making multiple port calls within the same location.

Map 2.4 Vietnam: Fragmentation of the Haiphong Port System

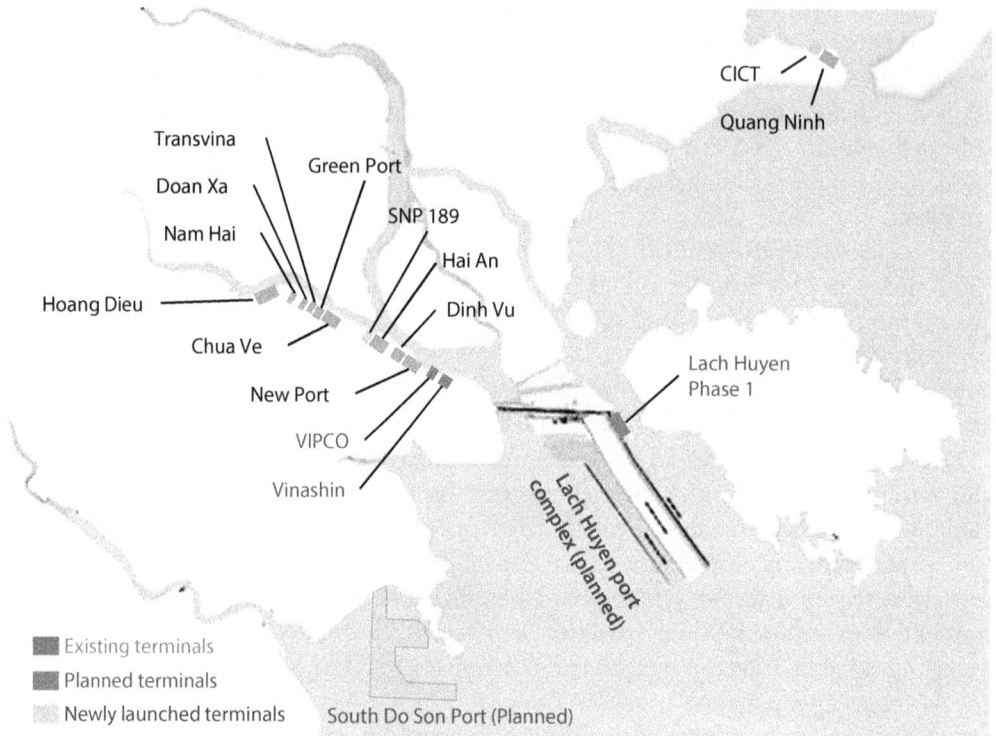

Transvina
Green Port
Doan Xa
SNP 189
Nam Hai
Hai An
Hoang Dieu
Dinh Vu
Chua Ve
New Port
VIPCO
Vinashin
CICT
Quang Ninh
Lach Huyen Phase 1
Lach Huyen port complex (planned)

Existing terminals
Planned terminals
Newly launched terminals   South Do Son Port (Planned)

Source: Liner Research Services.

The fragmentation of the port system in Vietnam is best illustrated when compared against the top 30 ports in the world (see table 2.12). The number of terminals in HCMC/Cai Mep and Haiphong/Cai Lan is higher than those at the world's major ports, while handling significantly lower volumes. In a majority of ports with multiple terminals (e.g., Shanghai, Busan, and Kaohsiung), the terminals are located within designated port zones and do not exhibit the same geographical, administrative, and operational fragmentation as in Vietnam.

Unwise Investment Emphasis: Van Phong

The current seaport Master Plan (2010–20) places particular emphasis on the development of the Van Phong transshipment port project in the South Central Coast region (see map 2.5). The port was originally designed to receive 6,000–9,000 TEU containerships based on a 2007 plan with a VND 1.1 trillion budget. After failing to secure foreign investor interest, the project was assigned to be fully funded by Vinalines, and construction started in October 2009. The budget was continuously adjusted until the total investment increased sixfold to nearly VND 6.2 trillion ($3.6 billion), with the design amended to receive 12,000–15,000 TEU ships.

Table 2.12 Vietnam: Top 30 Global Container Ports in 2011 and Fragmentation of Vietnamese Ports

2011 rank	Port	Country	TEU volume in millions	No. of terminals
1	Shanghai	China	31.7	8
2	Singapore	Singapore	29.9	5
3	Hong Kong SAR	China	24.4	5
4	Shenzhen	China	22.6	5
5	Busan	Korea, Rep.	16.2	11
6	Ningbo-Zhoushan	China	14.7	8
7	Guangzhou Harbor	China	14.3	5
8	Qingdao	China	13.0	4
9	Jebel Ali, Dubai	United Arab Emirates	13.0	1
10	Rotterdam	Netherlands	11.9	5
11	Tianjin	China	11.6	10
12	Kaohsiung	Taiwan	9.6	10
13	Port Klang	Malaysia	9.6	2
14	Hamburg	Germany	9.0	5
15	Antwerp	Belgium	8.7	7
16	Los Angeles	United States	7.9	8
17	Keihin Ports	Japan	7.6	n.a.
18	Tanjung Pelepas	Malaysia	7.5	1
19	Xiamen	China	6.5	6
20	Dalian	China	6.4	3
21	Long Beach	United States	6.1	6
22	Bremen-Bremerhaven	Germany	5.9	4
23	Laem Chabang	Thailand	5.7	7
24	Tanjung Priok	Indonesia	5.6	6
25	New York–New Jersey	United States	5.5	6
26	Lainyungung	China	4.9	1
27	Hanshin Ports	Japan	4.8	3
28	Suzhou	China	4.7	n.a.
29	Ho Chi Minh Cai Mep-Thi Vai	Vietnam	4.5	11 in 2011 18 by 2015
30	Jawaharlal Nehru	India	4.3	3
50+	Haiphong Cai Lan	Vietnam	2.7	10 in 2011 15 by 2016

Source: Compiled by authors with data from Journal of Commerce and Liner Research Services.
Note: n.a. = not available; TEU = 20-foot equivalent unit container.

The Van Phong project has been divided into four phases:

Phase 1: Two berths with a total length of 690 meters (41.5 hectares) by 2013, total capacity 710,000 TEUs/year

Phase 2: Nine berths with a total length of 2,260 meters (125 hectare) by 2015; total capacity 2.1 million TEUs/year

Phase 3: Sixteen berths with a total length of 5,170 meters (405 hectares) by 2020, total capacity 4.5 million TEUs/year and

Phase 4: Thirty-seven berths with a total length of 12,590 meters (750 hectares) after 2020, total capacity 17 million TEUs/year.

Map 2.5 Location of Van Phong in Vietnam's Main-Port Network

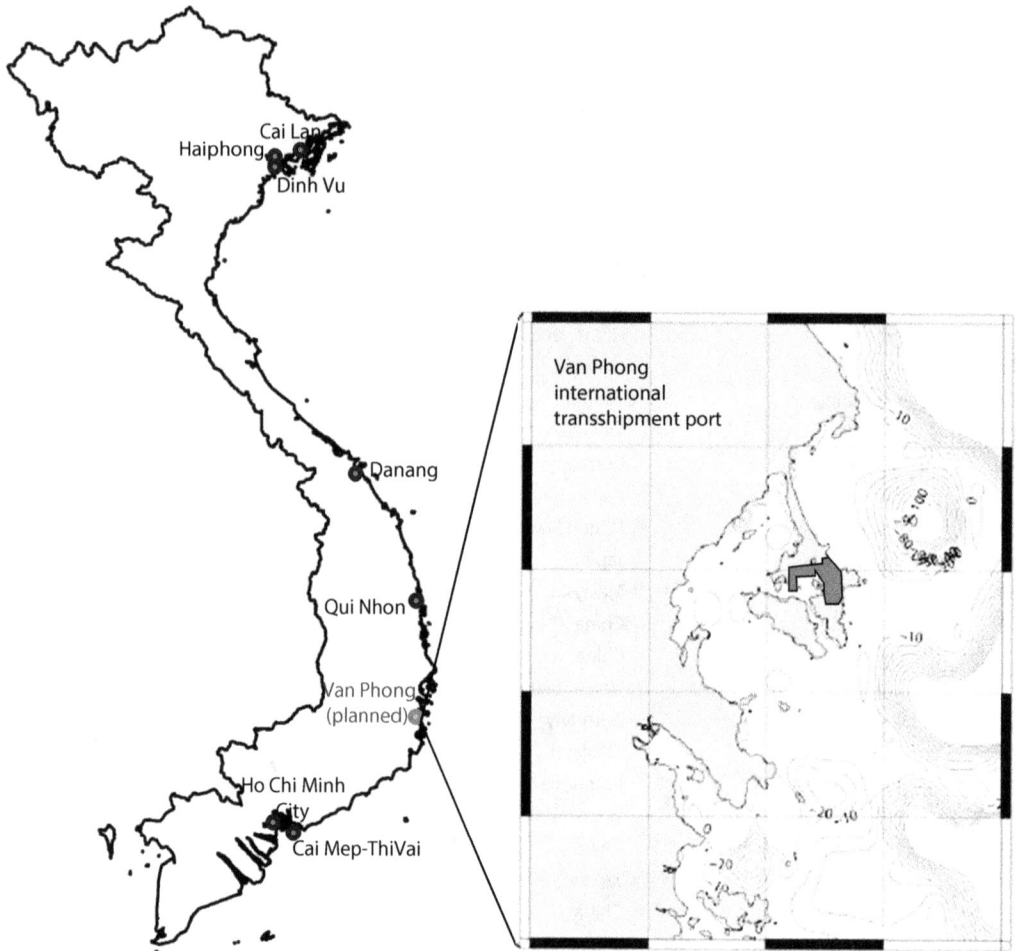

Source: Liner Research Services.

The project has weak economic justification and holds limited potential to develop into a major container hub. The investment premise for the port was based on mistaken assumptions that large containerships serving intercontinental routes to Europe and the United States can be enticed to call at a deep-water port along the central Vietnam coast where Van Phong is located.

Although Van Phong Bay offers natural water depths of up to 20 meters, the conditions for Van Phong to develop into a container transshipment hub are not present for the following reasons:

1. The development of Cai Mep-Thi Vai in the South of Vietnam and the planned development of Lach Huyen in the North of Vietnam negate the need for a transshipment hub for Vietnamese cargo. Direct linehaul services to both

Efficient Logistics • http://dx.doi.org/10.1596/978-1-4648-0103-7

Europe and the United States are already calling at Cai Mep and are also expected to call at Lach Huyen when the port is ready.

2. There is limited cargo potential in the central Vietnam region, with total throughput of container volumes in the Central region accounting for only 3 percent of total Vietnamese container volumes (or 219,000 TEUs) in 2011. Future transshipment of Central Vietnam cargo is better served through existing ports.

3. Apart from the limited cargo potential of Central Vietnam, Van Phong offers no other natural cargo catchment for international transshipment for cargo to and from the main gateway ports of Cambodia, Indonesia, Malaysia, the Philippines, Singapore, and Thailand, with a longer sailing distance required compared with existing transshipment hubs (see table 2.13).

Other than Muara in Brunei, Van Phong is situated further from the hub ports of Singapore, Tanjung Pelepas, Port Klang, Kaohsiung, Hong Kong SAR, China, and Shenzhen, which would be its main competitors for regional transshipment cargo. Even for Cambodian cargo, which is the closest gateway origin or destination for Van Phong, the existing facilities at Cai Mep offer a more attractive option for cargo for Sihanoukville and Phnom Penh.

Apart from geographical limitations, cargo flows are limited between ports in East Malaysia, Brunei, or southern Philippines and Vietnam, and these ports are better served by existing connections to Malaysian and Singapore hubs.

After continuous delays to the planned construction schedule, the GoV formally suspended the Van Phong project in September 2012. However, construction had already stopped since August 2011, after initial piling works had been completed by a Korean contractor at a cost of VND 146 billion.

Table 2.13 Distance from Main Southeast Asia Gateway Ports to Van Phong

Distance in nautical miles	TEUs (2011) (millions)	Distance to Van Phong	Distance to nearest hub
Jakarta	5.6	1,132	629 (Singapore)
Manila	3.4	699	610 (Kaohsiung)
Surabaya	2.7	1,284	758 (Singapore)
Bangkok	2.0	885	848 (Singapore)
Penang	1.2	1,202	245 (Port Klang)
Belawan	1.2	1,134	167 (Port Klang)
Pasir Gudang	0.8	783	46 (Singapore)
Davao	0.7	1,199	1,166 (Kaohsiung)
Semarang	0.4	1,191	670 (Singapore)
Kota Kinabalu and Sabah	0.4	559	785 (Singapore)
Kuching	0.2	666	448 (Singapore)
Sihanoukville	0.2	616	424 (Cai Mep)
Muara	0.1	562	740 (Singapore)

Source: Liner Research Services.
Note: TEU = 20-foot equivalent unit container.

Efficient Logistics • http://dx.doi.org/10.1596/978-1-4648-0103-7

The suspension came at the request of the MoT, because of Vinalines's financial difficulties. Despite this, the GoV continues to emphasize the development of the port at Van Phong, with the MoT directing the Vietnam Maritime Administration (Vinamarine) and local provincial authorities in Khanh Hoa to set up plans to call for domestic and foreign investments in the construction of the port.

Airports

Two Vietnamese airports handle cargo for international markets: Tan Son Nhat Airport (TSNA) in HCMC and Noi Bai Airport (NBA) in Hanoi. A third facility, Long Thanh Airport, is under construction in HCMC, with a completion date scheduled for 2015. However, LSPs interviewed believe it will be delayed to 2020 and that foreign companies should be allowed to participate in the construction to minimize further delays.

TSNA has two cargo terminals. Tan Son Nhat Cargo Services (TCS), the oldest of the two, is owned in joint venture by three partners: Vietnam Airlines, Vietnam's national air carrier and a state-owned enterprise (SOE) of the Ministry of Defense; Singapore Airport Terminal Services Ltd., the ground handling agent; and Southern Airports Services Company Ltd. BCOs and LSPs consider TCS to be crowded and inefficient with cargo-handling equipment that is substandard relative to other Asian countries. All air carriers utilize this terminal.

The other terminal, Saigon Cargo Service Corporation (SCSC), was established by four groups of investors in April 2008: Southern Airport Corporation, 25 percent; Gemadept Corporation, 23 percent; the Vietnamese military, 24 percent; and ACB, 28 percent. This terminal is more modern and efficient and has sufficient capacity. However, to reduce competition, Vietnam Airlines has applied pressure to air carriers to focus their operations at TCS, which makes air carriers reluctant to sign agreements with SCSC.

The terminal at NBA is also owned by Vietnam Airlines, and the operating environment is similar as at TSNA's TCS. The ground handling agent is Noi Bai Cargo Terminal Services, JSC, a subsidiary of Vietnam Airlines.

In general, LSPs view the skill level of air cargo terminal operator workers as low, which results in delays, cargo damage, and increased costs for LSPs and BCOs. Security is also lax.

LSPs reported during interviews that if TSNA's TCS and NBA terminals were owned and operated by private companies rather than SOEs, Vietnam's airports would be more competitive with comparable countries. LSPs estimated that their logistics and operating costs could be decreased by approximately 50 percent because private companies would operate air cargo terminals more efficiently.

LSPs are not permitted to engage in cargo consolidation activities at airports. All loading is done by the terminal operators. It would be beneficial for LSPs to be allocated space and be allowed to load build-up pallets at airports so that light and dense cargo could be combined for better pallet utilization. This would allow LSPs to offer their customers more competitive rates.

Air carriers offer a limited number of regularly scheduled air freighter services at TSNA and NBA. Most freighters serve the airports on an ad hoc basis, and since all aircraft stop in the Middle East, Korea, Singapore, or Taiwan, capacity in Vietnam is often tight, particularly at the end of the month. As a result, much air cargo moves in the underbellies of passenger aircraft, but this capacity is limited. Since the decision to move orders as airfreight is usually made by buyers at the last minute, they often have to pay higher rates to move cargo out of Vietnam than from other Asian countries.

Cargo-Handling Facilities and Logistics Parks

The concept of logistics parks—clustering cargo-handling facilities operated by LSPs in an area nearby a port, airport or industrial zone to promote operating efficiencies—is not widely understood or prevalent in Vietnam. Most cargo-handling facilities are developed by the private sector and are standalone warehouses usually located near factories, ports, or airports.

According to LSPs interviewed, the GoV tightly controls issuance of Container Freight Station (CFS) licenses, particularly of bonded facilities, and the rules for applying for licenses are onerous and difficult for LSPs to comprehend.

Most existing facilities are substandard relative to what can be found in other Asian countries. General standards, such as fire protection and security, are low. Many lack full concrete floors and are built with bricks over sand that settles, resulting in uneven floors that can lead to cargo damage. Ventilation is limited, which impacts product quality when cargo is stored for any length of time. The skill level of workers also needs improvement. All these factors reduce LSP efficiency and increase operating costs.

Although some LSPs desire to build and operate their own, modern facilities, land parcels of adequate size are not readily available, so lease arrangements are common.

Central and provincial government authorities do not seem to have reasonable plans for locating cargo-handling facilities where they would be the most effective. According to BCOs and LSPs, the GoV should plan logistics parks in HCMC, Hanoi, Nha Trang, Lam Dong, and the Mekong Delta, and invest in adequate infrastructure like access roads in these areas to make cargo flows smoother.

Strategic Freight Corridors

The concept of strategic freight corridors has proven to be an effective way for government entities around the world to look more holistically at land-side transportation infrastructure. Corridor approaches to improving logistics

Efficient Logistics • http://dx.doi.org/10.1596/978-1-4648-0103-7

performance respond to the fact that most freight shipments move on multiple modes (water, air, truck, and rail) and large land-side infrastructure projects generally pass through numerous jurisdictional boundaries within a freight corridor. For example, the HCMC–Vung Tau Corridor comprises three provinces—Binh Duong, Dong Nai, and Ba Ria-Vung Tau—and the HCMC municipal government. These jurisdictions need to work cooperatively to effectively plan, fund, and implement land-side infrastructure that will be routed through their individual demarcations to deliver the highest benefit for transportation system users, including freight stakeholders. For the purpose of this report, six critical freight corridors have been identified (see map 2.6).

As this report is primarily concerned with containerized freight, emphasis has been placed on those corridors currently handling the highest volume of container flows today and through 2020. As a result, the report zeroes in on the two highest-volume freight corridors: the HCMC–Vung Tau Corridor and the Hanoi-Haiphong Corridor. Less detailed overviews of the rest of the corridors follow overviews of the chosen major corridors.

HCMC–Vung Tau Freight Corridor

This corridor handled 4.8 million TEUs in 2011, and 9.5 million TEUs are projected for 2020. This corridor has 11 primary container-handling marine terminals, including five deep-water terminals and numerous ICDs. These terminals are served by highways and barge service on a major inland waterway system. Presently barges transport about 95 percent of the containers from the HCMC area to the Cai Mep-Thi Vai terminals. The inland waterway system also transports heavy bulk products ranging from food to construction materials. This waterway transportation system is critical to the economic growth in this corridor and the entire Southern Economic Zone.

While significant highway and bridge developments have been made in this corridor over the past 10 years, major unfinished road projects remain. Specifically, plans for additional highways—including ring roads, connector roads, and port access roads—over the next 20 years are as follows:

1. *NH 51:* The expansion from four lanes to six lanes is scheduled to be completed by the end of 2012.
2. *Bien Hoa–Vung Tau Highway (Parallel to NH 51):* Construction is scheduled to commence in early 2013 and planned to be completed at the end of 2017, although these dates are likely to be pushed out. This is expected to be a limited-access, tolled expressway system that will allow heavy container trucks to travel at high speeds to Cai Mep-Thi Vai terminals.
3. *HCMC–Long Thanh–Dau Giay Highway:* Currently under construction, this is a controlled-access, tolled expressway system that will cut travel distances and allow heavy container trucks to travel at higher speeds. It was scheduled to

Map 2.6 Vietnam: Six Primary Freight Corridors

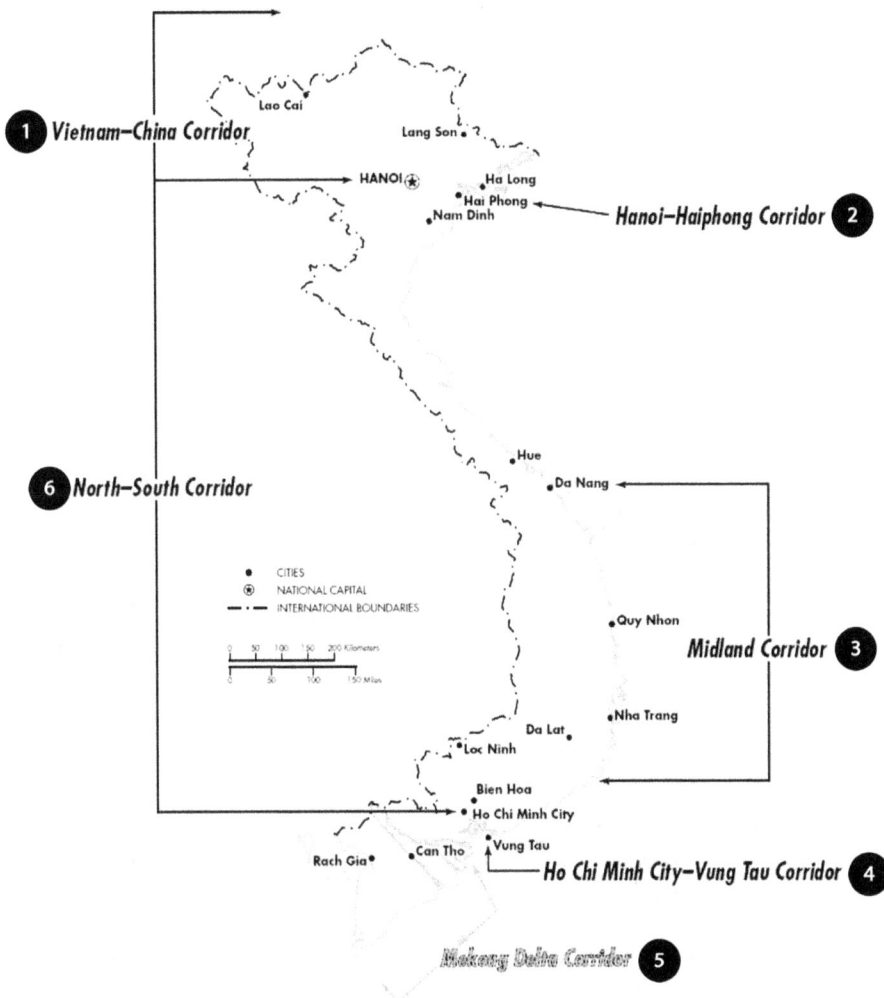

This map was produced by the Map Design Unit of The World Bank. The boundaries, colors, denominations and any other information shown on this map do not imply, on the part of The World Bank Group, any judgment on the legal status of any territory, or any endorsement or acceptance of such boundaries.

Source: Authors.

be completed at the end of 2012. However, this will likely be pushed back to late 2013 or early 2014.

4. *Beltway 2:* Currently under construction, the beltway is scheduled to be completed in late 2014.

5. *Beltway 3:* The construction plan (three phases) was approved by the prime minister in September 2011. Construction has not started. Phase 1 is scheduled to be completed before 2017.

6. *Beltway 4:* The construction plan (five phases) was approved by the prime minister in September 2011. Construction has not started. Phase 1 is scheduled to be completed before 2017.
7. *Cho Tho–HCMC Expressway:* This will complete the expressway network (HCMC–Long Thanh–Dau Giay Highway and HCMC–Trung Luong Expressway [completed]) from Cho Tho to NH 1 north of HCMC.
8. *Long Thanh International Airport:* Construction has not started. Phase 1 is scheduled to be completed and operational in 2020.

Increasing highway and road capacity is critical for the rapidly growing HCMC area. Road congestion in the corridor results from much the same challenges that impact other corridors in the country (and notably the Hanoi-Haiphong corridor): rapidly expanding urbanization, increasing levels of car ownership, higher volumes of freight, a shortage of road capacity, and poorly designed highway and road intersections.

The use of more modern highway design could substantially reduce overall highway congestion and, by extension, logistics costs. Most Vietnamese highways intersect at traffic circles. There are few overpasses or flyovers that allow traffic from one highway system to merge with another highway system to maintain traffic flow. Access roads leading to ports use traffic lights instead of ramps. The municipality of HCMC plans to construct overpass bridges at two major traffic circles on the main highways to industrial areas in Binh Thanh and Dong Nai, and to NH 51 and the Cai Mep-Thi Vai terminals. The implementation of this type of civil works projects should be extended.

Improvements in highway congestion (e.g., through increases in average truck speeds and/or reductions in travel time variability) reduces the transport cost dimension of logistics costs through improvements in trucking operational efficiency. Using information from Vietnamese trucking companies interviewed for this report, it is estimated that annual savings in trucking costs in this corridor can reach $121 million by 2020 if more truck trips per truck per day can be generated through better highway and road designs (see table 2.14). Given the competitive nature of Vietnam's trucking sector, it is expected that most of these savings would be passed on by truck carriers to BCOs.

But the bulk of logistics cost savings to be obtained from less congested highways and more predictable trucking itineraries is associated with inventory

Table 2.14 Truck Cost Savings from Decreasing Congestion in the HCMC Area
Millions of dollars (unless otherwise specified)

Location	2012	2015	2020
HCMC terminals	70.9	84.5	113.0
Percentage barge service to Cai Mep-Thi Vai	95%	90%	90%
Cai Mep-Thi Vai terminals	1.3	4.1	8.2
Total truck cost savings: HCMC/Cai Mep-Thi Vai Port range	72.3	88.5	121.2

Source: Authors. See table A.4 for details.

carrying cost reductions. It is estimated that truck-related congestion on road-ways has an estimated total cost impact[23] of $487 million on the Vietnamese economy (see table 2.15).

The cost of congestion when all motor vehicle highway users are included (i.e., beyond freight trucks), has an estimated cost of $1.7 billion on the Vietnam economy (see table 2.16).

Table 2.15 Estimates for Costs of Truck-Related Congestion in Vietnamese Cities and Regions (2010 Data)

Urban area	Population (million)	GDP[a] (VND trillion)	GDP ($ billion)	Cost of congestion[b] ($ million)	Congestion costs (% of total country)
Whole country	87.8	1,981	104	487	100%
Red River Delta	20.0	475	25	121	25
Of which: Hanoi	6.7	160	8	97	20
Northern Midlands and Mountain Areas	11.3	57	3	8	2
North Central Area and Central Coastal Area	19.0	185	10	19	4
Central Highlands	5.3	15	1	2	0.4
Southeast	14.9	1,050	55	268	55
Of which: HCMC	7.5	399	21	215	44
Mekong River Delta	17.3	199	10	68	14

Source: Authors' estimates. See appendix D for details.
Note: GDP = gross domestic product.
a. General Statistics Office of Vietnam.
b. Cost of congestion is derived from applying GDP factors from comparable U.S. cities. The GDP factor accounts for the value of truck commodities and truck delays and in the U.S. ranges from 0.16% of GDP to 0.47% of GDP.

Table 2.16 Estimates for Total Costs of Congestion (by All Vehicles) in Vietnamese Cities and Regions (2010 Data)

Urban area	Population	GDP[a] (VND trillion)	GDP ($ billion)	Cost of congestion[b] ($ million)	Congestion costs (% of total country)
Whole country	87.8	1,981	104	1,709	100%
Red River Delta	20.0	475	25	426	25
Of which: Hanoi	6.7	160	8	341	20
Northern Midlands and Mountain Areas	11.3	57	3	27	2
North Central Area and Central Coastal Area	19.0	185	10	68	4
Central Highlands	5.3	15	1	7	0.4
Southeast	14.9	1,050	55	942	55
Of which: HCMC	7.5	399	21	753	44
Mekong River Delta	17.3	199	10	239	14

Source: Authors' estimates. See appendix D for details.
Note: GDP = gross domestic product.
a. Vietnam General Statistics Office 2011.
b. Cost of congestion is derived from applying GDP factors from comparable U.S. cities. The values for cities in the U.S. range from 0.76% of GDP to 1.65% of GDP.

Map 2.7 HCMC-Long Thanh-Dau Giay Expressway

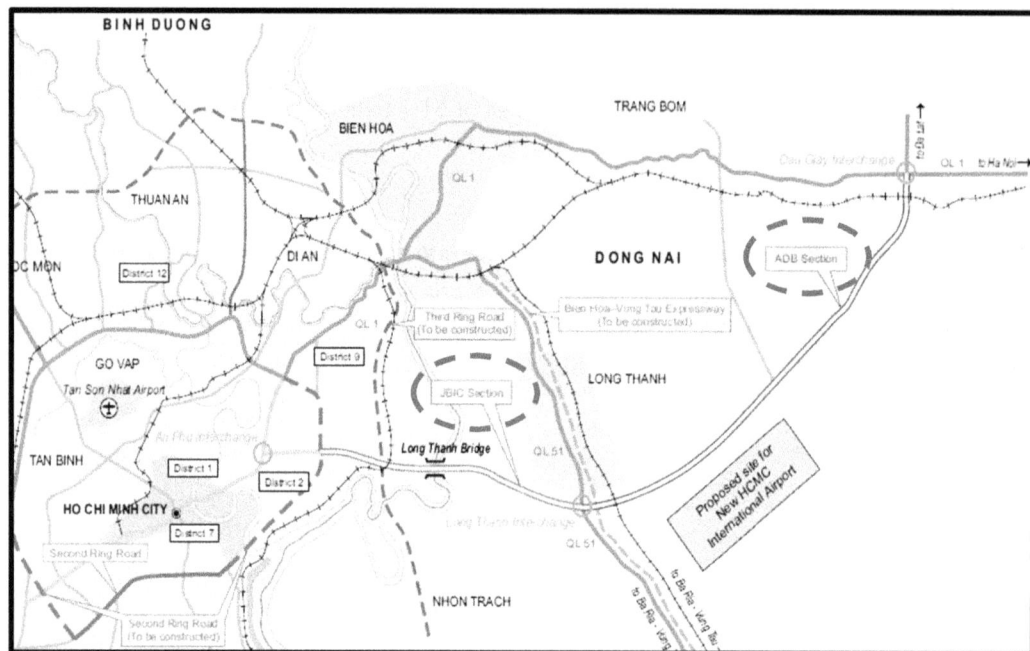

Source: Asian Development Bank.

One of the future key highway developments to improve freight flows in the corridor is the planned HCMC–Dau Giay Expressway. Cofinanced by the Asian Development Bank and the Japan Bank for International Cooperation, it will link the junction of the Second Ring Road in District 9 to the junction of NH 1 at Dau Giay (see map 2.7). The project (1) is scheduled to be completed in early 2014, (2) will eventually serve the new Long Thanh International Airport, and (3) will offer a shorter distance from HCMC to NH 51 and to the Cai Mep-Thi Vai terminals. This project will provide approximately 51 kilometers of four-lane, tolled expressway with only three highway access points. It is unclear whether such access points will be equipped with efficiently designed overpasses and on-off ramps.

Map 2.8 depicts the HCMC–Dau Giay Expressway (represented in green) eventually connecting with the planned Can Tho–HCMC Expressway (shown in magenta and orange), which has yet to be approved. This highway would help expedite the shipments of two of Vietnam's largest export commodities—rice and seafood—to the HCMC and Cai Mep-Thi Vai terminals.

During the planning and construction of Cai Mep-Thi Vai, the expansion of NH 51 and access roads to the Cai Mep-Thi Vai terminals was a critical part of this corridor's planned multimodal improvements. Today it serves as a good example of a poorly executed multimodal strategy. The first Cai

Map 2.8 HCMC-Long Thanh-Dau Giay Expressway Link to Can Tho

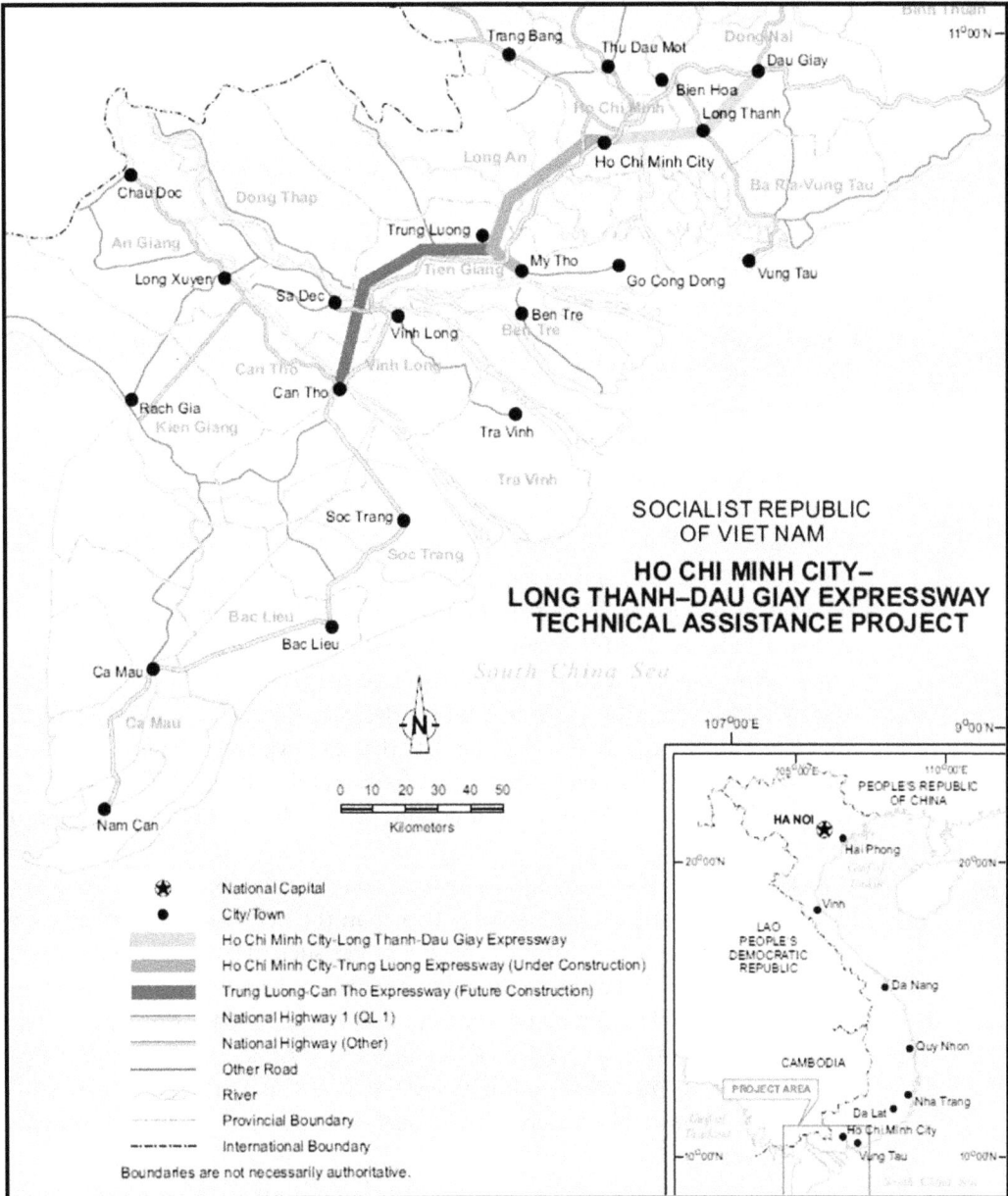

Source: Asian Development Bank.

Mep-Thi Vai marine terminal was open in 2009, and yet the planned expansion of NH 51[24] to three lanes for freight and vehicles and a separate lane for motorcycles in each direction was not expected to be completed until the end of 2012, as was the access Road 965[25] from NH 51 to the Cai Mep-Thi Vai terminals.

Because of the continued excess capacity in HCMC terminals, and especially the Cai Mep-Thi Vai terminals, the current plans to develop the new Bien Hoa–Vung Tau Expressway as a parallel structure to NH 51 (see map 2.7) will likely not be needed by 2020 to handle the expected landside transport of containers to Cai Mep-Thi Vai. That is because barge service is expected to continue handling between 80 and 90 percent of all containers transported between HCMC and Cai Mep-Thi Vai through the year 2020,[26] primarily because the cost of barging containers to and from Cai Mep-Thi Vai is one-third the cost of trucking (which is generally paid by the ocean carriers and is not a direct pass-through cost to BCOs). It is estimated that there were 80 truck trips per day to transport containers to and from Cai Mep-Thi Vai in 2012, and that this will climb to approximately 500 trips per day in 2020 (see table 2.17).

As stated in interviews with Cai Mep-Thi Vai terminal operators, barge service is not expected to interfere with mother vessel berthing operations until these terminals' overall utilization approaches 70 percent. Assuming SSIT, CMCT, and Gemalink Phase 1 (see table 2.8) are operational by 2020, the combined capacity at Cai Mep-Thi Vai would be 8 million TEUs, and 70 percent of that number would bring total demand to 5.6 million TEUs. If the projected demand level is 1.5 million TEUs by 2015 (see figure 2.7), the 5.6 million TEUs could be achieved only by 2020 if annual demand was to grow by 31 percent per year, which seems unrealistic. It is on this basis that barge service will likely continue to handle the majority of the containers transiting between HCMC and Cai Mep-Thi Vai through 2020. This suggests that the expanded NH 51 should be able to accommodate container truck trip demand between HCMC and Cai Mep-Thi Vai through 2020 without adding appreciably to traffic congestion on this artery.

Based on the above scenario, justification for the Bien Hoa–Vung Tau Expressway may be based on factors other than the need to transport large volumes of containers to and from Cai Mep-Thi Vai, such as strategically to provide network resiliency.[27] Furthermore, additional truck trips in the HCMC–Vung Tau Corridor could be generated from the development of a major logistics park at the junction of the Long Thanh–Dau Giay Highway and NH 51 and/or from the expansion of manufacturing between HCMC and Qui Nhon. This would increase the volume of containers specifically routed by truck to and from Cai Mep-Thi Vai.

Table 2.17 Cai Mep-Thi Vai Terminals, Daily Truck Trips

Cai Mep-Thi Vai terminals truck volume	2012	2015	2020
Total container volume (TEUs)	965,000	1,500,000	3,000,000
Percentage barge service to CM-TV	95	90	90
Total containers trucked (FEUs)	24,000	73,500	148,000
Daily truck trips	80	250	500

Source: Authors. See table A.4 for details.
Note: CM-TV = Cai Mep-Thi Vai; FEU = 40-foot equivalent unit container; TEU = 20-foot equivalent unit container.

Hanoi–Haiphong Corridor

This corridor handled 2.7 million TEUs in 2011, and 5.5 million TEUs are projected for 2020. This corridor has three port complexes: (1) Haiphong port, with five container terminals, (2) Dinh Vu port, with five container terminals (and two more container terminals to be opened by 2014) along with other terminals for bulk and liquid cargo, and (3) Cai Lan port, with two container terminals. A fourth port, Lach Huyen, is planned to open its phase one terminal in 2016. Lach Huyen will be able to accommodate larger, mother vessels with its channel depth of 14 meters (see map 2.4 for a diagram of these ports and terminals).

Haiphong is 100 kilometers from Hanoi, where the majority of manufacturing is done in Northern Vietnam. The Haiphong-Dinh Vu terminals are served by NH 5, which has three lanes for vehicles and a separate motorcycle lane in each direction. However, part of the Dinh Vu road connection to Haiphong City and NH 5 is currently still unpaved and highly congested.

Cai Lan is served by NH 18, but about 80 percent of Cai Lan's container traffic is barged to Haiphong terminals due to weight restrictions on Highway 18 and customers' preference to use Haiphong's freight infrastructure. Although improvements to the highway have been made, truck weight limits have continued to divert a significant part of Cai Lan's container traffic to Haiphong via barges.

There is rail service from Hanoi to Haiphong, but trucking is the preferred mode of transit. It typically takes about four hours to truck containers to or from Haiphong–Dinh Vu terminals; this is about two hours more than in noncongested periods. There is also significant congestion in the Haiphong terminal area.

The Red River provides small barge transport for bulk materials from Haiphong to Hanoi and beyond, but its shallow draft cannot accommodate barges with containers at this time. Based on background studies for the World Bank–financed Northern Delta Transport Development Project (Royal Haskoning Nederland B.V. 2008), the GoV does have plans to improve channel depth and improve ports and landings along the Red River. Even if these improvements are implemented, transit time will be the determining factor whether the Red River becomes a meaningful transport mode for containers from the Hanoi area to and from Haiphong.

A new Hanoi to Haiphong Expressway[28] is planned to be completed by 2015. It will accommodate trucks up to 30 metric tons compared with an 18 metric ton limit on NH 5. This tolled expressway is among the first such facilities in Vietnam to be built to international technical standards. It will be 105.5 kilometers in length and 33 meters in width on average, allowing a maximum speed of 120 kilometers per hour. This highway will likely be a significant game changer for Vietnam in terms of modern highway infrastructure development to support heavier trucks and the use of exit lanes and overpasses to keep traffic from bottling up at intersections.

Improving the rail link to Haiphong is an important strategy if properly designed. The distance of 100 kilometers between Hanoi and Haiphong is very similar to the Lat Krabang IDC near Bangkok to the port of Laem Chabang (JETRO 2008). However, because of the fragmentation of the ports in Haiphong, only one terminal (Chua Ve) offers an on-dock rail facility. A near-dock rail yard where containers can be transported from double-stacked railcars to the terminals with minimal delays and cost could make rail a viable option that is cost-competitive and removes a portion of the current container cargo from the congested road network. (In the United States, Seattle and Tacoma, Washington, are good examples of how near-dock rail yard operators worked with marine terminals to develop an attractive service.) Although a direct rail link to the new Lach Huyen terminals is planned, there needs to be a stronger commitment to promote this as a cost-efficient and effective rail option since it would also benefit the China–Vietnam corridor.

Although a Hanoi–Cai Lan rail connection (the Yen Vien Pha Lai–Ha Long–Cai Lan Railway Project) has been proposed since 2004, actual construction was delayed until 2008 and scheduled to be complete by the end of 2012. Delivery of this project will most likely be delayed further.

Vietnam-China Corridor

The cross-border trade with southern China transits through the border gates at Lang Son, Lao Cai, and Mong Cai. Vietnam's annual exports are primarily fresh fruits, seafood, and rubber. China's primary exports include machinery, raw materials for manufacturing, and finished goods. In 2011 Vietnam exported approximately 20 million metric tons (or 1.8 million TEUs) to China across these border gates. About 400,000 of the TEUs shipped to China transited through the Haiphong and Cai Lan terminals in 2011. Vietnam imported approximately 25 percent of its export volume, which translates into 250,000 TEUs in 2011.

The main freight border crossing point in this corridor is the Friendship Gate near Lang Son. This is one of the busiest border trading points of Vietnam and the point where NH 1 begins. Effective August 2012, Vietnamese trucks have been allowed to dray containers to the Ping Xiang ICD, 50 kilometers inside China. Chinese trucks are permitted to dray containers to Tien Son ICD, about 150 kilometers inside Vietnam. At these ICDs, container contents are customs-cleared and transloaded into the other country's containers[29] and trucked to final destinations by trucks registered in that country. Lightweight containers can be lifted off and on chassis; otherwise, the contents of containers are physically transloaded between containers.

Midland Corridor

The Central Corridor ports of Danang, Qui Nhon, and Nha Trang accounted for only 3 percent of Vietnam's container throughput in 2011. Danang is the largest port (Tien Sa), with a channel depth of 11 meters and the ability to handle ships up to 2,000–2,500 TEUs. However, as a result of relatively small volumes, the port receives only vessels of 700–1,700 TEUs. In 2011 Danang's throughput was 114,373 TEUs, or 1.5 percent of Vietnam's total container volumes. Besides being a gateway for domestic cargo, Danang lies at one end of the East-West Economic Corridor, which connects Vietnam with Lao PDR, Myanmar, and Thailand, but the volumes moving on this corridor are insignificant. Given the low cargo volume in this corridor, no strategic infrastructure issues are relevant to this region at this time.

Mekong Delta Corridor

The region is famous as a large rice-growing area. It produces about half of the total of Vietnam's rice output. Vietnam is the second largest exporter of rice globally after Thailand. Seafood is the second largest export commodity from the region.

The port of Can Tho is 65 nautical miles upriver from the sea and has a maximum draft of 7.5 meters with a tidal surge of three to four meters. The maximum vessel size at Can Tho port is 10,000 DWT. As Can Tho primarily handles breakbulk cargo, the total number of containers handled by Can Tho in 2011 was only 3,196 TEUs, a decrease of more than 12,000 TEUs from its 2004 volume (this is mainly because of the new Can Tho bridge over the Mekong River). For containerized shipments, trucks are now the primary mode of travel from the Mekong Delta region to HCMC.

The primary mode for container freight transport from the region is on the NH 1 to HCMC ports. Seafood is mostly trucked in refrigerated containers or trucks from the Mekong Delta to HCMC ports. Trucking is done at night to avoid HCMC's truck restriction hours, thus allowing containers to be delivered directly to HCMC marine terminals. Night trucking also reduces the transit time to four hours compared with the daytime average travel time of seven to eight hours, because the highway is two lanes in each direction with no divider for motorcycles. Some of the containers delivered to VICT and Cat Lai are barged to Cai Mep-Thi Vai. The port of Can Tho is not used because the cost savings over truck transport do not offset faster truck delivery times, and it was reported that container service from Can Tho is not available year round. The construction of the Can Tho Bridge over the Mekong River in 2010 has definitely increased the volume of container and truck freight shipments to HCMC ports. As noted in map 2.6, there are plans to construct a Can Tho to HCMC Expressway in the future, but the project has not yet been approved.

The Cho Gao Canal (see map 2.9) is a critically positioned, narrow waterway linking the much wider, higher-capacity Tien and Vam rivers at each end, providing a critical freight link between the Mekong Delta region and HCMC. This navigable waterway is the main channel for barges carrying loose cargo from the Mekong Delta region to HCMC ports. This narrow

Efficient Logistics • http://dx.doi.org/10.1596/978-1-4648-0103-7

Map 2.9 Cho Gao Canal

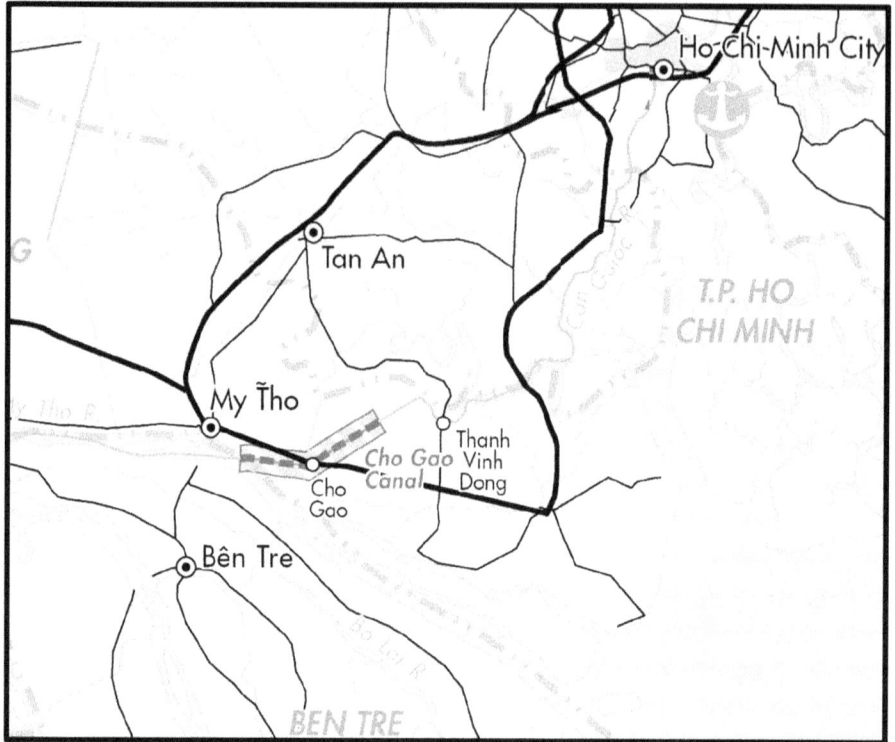

Source: World Bank.

canal has become a major bottleneck for waterway cargo transport in the region due to increased traffic levels and larger-sized vessels over the past several years. It is a safer method than open sea navigation from HCMC ports to Can Tho. The resulting congestion has not only increased logistics costs for regional BCOs, importers and exporters, but has also led to unsafe navigation. As a result, the GoV has made the upgrading of the Cho Gao Canal a transport efficiency and competitiveness priority network-wide (World Bank 2012b).

The GoV considers barge shipments between Cambodia and Vietnam to be "transit" rather than "transshipment" because the border is an inland border. This reduces the potential volume of commodities like second-hand machinery and used autos from moving on the barge system because it is illegal to import them into Vietnam.

North-South Corridor

Table 2.18 shows that in 2008 approximately 29,000 tons of containerized cargo were transported every day between the two delta regions (Red River and Mekong Delta), of which about 13,000 tons per day traveled the southbound leg

Table 2.18 Road and Coastal Containerized Cargo Flows on Vietnam's North-South Trade Axis

Tons per day

	2008	2020	2030	CAGR 2008–20	CAGR 2020–30
Road					
North-South	3,341	22,923	39,241	17.4%	5.5%
South-North	7,624	20,347	30,950	8.5	4.3
Both	10,965	43,270	70,191	12.1	5.0
Coastal					
North-South	9,611	65,945	112,889	17.4	5.5
South-North	8,642	23,064	35,083	8.5	4.3
Both	18,254	89,009	147,972	14.1	5.2
Total					
North-South	12,952	88,868	152,130	17.4	5.5
South-North	16,266	43,411	66,033	8.5	4.3
Both	29,219	132,279	218,163	13.4	5.1

Source: Blancas and El-Hifnawi 2013 using data from JICA 2009.
Note: CAGR = Compounded annual growth rate.

while slightly more than 16,000 tons per day traveled the northbound leg. In other words, the North-South trade is directionally imbalanced overall, with more volumes traveling from Southern to Northern Vietnam. However, the story changes when volumes are segregated by mode: The southbound leg is the dominant leg for coastal shipping while the northbound leg is the dominant leg for highway shipping. This imbalance continues today but is projected to become dominated by southbound trade in 2030.

The volume of containers moving South-to-North and North-to-South will expand significantly beyond present levels because of the dominant domestic production base in the HCMC area and to a lesser degree in the Hanoi area. One of the key drivers for Vietnam's export growth, as noted in section 2.1, is Vietnam's young and comparatively less expensive workforce. Between manufacturers in the HCMC area looking for additional low-cost, semiskilled workers to expand their Vietnamese operations, and the expectation that the GoV will encourage new FDI export-based manufacturing to locate in the less-developed Central Vietnam area, these new manufacturing locations will need to draw upon the domestic production bases in HCMC and Hanoi for the raw materials needed for the production of export products. Therefore, these manufacturers will need a multimodal infrastructure system to provide timely and cost-efficient transport for their raw materials.

The three transport options for freight in this corridor are NH 1, coastal ocean shipping, and rail. NH 1 is 1,726 kilometers in length between Hanoi and HCMC, with Danang located roughly at the midpoint.

It takes about 72 hours to truck freight from Hanoi to HCMC. For the most part, NH 1 is a two-lane highway. Being a National Highway, it falls under the exclusive control of the MoT. Currently an ongoing road-widening

Map 2.10 Vietnam National Railway System

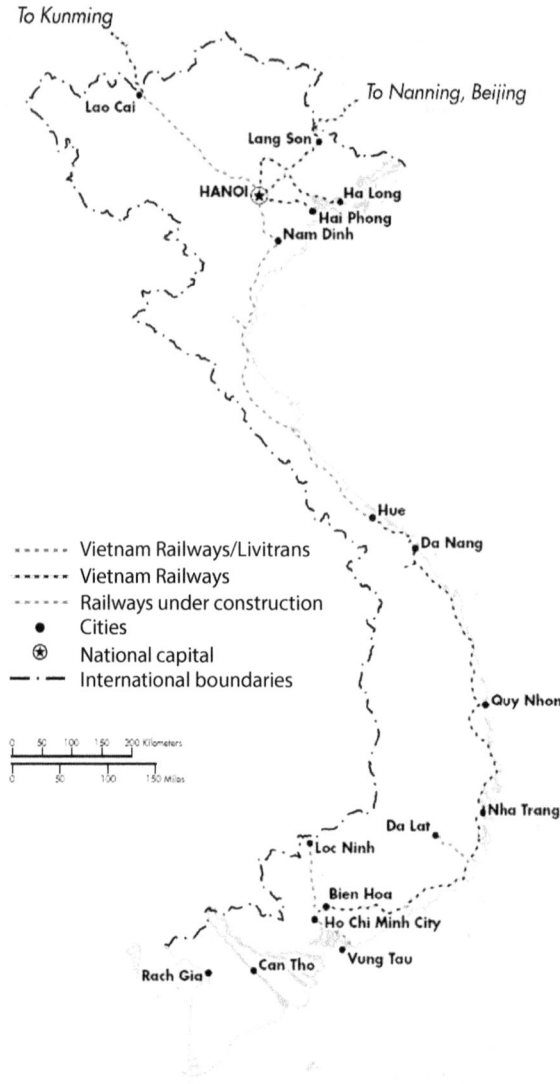

This map was produced by the Map Design Unit of The World Bank.
The boundaries, colors, denominations and any other information
shown on this map do not imply, on the part of The World Bank
Group, any judgment on the legal status of any territory, or any
endorsement or acceptance of such boundaries.

Source: World Bank with data from TrainTicketDeliver.

project is underway from Hanoi south to Ha Tinh, which has significant
congestion. One BCO using NH 1 regularly for shipments of domestic products from HCMC to distribution facilities in Danang and Hanoi stated there
are two major congestion points between HCMC and Danang at the Deo Ca
mountain pass (between Phu Yen and Khanh Hoa) and at the Cu Mong

mountain pass (between Phu Yen and Binh Dinh). This area should be studied for possible lane expansion such that trucks do not divert around these two points by using secondary roads, which can cause additional safety and road-weight bottlenecks.

Besides coastal ocean shipping, another option in the North-South corridor is to move freight between Hanoi and HCMC via the National Railway system (see map 2.10). Rail service provides a single track between Hanoi and HCMC and carries only about 4 percent of Vietnam's freight. Freight is moved in two types of boxcars: "green" cars (shorter transit time, less cargo damage, and more reliable schedule) and "red" cars (longer transit time and lower cost). Transit time from HCMC to Hanoi using "green" boxcars is seven days, compared with 10 days for "red" boxcars. The railroad offers no tracking of cargo during transit, and BCOs are not advised in advance of arrival as to what boxcars contain their products. Rail transport, as reported by one BCO, is about 20–30 percent less expensive than ocean transport. However, there is no appreciable difference in total transit time from inland pick-up location in HCMC to inland delivery location in Hanoi between rail and ocean shipping, hence the low usage of rail as a mode in Vietnam.

Notes

1. The *Doi Moi* economic reforms of 1986 in Vietnam were explicitly implemented to develop a socialist-oriented market economy and have been credited with current-day economic growth in the country.
2. Vietnam General Statistics Office (2011), by Standard International Trade Classification (SITC) Code 2010 data.
3. The term "demographic dividend" was popularized by Bloom, Canning and Sevilla (2001).
4. Interview testimonies by the European (EuroCham) and American (AmCham) Chambers of Commerce in Vietnam, the US-ASEAN Business Council and the Vietnam Competitiveness Initiative (VNCI).
5. Cambodia, Indonesia, the Lao People's Democratic Republic, Malaysia, the Philippines, and Thailand. None of these countries registered double-digit inflation over the period.
6. Fitch Ratings Sovereigns Division (2012), "Vietnam Trade Balance, Inflation Improves, Risks Remain," February 27.
7. Although inflation risks remain heightened, by August 2012 inflation nationwide had fallen to 5 percent from its peak of 23 percent in August of 2011.
8. For a comprehensive, survey-based look at corruption in Vietnam specifically in the interface between government officials (e.g., Customs) and the public (citizens and firms), see World Bank and Government Inspectorate of Vietnam (2012). That report observes that "the top four most corrupt sectors, according to [survey] respondents, are the traffic police, land administration, customs and construction," and that, among firms facing difficulties created by state organizations, "59% chose to give gifts and/or money to the officials to settle the work." A separate survey of 246 Vietnam-based trucking companies and owner-operators conducted by the World Bank (2011) found

that corruption was perceived by respondents as the most pressing obstacle to inter-city trucking. The testimonies gathered by the present study from Vietnam freight stakeholders are consistent with these earlier findings.

9. Opaquely defined allowances are a typical (and in many cases substantial) supplement to base salaries for public sector officials in Vietnam, which weakens the merit orientation of the civil service body. Furthermore, citizens have reported making large unofficial payments in exchange for access to job applications in the public sector.

10. Particularly those domiciled in countries where facilitation payments are exempt from national antibribery laws (there are five such countries—including the United States and the Republic of Korea, home to large multinational LSPs). This stance, of course, ignores the more important point that the practice is nonetheless illegal under Vietnamese law. Increasingly emphatic calls are being made by the international community (notably by the OECD) to universally ban facilitation payments.

11. Import costs include origin costs (fees for delivery order, container imbalance charge, document administration, Customs and cargo inspection, terminal handling charge, and trucking costs for a 100-km drayage dispatch) and ocean freight from Busan, Korea.

12. Export costs include origin costs (fees for full container processing, document administration, Customs, port construction and security, container seal, terminal handling charge, container lift-on-lift-off chassis, advance manifest security filing, and trucking costs for a 100-km drayage dispatch) and ocean freight to Los Angeles, California.

13. Boston Logistics Group, in NCF (2008).

14. For a comprehensive survey of this type of reports and studies globally, see Rantasila and Ojala (2012).

15. Under the World Bank–financed Mekong Delta Transport Infrastructure Development Project (2007–14) efforts are being made to measure Vietnam's logistics costs as a percentage of GDP based on a survey-based methodology developed by a global logistics research firm in conjunction with technical inputs from the World Bank.

16. World Bank (2011) found that in a sample of 852 origin-destination trucking routes, the average truck age was 16.6 years. By way of comparison, the average age of the U.S. active Class 8 truckload fleet is approximately seven years.

17. The Central Region ports of Danang and Qui Nhon account for only 3 percent of the total throughput at Vietnamese ports.

18. For this and similar references throughout the report, volume forecasts conducted by this study are based on inputs from the Vietnam Port Association, interviews with port operators, Liner Research Services data, and study team estimates.

19. Estimates provided by two foreign-flag ocean carriers.

20. Members of CKYH are Costco, K Line, Yang Ming and Hanjin. The Grand Alliance comprises Hapag-Lloyd, NYK, and OOCL. The New World Alliance is made up of APL, Hyundai, and MOL.

21. Phu My Bridge provides a more direct routing from South HCMC area in District 7 and other southern provinces to the Cat Lai Industrial Park and Cat Lai Port in District 9. The bridge also provides a north-south link to NH 1, allowing traffic to bypass the center of HCMC. It is also a land bridge link to VICT and to SPCT/Hiep Phuoc ports, bypassing the HCMC center and its container transit-hour restrictions.

22. The issue of conflicts of interests in Vietnam's port sector extends far beyond Vinalines and is directly connected with many of the issues this report has dealt with,

including supply-demand mismatches, port fragmentation, and poor service levels. See Pincus and Nguyen (2011) for a detailed account of conflicts of interest in the planning and management of port projects in Southern Vietnam.

23. Cost of congestion is based on key statistics from several U.S. cities. Although data have not been collected for validation of the Vietnam situation (this lay beyond the scope of this study), the analysis provides an order of magnitude understanding of the cost of annual hours of delay for commuters and trucks, including inventory costs, excess fuel consumed, vehicle operating costs and commuter stress. Bespoke analysis of the cost of congestion in the Vietnamese context is an area in need of further study.

24. Under the credit agreement signed on June 9, 2010, the six banks financing the expansion of NH 51 have invested close to VND 2.4 trillion, or $125 million, equivalent to 72 percent of the total invested capital. The expansion of the 72.7-kilometer road running through Dong Nai and Ba Ria-Vung Tau provinces will take three years to build from August 2. It will be widened from 32.9 meters to 39.3 meters to have eight lanes and allow for a design speed of 80 kilometers per hour.

25. Road 965 will be a divided, two-lane road in each direction from NH 51 to the interport road to all the Cai Mep-Thi Vai terminals.

26. Based on interviews with terminal operators and ocean carriers.

27. It is recommended that a careful evaluation is conducted by the GoV to study the potential traffic volumes on NH 51 and determine when conditions warrant the construction of the Bien Hoa–Vung Tau Expressway.

28. Two major Japanese banks will provide preferential credit for the $1.5 billion Hanoi-Haiphong Expressway project under an agreement signed in Tokyo on February 22, 2012, by the Vietnam Development Bank (VDB), Japan's Sumitomo Mitsui Banking Corporation (SMBC), and Citibank Japan. SMBC and Citibank will provide VDB with $270 million to finance the contract packages nos. 3 and 8 of the project at preferential interest rates.

29. Since trucking companies purchase their own containers, Chinese trucking companies are not inclined to surrender their containers to a Vietnamese trucking company (and vice versa). In addition, a country's chassis would not be properly licensed to travel in the other country beyond the designated border area.

References

Arvis, Jean-François, Monica Alina Mustra, Lauri Ojalam, Ben Shepherd, and Daniel Saslavsky. 2012. *Connecting to Compete 2012: Trade Logistics in the Global Economy.* Washington, DC: World Bank.

Blancas, Luis C., and M. Baher El-Hifnawi. 2013. *Facilitating Trade through Competitive, Low Carbon Transport: The Case for Vietnam's Inland and Coastal Waterways.* Washington, DC: World Bank.

Bloom, David E., David Canning, and Jaypee Sevilla. 2001. "Economic Growth and the Demographic Transition." NBER Working Paper 8685, National Bureau of Economic Research, Cambridge, MA.

Breu, Marco, and Richard Dobbs. 2012. "The New Asian Tiger?" *Foreign Policy,* February 23. http://www.foreignpolicy.com/articles/2012/02/23/the_new_asian_tiger.

Brummit, Chris. 2012. "Vietnam Nabs Former Boss at Shipping Company." *Associated Press,* September 5.

EuroCham (European Chamber of Commerce in Vietnam). 2012. *Trade/Investment Issues and Recommendations 2012*. Ho Chi Minh City: EuroCham.

Fitch Ratings Sovereigns Division. 2012. "Vietnam Trade Balance, Inflation Improves, Risks Remain." February 27. http://www.fitchratings.com/gws/en/fitchwire /fitchwirearticle/Vietnam-Trade-Balance,?pr_id=743735.

JETRO (Japan External Trade Organization). 2008. *Study on Railway Freight Transport System Construction Project for the Improvement of Distribution Efficiency in the Southern Focal Economic Zone in the Socialist Republic of Vietnam*. Tokyo: Overseas Research Department.

———. 2012. *The 22nd Survey of Investment Related Costs in Asia and Oceania (FY 2011 Survey)*. Tokyo: Overseas Research Department.

JICA (Japan International Cooperation Agency). 2009. *The Comprehensive Study on the Sustainable Development of Transport System in Vietnam* (VITRANSS-2). Hanoi: JICA.

KPMG. 2010. "Fast Forward: What's Next for China's Logistics Sector." http://www.kpmg .de/docs/China-logistics-sector-O-201009.pdf.

Kulisch, Eric. 2012. "Right Shoring: Global Cost Structures Have Manufacturers Reevaluating Outsourcing Phenomenon." *American Shipper* 54 (6): 8–15.

Meyrick and Associates, Transport Development and Strategy Institute (TDSI), and Carl Bro. 2006. *Vietnam: Multimodal Transport Regulatory Review*. Washington, DC: World Bank.

NCF (National Chamber Foundation). 2008. *The Transportation Challenge: Moving the U.S. Economy*. Washington DC: NCF.

Pham, Duc Minh, Deepak Mishra, Kee-Cheok Cheong, John Arnold, Anh Minh Trinh, Huyen Thi Ngoc Ngo, and Hien Thi Phuong Nguyen. 2013. *Trade Facilitation, Value Creation, and Competitiveness: Policy Implications for Vietnam's Economic Growth*. Washington, DC: World Bank.

Pincus, Jonathan, and Nguyen Xuan Thanh. 2011. *Ho Chi Minh City Sea Port Relocation: A Case Study of Institutional Fragmentation*. Ho Chi Minh City: Fullbright Economics Teaching Program.

Rantasila, Karri, and Lauri Ojala. 2012. "Measurement of National-Level Logistics Costs and Performance." Discussion Paper 2012-4, International Transport Forum Discussion Papers Series, Organization for Economic Co-operation and Development (OECD), Paris.

Royal Haskoning Nederland B.V. 2008. *Northern Delta Transport Development Project (NDTDP) Feasibility Study*. Nijmegen: Royal Haskonig Nederland.

Schwarz, Matthew G. 2010. "Project 30: A Revolution in Vietnamese Governance?" Brookings Northeast Asia Commentary Series 41, Brookings Institution, Washington, DC.

TDSI (Transport Development and Strategy Institute). 2012. *Corridor Study for Trade and Transport Facilitation*. Hanoi: Vietnam Ministry of Transport.

Vietnam Chamber of Commerce and Industry. 2012. "Road Maintenance Fees: Unreasonable," May 18. http://vccinews.com/news_detail.asp?news_id=26013.

Vietnam General Statistics Office. 2011. *Age-Sex Structure and Marital Status of the Population in Viet Nam, Viet Nam Population and Housing Census 2009*. Hanoi: Vietnam General Statistics Office.

Williams, Brock R. 2013. "Trans-Pacific Partnership Countries: Comparative Trade and Economic Analysis." Congressional Research Service 7-5700. http://www.fas.org/sgp/crs/row/R42344.pdf.

World Bank. 2009. *Vietnam Development Report: Modern Institutions*. Joint Donor Report to the Vietnam Consultative Group Meeting. Washington, DC: World Bank.

———. 2011. *Vietnam Urbanization Review: Technical Assistance Report*. Hanoi: World Bank.

———. 2012a. *Doing Business in 2013*. Washington, DC: World Bank. http://www.doingbusiness.org/data/exploreeconomies/vietnam/.

———. 2012b. "Technical Note on the Proposed Cho Gao Canal Improvement Project." World Bank, Hanoi.

World Bank and Government Inspectorate of Vietnam. 2012. *Corruption from the Perspective of Citizens, Firms, and Public Officials—Results of Sociological Surveys*. Hanoi: National Political Publishing House.

CHAPTER 3

Freight Stakeholder Challenges and Opportunities

In August 2012, the authors conducted face-to-face interviews with a broadly defined set of freight stakeholders engaged in Vietnam's logistics. The results are presented in this section. Interviews were held with 25 international beneficial cargo owners (BCOs), two domestic BCOs, four Vietnamese apparel and footwear factories, 11 international logistics service providers (LSPs), four containerized ocean carriers, 15 marine terminal operators (MTOs), four Vietnamese trucking companies, four trade associations, and four national-level agencies of the Government of Vietnam (GoV) (Appendix C lists the names of these stakeholders). With the exception of four international BCOs interviewed in the United States, all interviews took place in Vietnam. The interviews were conducted by seasoned industry practitioners with significant direct exposure to Vietnam, aided by detailed, sector-specific questionnaires. They comprised open and closed questions and gave ample opportunity for respondents to provide candid comments and opinions, which were later collated, assessed, and summarized for this report.

Marine Terminal Operators

Managing Capacity Utilization at Cai Mep-Thi Vai

Conversations with Cai Mep-Thi Vai MTOs[1] quickly revealed that their most pressing short-term challenge is the issue of low utilization rates. What follows are potential ways, as suggested by these MTOs, to improve facility utilization (and therefore strengthen supply chain reliability).

Seaport master plan parameters that limit the size of vessels calling at Cai Mep-Thi Vai ports to only 80,000 deadweight tons (DWT) should be adjusted to reflect current operational practice. The size of the largest containerships already calling at Cai Mep-Thi Vai terminals has exceeded the 80,000 DWT (about 7,000 TEUs) limit since 2010—by up to a factor of two (table 3.1). Moreover, it is expected that vessels above 80,000 DWT will continue be deployed on both Asia–North Europe (see figure 3.1) and Asia–North America services for years

Table 3.1 Largest Container Vessels at Cai Mep-Thi Vai Terminals since 2009

Date	Terminal	Vessel name	DWT[2]	GT[3]	TEU	LOA[4] (m)
Dec. 19, 2011	CMIT	CMA CGM Laperouse	157,092	150,269	13,830	366
Mar. 30, 2011	CMIT	CMA CGM Columba	131,263	131,332	11,388	363
Mar. 21, 2011	TCIT	HANJIN Germany	122,900	114,144	10,114	349
Nov. 16, 2010	SP-PSA	CMA CGM Pelleas	120,853	111,249	9,661	350
Feb. 12, 2010	SP-PSA	Albert Maersk	109,000	93,496	8,650	352
June 3, 2009	TCCT	MOL Premium	72,968	71,776	6,350	293
May 29, 2009	SP-PSA	APL Alexandrite	59,603	49,716	3,821	288

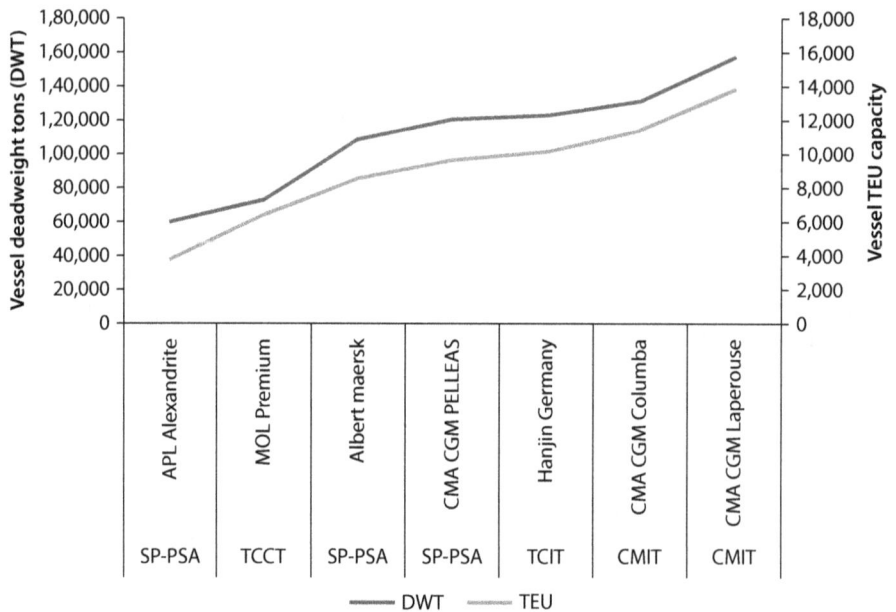

Source: Liner Research Services.
Note: DWT = Deadweight Tons; GT = Gross Tonnage; LOA = Length Overall; TEU = 20-foot equivalent unit container.

to come. This will require Vietnamese ports to ensure the safe navigation of such vessels, especially at Cai Mep-Thi Vai. Artificial operating limits should be removed, and infrastructure needs should be assessed based on actual demand.

Financial incentives could be provided to ocean carriers to promote additional vessel calls at Cai Mep-Thi Vai. At present, the average number of container moves per port call at Cai Mep-Thi Vai (1,000–2,000 TEUs) is significantly lower than the corresponding number at most other deep-water ports in the region (3,000 TEUs). As a result, tonnage and pilotage fees constitute a higher percentage of operating costs, on a per-TEU basis, for carriers calling Cai Mep-Thi Vai. One way to alleviate this extra burden, at least temporarily while volumes remain depressed, is through volume discounts assessed on vessel tonnage. The suggested discounts should be targeted, for example by establishing a container move threshold that would trigger them (e.g., below 3,000 TEUs). It is estimated that additional incentives along these lines, coupled with the lifting of current

Figure 3.1 Asia-North Europe Services: Average Vessel Size, October 2012

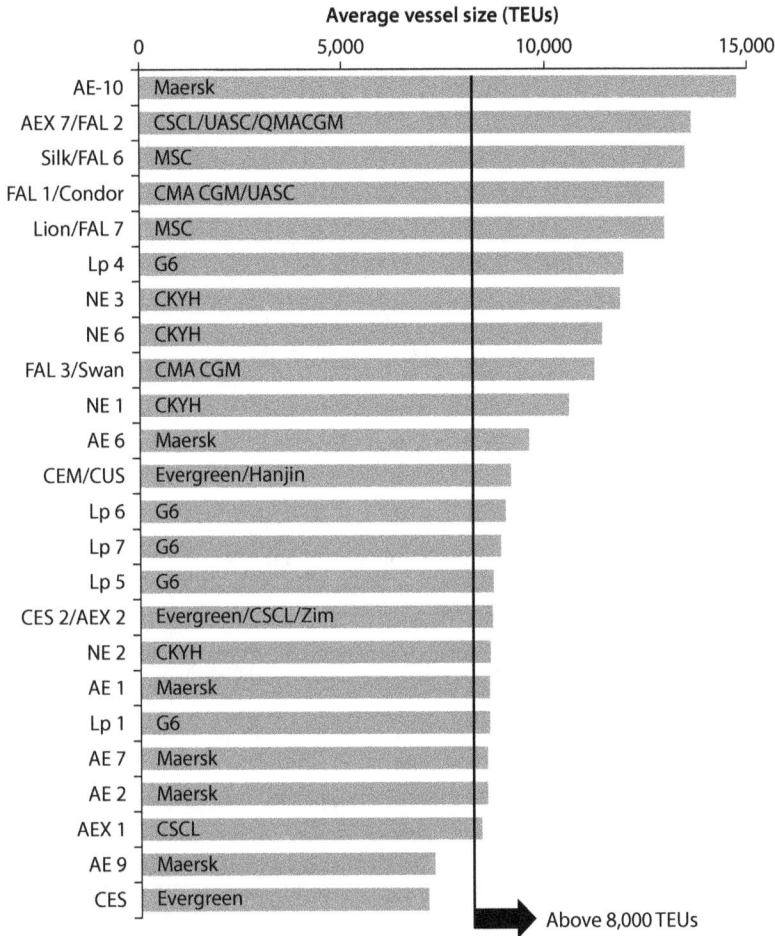

Average vessel size (TEUs)

Service	Carrier	Size
AE-10	Maersk	
AEX 7/FAL 2	CSCL/UASC/QMACGM	
Silk/FAL 6	MSC	
FAL 1/Condor	CMA CGM/UASC	
Lion/FAL 7	MSC	
Lp 4	G6	
NE 3	CKYH	
NE 6	CKYH	
FAL 3/Swan	CMA CGM	
NE 1	CKYH	
AE 6	Maersk	
CEM/CUS	Evergreen/Hanjin	
Lp 6	G6	
Lp 7	G6	
Lp 5	G6	
CES 2/AEX 2	Evergreen/CSCL/Zim	
NE 2	CKYH	
AE 1	Maersk	
Lp 1	G6	
AE 7	Maersk	
AE 2	Maersk	
AEX 1	CSCL	
AE 9	Maersk	
CES	Evergreen	

Above 8,000 TEUs

Source: Liner Research Services.
Note: G6 Alliance members are APL, Hapag-Lloyd, Hyundai Merchant Marine, MOL, NYK Line and OOCL; TEU = 20-foot equivalent unit container.

restrictions on vessels of over 80,000 DWT, could potentially increase the number of direct Vietnam-to-Europe services from one (as of September 2012) to four or five weekly service strings.

Transshipment traffic at Cai Mep-Thi Vai should be promoted as an additional, more permanent means to improving capacity utilization. Due to the very competitive nature of current handling tariffs at Vietnamese ports, there is strong unmet demand for additional transshipment cargo volumes at Cai Mep-Thi Vai. However, actual transshipment volumes remain limited, with little incentives provided to attract volumes from the natural catchment regions of Cambodia and Northern and Central Vietnam.

In particular, a relaxation of cabotage rules would increase the attractiveness of Cai Mep-Thi Vai as a national transshipment hub. This would enable foreign flag carriers to carry transshipment containers to and from Haiphong, Danang, and Quinhon into Cai Mep-Thi Vai.

As of September 2012, no domestic Vietnamese flag carrier serving the main cabotage routes calls at Cai Mep-Thi Vai terminals. Instead, these carriers call at inner-city terminals at Saigon Port, Ben Nghe, Tan Thuan Dong, VICT and Bong Sen, which are not specifically geared to handle transshipment cargo volumes with regular connections to mother vessels calling at Cai Mep-Thi Vai (see table 3.2).

The relaxation of cabotage rules for international transshipment containers would have little impact on existing Vietnam-flag carriers' share of the domestic container market. This is because Vietnam-flag carriers cannot deliver the service needed for transshipped international containers. Instead, Vietnam forgoes port revenue at Cai Mep-Thi Vai as these international containers will be trans-shipped through hubs external to Vietnam when the cabotage rules become enforced in January 2013.

Table 3.2 Domestic Carriers Serving the Haiphong-Quinhon-Danang-HCMC Coastal Trades, September 2012

Operator	Vessel	TEU	Route
Vinalines	Vinalines Diamond	1,118	HCMC-Haiphong-HCMC
	Me Linh	594	
	Van Xuan	594	Singapore-HCMC-Haiphong-HCMC-Singapore
	Vinalines Pioneer	588	
Bien Dong	Bien Dong Navigator	1.016	Haiphong-HCMC-Singapore-Haiphong
	Bien Dong Mariner	1,016	
Gemadept	Pacific Pearl	699	Haiphong–Hong Kong SAR, China–Haiphong-
	Pacific Express	749	HCMC–Danang (1/3)–Haiphong
	Pacific Gloria	699	
NASICO	Nasico Navigator	336	HCMC-Haiphong-HCMC
	Nasico Sky	260	
	Nasico Ocean	260	
VSICO	Prudent	436	HCMC-Haiphong-HCMC
	Vsico Pioneer	420	
Duong Dong	Duong Dong	404	HCMC-Haiphong-HCMC
Viet Sun	Tai Ping	602	Haiphong–Cua Lo–HCMC-Haiphong
VOSCO	Fortune Navigator	580	HCMC-Haiphong-HCMC
	Fortune Freighter	570	
Vinafco	Vinafco 25	252	HCMC-Haiphong-HCMC
	Dong Du	561	
Truong Hai	Truong Hai Star 2	228	HCMC–Chu Lai–HCMC
	Duong Dong	404	
Hub Line (foreign flag)	Hub Stellar	714	HCMC-Haiphong-HCMC–Port Klang–HCMC
	Hub Grandiose	714	

Source: Liner Research Services.
Note: Danang and Quinhon port calls also served on an irregular basis by all operators. HCMC = Ho Chi Minh City;
TEU = 20-foot equivalent unit container.

Table 3.3 Comparison of Transshipment Costs at Cai Mep Relative to Key Regional Hubs
Dollars

Port	Estimated transhipment cost per TEU	Difference vs. Singapore	Difference vs. Hong Kong SAR, China
Cai Mep	40	−60/TEU	−80/TEU
Singapore	100	n.a.	n.a.
Hong Kong SAR, China	120	n.a.	n.a.

Source: Authors based on interviews with ocean carriers.
Note: Handling rates are estimates only, and would differ in practice based on individual carriers' contracts with terminals at the various hub ports. TEU = 20-foot equivalent unit container; n.a. = not applicable.

Transshipment volumes to or from other countries in the region can benefit from accessing Cai Mep-Thi Vai while meaningfully contributing to these ports' financial footing. Incentives such as transshipment rebates and streamlined customs regulations for transshipment cargo on international routes, including those linked to Cambodia, Malaysia, the Philippines, and Thailand, could potentially increase the container throughput at Cai Mep-Thi Vai by between one and two million TEUs per annum by 2020.

A more open policy for transshipment volumes could also generate significant cost efficiencies for container shipping carriers. Specifically, potential savings from shifting transshipment volumes from existing hubs in Singapore and Hong Kong SAR, China, to Cai Mep-Thi Vai could be between $60 and $80 per TEU, to be realized from the lower costs of transshipment at Cai Mep (see table 3.3).

Land and inland waterway connections at Cai Mep-Thi Vai need to be improved or developed. In particular, the upgrading and completion of the NH 51 expansion and the connector Road 965 from NH 51 to the Cai Mep-Thi Vai terminals should be prioritized. At present, a traffic signal controls the intersection of NH 51 and Road 965. When completed (completion was originally planned for early 2013), Road 965 will be a divided highway with two lanes in each direction and connecting to the Cai Mep-Thi Vai Interport Road,[5] construction of which is also behind schedule.

Inland waterway connections between Cai Mep-Thi Vai and the various Inland Container Depots (ICDs) in the port's hinterland are currently provided to the following locations:

- ICD Tang Cang
- ICD Transimex
- ICD Sotrans
- ICD Tanamexco
- ICD Phuoc Long/Phuoc Long 3 and
- ICD Phuc Long.

These ICDs, which store empty and full containers with customs clearance and container maintenance facilities located on site, are located throughout the Ho Chi Minh City (HCMC) area. Some are situated along the inland waterway system for direct loading on to barges. Other ICDs are located near industrial areas, and containers must be drayed directly to a port or to another ICD, owned by the same company, located on an inland waterway for barge loading. The size of ICDs can range from 500 TEUs to 1.4 million TEUs.

As previously reported, 95 percent of containers to and from Cai Mep-Thi Vai are barged to or from HCMC area ICDs. Because of traffic restrictions on containers transiting through HCMC, between 40 and 80 percent of the container volumes to or from the inner-city terminals (SPCT and VICT) are barged from ICDs located on the opposite side of HCMC.

Highway connectors and access roads to many ICDs contribute to overall highway congestion in the HCMC area. There is also concern about navigational safety on the local inland waterways due to the number of barges transporting containers to or from marine terminals. The improvement of these land-side and inland waterway infrastructures would significantly improve the operating efficiency of the ports in the Southern region and provide lower operating costs for ocean carriers and BCOs.

Ocean Carriers

Doing Business in Vietnam Today

As of September 2012, 46 containerized ocean carriers,[6] foreign and domestic flag, made port calls in Vietnam as part of regular, scheduled services (see table 3.4).

Apart from Cai Mep-Thi Vai ports, which are able to receive ships of up to 14,000 TEUs, no Vietnamese port is able to receive ships above 3,000 TEUs. From a cost-competitiveness perspective, the four foreign carriers were unanimous in identifying their highest operating costs to be utilities and expatriate

Table 3.4 Containerized Ocean Carriers Calling Vietnam

Vietnamese-flagged carriers	Foreign-flagged carriers	
Bien Dong Shipping Co.	APL	Maersk Line
Duong Dong	Asean Seas Line Co.	MCC
Gemadept	CNC	Mariana Express Lines
Nasico	China United Lines	MOL
Truong Hai	CK Line	MSC
Vietsun	CMA CGM	Namsung Shipping
Vinafco	COSCO	NYK
Vinalines	CSCL	OOCL
VOSCO	Evergreen	PIL
VSICO	Gold Star Line	RCL
	Hainan PO Shipping	Samudera
	Hanjin	Sinokor
	Heung-A	Sinotrans
	HMM	SITC
	Hubline	STX Pan Ocean
	Interasia	TS Lines
	K Line	Wah Hai
	KMTC	Yang Ming

Source: Liner Research Services.

Figure 3.2 Ocean Carriers: Relative Cost of Operations in Vietnam

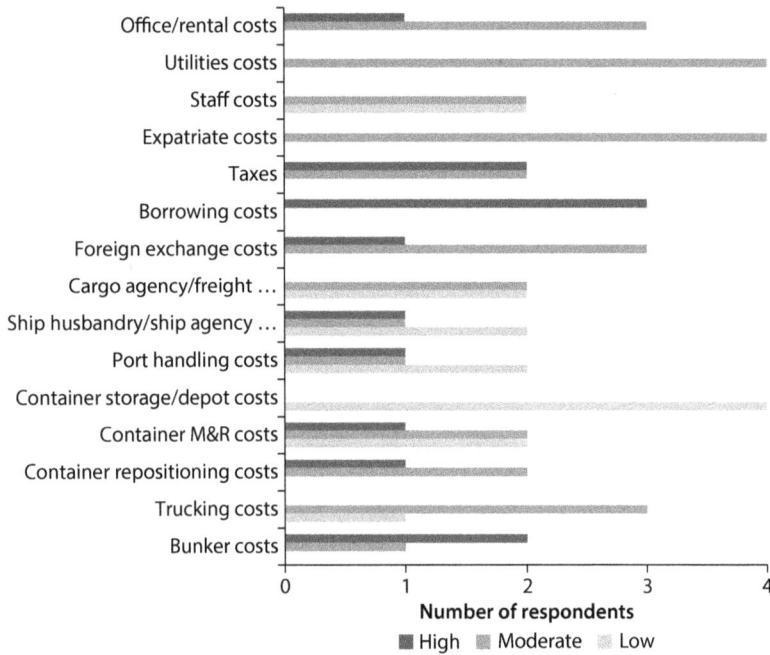

Note: M&R = Maintenance and repair.

costs (see figure 3.2). Three carriers identified the cost of borrowing money, taxes, and bunker costs to be high compared with other costs. The high expatriate cost refers to the need to bring in foreign nationals for senior management positions (e.g., country general managers, directors of sales and marketing and other key director-level positions). This issue will be discussed in more detail later in this report.

Some cost drivers affect operating costs more than others (see figure 3.3). Issues with the greatest impact on operating costs include the high inflation rates prevailing at the time of the survey (which lead to wage inflation) and the perceived incidence of taxation. Road congestion and government regulations are also stated as having a higher than average impact on operating costs.

The quality of carriers' Vietnamese staff is believed to be above average (see figure 3.4). Regarding sales, one respondent noted that its office staff is competent and often used as a "beta site" to test new processes before implementing them in other Asian offices. Another respondent mentioned that sales staff at the manager level and below is adequate, but its sales team is not sufficiently customer service oriented. Although not shown in figure 3.4, carriers reported that Vietnam lacks experienced executive level managers and directors who have sufficient supply chain and logistics experience to replace expatriate staff.

Figure 3.5 shows how carriers rated port operations for HCMC, Cai Mep-Thi Vai, Haiphong, and Danang ports. Cai-Mep-Thi Vai ports rank the highest in all categories simply because of the tremendous amount of excess capacity at those

Figure 3.3 Challenges That Impact Ocean Carrier Operation Costs in Vietnam

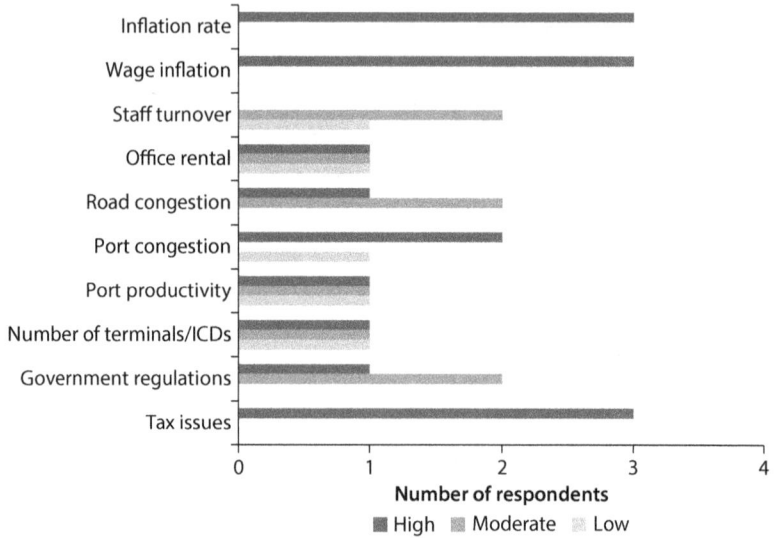

Note: ICD = inland container depot.

Figure 3.4 Qualities of the Ocean Carrier Staff Functions for the Industry

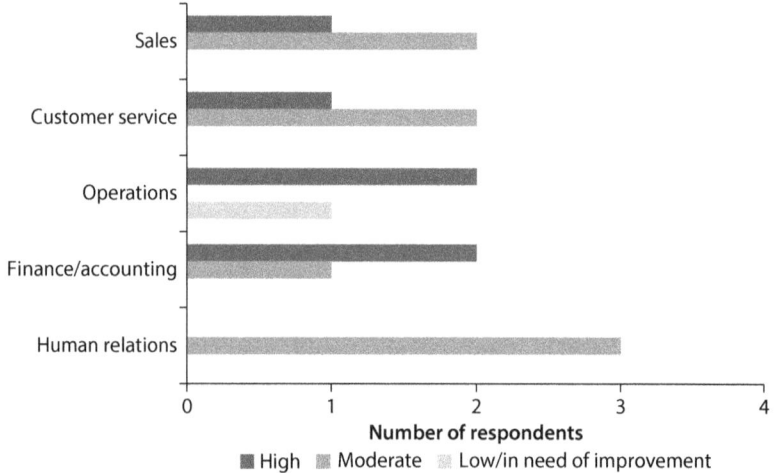

locations (with only six vessel strings currently calling those ports). The ratings for HCMC ports are for Cat Lai and VICT terminals. Given the significant volume of containers transiting through these two terminals, the ratings reflect above average performance. Although Haiphong terminals have the same performance for port congestion rating as HCMC ports, their overall performance is about average. Danang's ratings reflect a sporadic performance rating for a little used container terminal. One BCO said it stopped using Danang 18 months ago because of poor port operations and inadequate feeder service.

Figure 3.5 Perceived Port Operations Performance

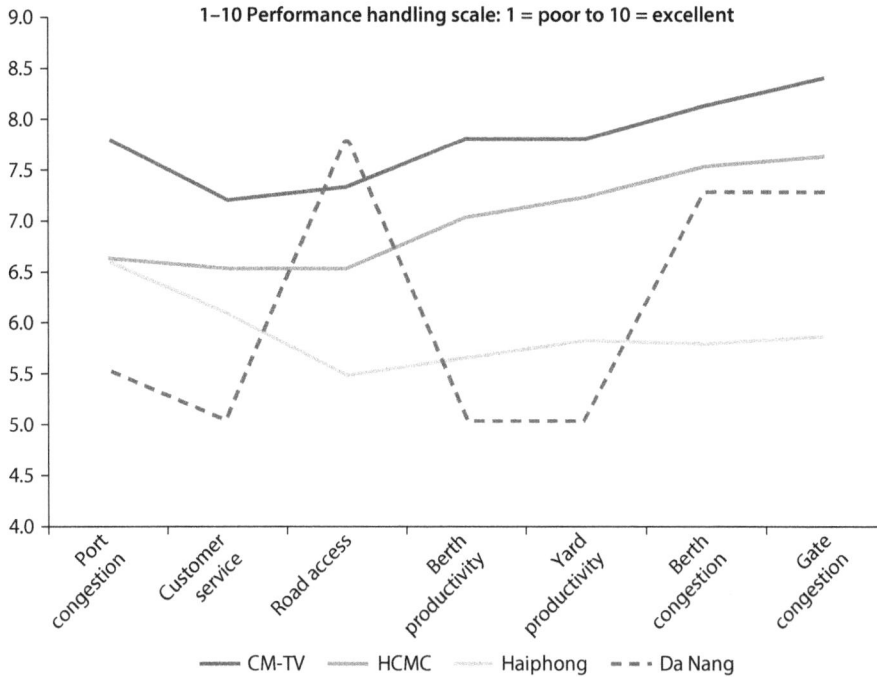

Table 3.5 Positive and Negative Aspects of ICDs

Positive aspects	Negative aspects
The current number of ICDs in the HCMC area provides a wider footprint for receiving containers closer to large manufacturing areas	Although the high number of IDCs around HCMC fosters competition, it is difficult for a carrier to monitor its inventory of loads and empties within the various ICDs.
Most BCOs prefer to use ICDs around HCMC because they have relationships with Vietnam Customs officials there.	BCOs have preferences about which ICDs to use (mainly for customs purposes), so carriers have to juggle operations to accommodate customer demands.
ICDs near inland waterways allow containers to be transported to marine terminals by barge as opposed to more expensive truck transport.	Highway connectors and access roads to many of the ICDs are generally poorly planned which contributes to the overall highway congestion within the HCMC area.
ICDs are especially helpful for transporting containers to VICT that would otherwise have to transit through HCMC during non–truck-traffic restriction hours.	Two to three small ICDs in HCMC should be merged into a single larger one with higher professional and quality standards.

Note: ICD = inland container depot; HCMC = Ho Chi Minh City; Vietnam Customs = General Department of Vietnam Customs.

Besides delivering containers direct to ocean terminals, carriers also interact with ICDs for positioning empty containers and picking up full containers. To the questions of (1) whether current locations and operation of off-dock depots were adequate for carriers' operational needs and (2) whether ICDs added significant extra costs to carriers' operations, mixed reactions were expressed, with two carriers agreeing with the questions while the other two disagreed. They all agreed, however, that trying to consolidate the ICDs would be nearly impossible. The perceived pros and cons on the number of ICDs are shown in table 3.5.

Efficient Logistics • http://dx.doi.org/10.1596/978-1-4648-0103-7

Table 3.6 Trucking Industry: Perceptions of Ocean Carriers

	Agree	Disagree
There is an adequate supply of trucking companies to meet our company's business needs.	1	2
The trucking industry in Vietnam is characterized by a number of small companies that lack the capacity to expand their businesses.	3	1
The majority of trucking companies use old and polluting trucks.	3	1
Trucking companies generally do a good job in minimizing loss or damage to cargo/ containers.	1	3

Responses to the statements shown in table 3.6 reflect viewpoints that are divided by carriers' operating setup, with three carriers outsourcing trucking services and one owning and operating its own trucks. Specifically, the company that invested in its own trucks had a markedly more positive view of the trucking industry than did the carriers relying on third-party truckers.

Ocean carriers reported that the state of the trucking industry in Vietnam has considerable room for improvement. Trucking companies generally are small, trucks old, and driver attitudes poor. Most trucking companies do not meet international standards, which led one of the four international ocean carriers interviewed for this report to invest in its own fleet of trucks to maintain the high service level demanded by its customers. It has become risky for this ocean carrier to purchase additional trucks, so it has to employ subcontracted trucking companies. Like the other ocean carriers, this ocean carrier found that its subcontracted trucking companies are not consistent in meeting international performance standards.

Cost Management Challenges

Containerized ocean carriers operating in Vietnam reported the following four key cost management challenges:

1. A fragmented trucking industry increases ocean carriers' operational costs. Fragmentation forces ocean carriers to manage numerous trucking contracts to be assured of service during peak shipping periods, as the number of trucks any one trucking company can commit to a carrier is limited. The use of multiple trucking companies may also be tied to the special arrangements they often have with the police on certain road sections. This may generate a need to use different trucking companies for different routes. Without such arrangements, trucks risk being delayed by unannounced road inspections, ostensibly for the purpose of exchanging undocumented facilitation payments.

2. Vietnam has a complex and costly process for international ocean carriers to file the necessary documents to avoid double taxation.[7] Even after filing the paperwork, the GoV does not fully exempt carriers from paying some Vietnamese taxes on freight. This is not the experience carriers have in other countries that have double freight taxation agreements. The additional tax costs for each international carrier are estimated to range from $50,000 to $200,000 per year. The GoV could simplify the tax filing exemption process

in order to align itself with the international standards designed to eliminate double taxation on freight.

3. The GoV considers barge shipments between HCMC/Cai Mep-Thi Vai and Cambodia as "transit" rather than "transshipment." This responds to the fact that the trade is linked by an inland border connection. Cambodia allows imports of second-hand machinery and cars originating in the United States and other foreign countries that are prohibited from being imported into Vietnam. Therefore, this type of restricted cargo cannot be transported to Cambodia via Vietnam. Currently the trade between Vietnam and Cambodia is imbalanced, with more cargo coming out of Cambodia than going in. Vietnam's economy loses potential revenue as a result of this restriction, and carriers could be more profitable in this barge trade by having a more balanced two-way flow of cargo.

4. The cargo insurance coverage of transportation partners involved in the domestic portion of container shipments is limited. For example, barge companies generally carry freight insurance with a maximum payment of $50,000 per occurrence (roughly the value of the goods inside a typical 20-foot container in Vietnam). As such, barges loaded with 20–80 such containers create a loss exposure for carriers, as they would not be able to recoup, in the event of loss, the full compensation they are required to pay the BCO from the barge operator that was responsible for the loss incident. A similar issue arises with underinsured trucking companies, although the exposure is limited to the truck's (typically single) trailer capacity. A root cause of these challenges is that obtaining cargo insurance in Vietnam is expensive (an average of $0.50 per $1,000) compared with regional peers (average $0.125 per $1,000).

BCO Supply Chain Impact

As Northern Vietnam attracts more manufacturing activity, the worsening port congestion in the Haiphong area could lead to longer cutoff times for manufacturers to deliver containers to ocean carriers. This in turn would increase BCOs' inventory carrying costs, especially for time-sensitive cargo. The same may occur as a result of increasing highway congestion in the HCMC area between ports, ICDs, manufacturing locations, and logistics parks.

Future Freight Flow Impacts

The future operating environment in Vietnam for ocean carriers will change (both positively and negatively) as a result of the following four anticipated impacts:

1. A strict enforcement of cabotage rules in 2013, which will prevent foreign flag carriers from carrying internationally destined containers from Northern and Central Vietnam to Cai Mep-Thi Vai to connect with mother vessels. This will increase carriers' operating costs, as they would be forced to incur higher transshipment costs at foreign hubs.

2. New infrastructure being developed in the HCMC area has the potential to generate higher container flows in and out of this region. The completion of

the HCMC–Long Thanh portion of the HCMC–Long Thanh–Dau Giay Expressway by 2014[8] will create a shortcut from HCMC to NH 51 and on to Cai Mep-Thi Vai. The remaining portion of the HCMC–Long Thanh–Dau Giay highway connecting NH 1 is also under construction. When the new Long Thanh Airport is completed, this triangle will become an important logistics area where new logistics parks could be built for closer access to ports and the new airport.

3. Some industries are likely to move out of the inner-HCMC area and into Nhon Trach and Long Thanh, closer to Cai Mep-Thi Vai. There are numerous steel mills and glass and chemical plants located in Phu My, which would allow manufacturers to source more raw materials in the Phu My area compared with the current heavy reliance on imported raw materials.

4. The GoV is considering setting up a coal center in HCMC where bigger vessels can call and transload to barges for distribution to electric plants locally and in the Mekong Delta region. The importance of the Cho Gao Canal, considered the most pressing bottleneck of the Mekong Delta inland waterway network connecting Can Tho and HCMC, is growing, and congestion due to vessel queuing is delaying cargo movement. Government plans to increase capacity at Cho Gao, with World Bank support, are ongoing.

Logistics Service Providers

Respondents' Profile

Ten LSPs were consulted and interviewed for this study. Nine are large international LSPs with operations in Vietnam and across the globe; one is a Vietnamese company. Two are integrators handling small package shipments. All LSPs provide service across Vietnam. Two LSPs are subsidiaries of ocean carriers; the rest are non–asset-based operators. These LSPs provide a wide range of services, including ocean and airfreight forwarding, customs brokerage, storage and value-added warehousing, and trucking.

Cost Management Challenges for LSPs Related to Customs Processes and Transportation Infrastructure

According to LSPs, their operating costs are generally lower in Vietnam compared with their operations in China, India, Malaysia, and Thailand (see figure 3.6). However, 70 percent of respondents noted that regulations negatively impact their business operations and cited inflation as a recurrent concern for them and their customers.

Customs and Import/Export Documentation

More than half of respondents consider Vietnam's customs requirements to be more stringent and expensive to comply with compared with other Asian countries where they operate (see table 3.7). All but one of the interviewees was concerned with the inconsistent manner in which customs regulations and fees are applied and with the cumbersome nature of working with the General

Figure 3.6 Comparison of Vietnam Operating Costs to Other Asian Countries

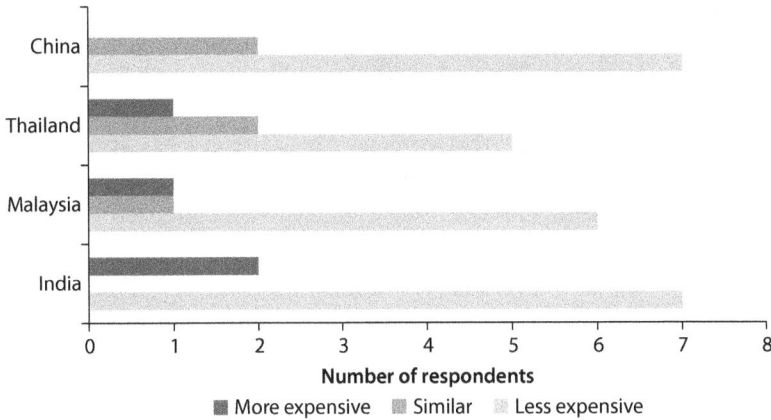

Number of respondents
■ More expensive ▨ Similar ░ Less expensive

Table 3.7 LSPs' Opinions about Vietnam Customs Processes

	Strongly agree	Mostly agree	Disagree	Strongly disagree
Customs decisions, policies, and/or directions are arbitrary and inconsistent.	6	3	1	
Customs is bureaucratic, but consistent among the various Customs districts.	1	6	2	1
Customs operations are consistent with other Asian countries.		3	6	1
Customs operations are better than in other Asian countries.		2	5	3
Customs officials work cooperatively with our company to address issues.		5	3	2
Customs fees are well publicized and consistently applied.		3	3	3

Note: Customs/Vietnam Customs = General Department of Vietnam Customs.

Department of Vietnam Customs (hereafter "Vietnam Customs" or simply "Customs"). Vietnam Customs is also viewed as being harder to conduct business with than with equivalent agencies in some of Vietnam's peer Asian countries.

From Table 3.7 it is evident that LSPs overwhelmingly believe that Customs rules are subjective and that dealing with Vietnam Customs is cumbersome and more difficult than in other Asian countries. Only half of the LSPs stated that Customs officials try to work cooperatively with them to solve problems. Two-thirds consider that Customs fees are not well publicized and are inconsistently applied.

Issues that LSPs brought up repeatedly during interviews include the following:

• As customs modernization is underway and the electronic e-Customs system has not been fully implemented, inefficient manual customs import and export clearance processes continue to result in clearance delays, increased administrative time and costs for BCOs and LSPs, and higher inventory carrying costs for BCOs.

- Regulations governing international trade need to be more transparent, less ambiguous, and easier to understand such that companies can more easily comply with them. Interpretation of rules is inconsistent among Customs agents across Vietnam. This includes commodity classification and valuation, product inspection, and licensing and certification of certain products. Several LSPs reported that, given that dealing with Customs is unpredictable and often cumbersome, they have larger numbers of staff members handling customs processing in Vietnam than in other Asian countries.

- Corruption is perceived to be endemic throughout the Customs ranks and with officials in other government agencies involved in international trade. LSPs believe it is common practice for Customs agents to solicit undocumented, nontransparent facilitation fees to accept such things as wrong data on documents (e.g., inaccurate weights or Harmonized Tariff System numbers) or missing documentation in order to clear the cargo in a timely manner. Since any facilitation paid by LSPs on behalf of their BCO customers is built into the overall LSP rates, facilitation cannot be easily tracked by BCOs. LSPs and BCOs that do not engage in facilitation firmly believe they are at a competitive disadvantage to those that do. Every LSP interviewed stated that corruption in customs needs to be tackled as the competitiveness area in most need of improvement, especially related to the import process.

- The skill level of government officials who work directly with the movement of cargo is perceived to be inadequate, especially in rural areas. These positions are often allocated on the basis of relationships with people in power or by sharing facilitation payments. GoV human resource systems are not merit-based. This suggests more ongoing training and testing for Customs officials is needed.

Addressing these critical customs-related issues would speed import and export clearance, have a direct and positive impact on customs clearance costs, decrease the amount of redundant safety stock BCOs keep in their supply chains, create a level playing field for BCOs and LSPs, and enable LSPs to provide better service to their customers at lower costs. Three LSPs indicated that if conditions were better, their companies would be more likely to expand operations in Vietnam.

From the specific perspective of the two international integrators interviewed for this report (companies that handle end-to-end express deliveries utilizing their own transportation and IT assets), Vietnam Customs is viewed as more progressive in some areas, for example:

- Customs deploys a team solely focused on the express industry; this team reports to the Department of General Customs in HCMC.
- Import shipments under $50 are not taxed; Vietnam is progressive in this regard relative to other Asian countries.
- Airfreight can be cleared for export at industrial parks, allowing it to be shipped directly to the loading area at the airport with an export declaration. In a

separate express processing center near the loading area for aircraft, the cargo is security-cleared (x-rayed) and weighed prior to loading.

However, it is reported that high-value express import shipments generally take between six and eight days to be processed (and can take up to four weeks in some instances). A root cause for this is that the import process for express shipments over $50 is a manual process subject to interpretation by Customs officials.

Vietnam, like China, is perceived by LSPs as administratively burdensome. Whereas India, Indonesia, and Malaysia all have more complex import regulations than Vietnam's, their processes are not as slow to navigate. Presentation of prearrival documents is not permitted in Vietnam, because it has not implemented a "trusted shipper" program. As a result, the customs clearance process may start only after the cargo arrives with the original documents. Import license requirements are based on commodity type rather than value.

According to one express interviewee, in handling express shipments, India is most restrictive, followed by Indonesia, the Philippines, Thailand, Vietnam, China, Malaysia, Japan, Korea, Taiwan, Hong Kong, and Singapore.

Trucking Industry

Most LSPs consider trucking costs to be higher in Vietnam than in China, India, Malaysia, and Thailand (figure 3.7). At the same time, trucking service delivery is considered to be substandard compared with India and Thailand, and similar to China and Malaysia (figure 3.8). This suggests that Vietnam's trucking industry generally offers a lower value proposition compared with most of Vietnam's key regional peers.

LSPs have concerns about the fragmented and unsophisticated nature of the trucking industry (table 3.8). No pan-Vietnam companies exist, and most

Figure 3.7 Vietnam Trucking Costs Compared with Other Asian Countries

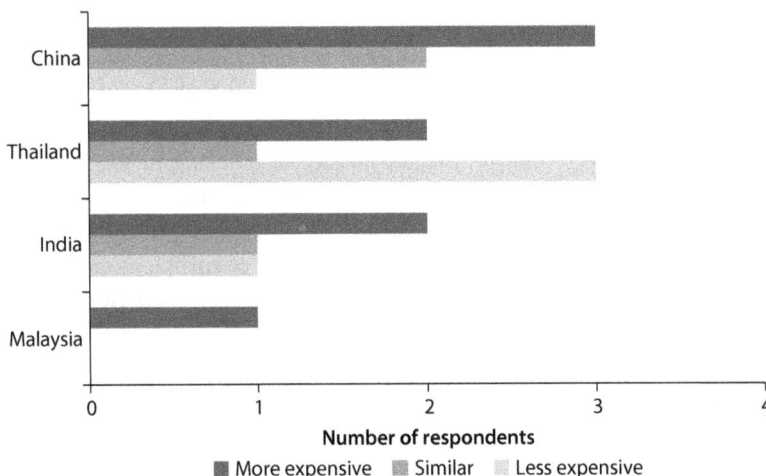

Figure 3.8 Vietnam Trucking Service Quality Compared with Other Asian Countries

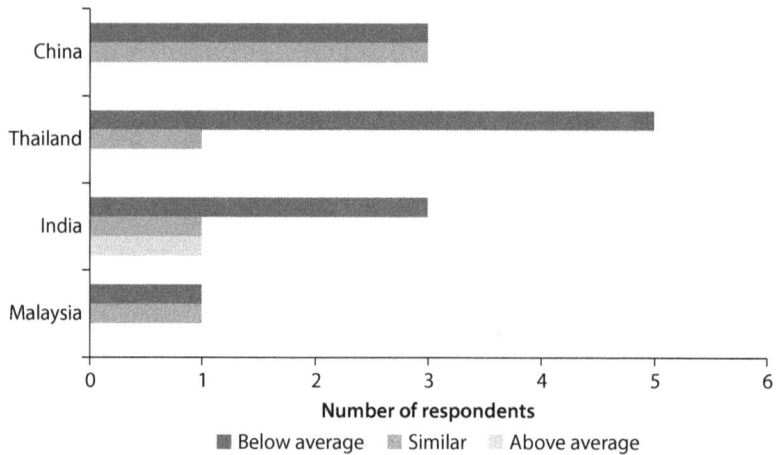

Number of respondents

■ Below average ▨ Similar ▨ Above average

Table 3.8 LSPs' Opinions about Vietnam's Trucking Industry

	Strongly agree	Mostly agree	Disagree	Strongly disagree
There is an adequate supply of trucking companies to meet our company's business needs.		2	5	2
The trucking industry in Vietnam is characterized by a number of small companies that lack the capacity to expand their businesses.	3	5	1	
The majority of trucking companies use old and polluting trucks.	5	2	2	
Shipment tracking is a requirement for us and/or our customers.	3	6		
Most trucking companies do not offer GPS tracking.	3	6		
Trucking companies generally do a good job in minimizing loss or damage to cargo.		4	4	1

trucking companies are small and use second-hand trucks that are inadequately maintained. Driver attitude is generally poor. In order to satisfy the requirements of their customers, several LSPs have invested in their own trucking fleet. Imposition of trucking regulations based on international standards would prompt consolidation in the trucking industry and enable the larger, more professional companies to be more price-competitive with the substandard trucking companies, while improving the overall quality of trucking in Vietnam. Stricter licensing and training of truck drivers would also help upgrade the industry and improve traffic safety.

Nearly 80 percent of LSPs do not believe there is sufficient capacity in the trucking industry to enable them to adequately service their BCO customers (table 3.8). All but one stated that trucking companies are small, with few resources to expand. All but two LSPs consider trucks used in Vietnam to be old and poorly maintained, contributing to air pollution. BCO customers of every LSP require shipment tracking, but few trucking companies offer Global Positioning System (GPS) support in trucks. More LSPs say that trucking companies do not take sufficient care to minimize cargo loss or damage than those who believe they do.

Logistics Parks and Cargo-Handling Facilities

LSPs stated that it is difficult to locate cargo-handling facilities in Vietnam of the quality adequate to satisfy their BCO customers—particularly in the Northern region. Specific challenges cited are as follows:

- Though LSPs generally feel cargo-handling facilities are physically similar to those in other Asian countries, it is reported that not enough are available today, and they are often not located near ports and areas of production (see table 3.9). Better (e.g., more demand-driven) location of cargo-handling facilities could contribute to improving the flow of products and reduce logistics costs for BCOs through synergies between transport modes and logistics services.
- Logistics parks have generally not been pursued by government officials, and as a result no strategy has been established to create efficient, well-placed logistics parks. Cargo-handling facilities are usually standalone facilities. Good quality container freight station (CFS) facilities are a scarce commodity in the country. Recently built facilities are modern, but older ones are substandard. Provision of good general international standards (e.g., fire protection, layered security, consistent supply of power, efficient warehouse management systems) is rare.
- As the process to secure CFS operating licenses is complex and difficult to navigate, these are often granted through facilitation payments and relationships, rather than clear rules.

LSPs suggested numerous examples of what they consider promising, underserved locations for logistics parks, including the following:

- Nonurban areas around HCMC, in Dong Nai, in Lam Dong, at the future intersection of the Long Thanh–Dau Giay Expressway and NH 51, and in Vung Tau
- In the Mekong Delta near Can Tho
- Near the ports in Danang and Nha Trang
- In the nonurban areas around Hanoi and in Bac Ninh and
- More generally, near key highways leading to ports and near the two major airports.

Table 3.9 Respondents' Opinions about Vietnam's Logistics Parks

	Yes	No
Are the numbers of locations adequate today?	1	7
Do you think they will be adequate in the future?	3	3
Are existing and planned sites located conveniently to factories and ports?	2	5
Are existing facilities built to standards comparable to those you operate in other Asian countries?	5	2

Logistics parks and cargo-handling facilities should be considered integral elements of end-to-end supply chains and, therefore, integrated into the transportation infrastructure network. Similar to the case of maritime terminals, access to logistics parks from highway arteries should be enhanced through the use of such tools as fly-overs or timed traffic signals that keep trucks moving with minimal delays. To enable use of rail, logistics parks should be adjacent to planned rail yards and/or have tracks for container and boxcar loading within the park. An excellent example of a multimodal logistics park concept is the CenterPoint Intermodal Center in Ellwood, Illinois (USA) (see box 3.1).

Marine Terminals

The majority of LSPs interviewed manage truck shipments between factories, cargo-handling facilities, ports, and airports on behalf BCOs, whether by using their own equipment or by subcontracting with trucking companies. As shown in figure 3.9, LSPs' most significant highway congestion challenges are associated with highway corridors to/from gateways and with access roads to marine terminals in the HCMC and Haiphong areas. Since there is still little truck traffic to Cai Mep-Thi Vai terminals, highway congestion is moderate in that area and is even less of a challenge in the Central region. BCOs have only moderate difficulty with the closing or cutoff times at terminal gates or in getting access to containers.

Airports

As shown in tables 3.10 and 3.11, LSPs see room for improvement at Vietnam's two cargo airports, Tan Son Nhat Airport (TSNA) and Noi Bai Airport (NBA). This is both in terms of reducing congestion and operating costs and improving service levels. They rank these airports as delivering substandard service relative to other Asian countries.

The two terminal operating companies at TSNA—Tan Son Nhat Cargo Services (TCS) and Saigon Cargo Service Corporation (SCSC)—have different ownership models. LSPs consider TCS's public ownership structure an impediment to modernization of the terminal and its operations. They also rated the service performance of the three SCSC terminals, operated under a joint venture arrangement, higher than TCS's. But because not all air carriers have signed contracts with SCSC, as they have with TCS, LSPs must continue to deal with TCS.

As production of high-tech goods has increased in the Northern region, NBA is considered to be too small, and current capacity is insufficient during certain seasons. This situation is likely to worsen over the medium term as high-tech production increases, making a strong case for the cargo-handling capacity at the airport to be expanded.

LSPs repeatedly stated that TSNA and NBA should have more competitive operations and modernized facilities and equipment. Many called for privatization of terminal operations because of their belief that private companies generally operate more efficiently than state-owned enterprises (SOEs). All LSPs desired to have areas to rent at both airports, where they could perform cargo

Box 3.1 CenterPoint Intermodal Center, Ellwood, Illinois

CenterPoint Intermodal is a freight logistics center that integrates direct rail, truck, transload, and intermodal services with distribution and warehousing. In operation since 2002, it is located 40 miles southwest of Chicago, near the intersection of I-55 and I-80 (see map B3.1.1). All levels of government, more than a dozen public agencies, and private industry came together during the planning of this facility to create a coherent, overarching plan. Over the past 10 years, CenterPoint has achieved the desired outcome of benefiting the community and freight stakeholders by consolidating a critical mass of multimodal cargo-handling activities in one location.

CenterPoint is one of the largest private developments ever undertaken in North America. It comprises approximately 1,000 hectares, with a total investment of $1 billion. It features a 312-hectare intermodal yard (BNSF Logistics Park–Chicago), has the capacity for up to 12 million square feet of industrial and distribution facilities, and provides easy on-off access to adjacent multilane interstate highways. CenterPoint's customers include BNSF Railway, Wal-Mart Stores, DSC Logistics, Georgia Pacific, Potlatch, Sanyo Logistics, Partners Warehouse, California Cartage, and Maersk.

This example demonstrates how rail and highway access makes a logistics park more valuable to BCOs by enabling multimodalism. In particular, it drives cost reductions in supply chains through rail transloading, value-added warehousing, and dedicated distribution. The example also illustrates the impact that public and private sector collaboration can have in enabling higher-service-level logistics.

Map B3.1.1 CenterPoint Intermodal Center, Ellwood, Illinois

Source: Authors, Google.

Efficient Logistics • http://dx.doi.org/10.1596/978-1-4648-0103-7

Figure 3.9 Average Rating of the Perceived Business Impacts of Inland Trucking Factors

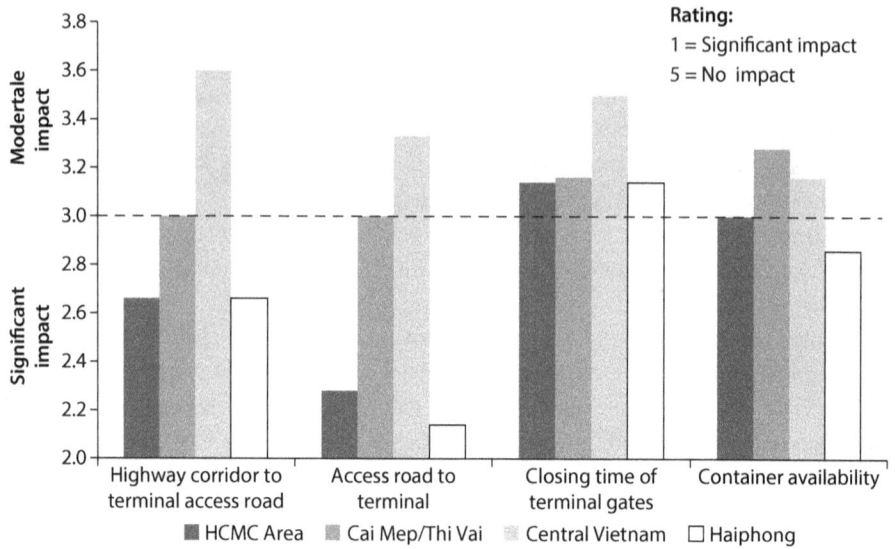

Rating:
1 = Significant impact
5 = No impact

HCMC Area   Cai Mep/Thi Vai   Central Vietnam   Haiphong

Table 3.10 Quality of Tan Son Nhat Airport

	Strongly agree	Mostly agree	Agree	Strongly disagree
The airport meets my service needs.			5	3
The airport freight area is congested so I experience delays in getting my products customs-cleared and out of the airport.	2	1	3	1
The cost of ground services is expensive and I would like to see improvements.	2	2	1	3
There needs to be more than one ground provider.	4	1	3	
I occasionally have damage to cargo due to storage conditions at the airport	1	3	2	2
I would like to see more freighter aircraft calling the airport.	4	2	2	

Table 3.11 Quality of Noi Bai Airport

	Strongly agree	Mostly agree	Agree	Strongly disagree
The airport meets my service needs.		1	3	3
The airport freight area is congested so I experience delays in getting my products customs-cleared and out of the airport.	2	2	3	
The cost of ground services is expensive and I would like to see improvements.	2	2	1	2
There needs to be more than one ground provider.	4		2	1
I would like to see more freighter aircraft calling the airport.	5	1	1	

consolidation and build pallets—an activity now performed by air carriers. This, they noted, would give them better control over the cargo and enable them to reduce airfreight rates for the exporting community. One LSP estimated that its operating costs for handling airfreight could go down by up to 50 percent if it had the ability to consolidate cargo at the terminal.

LSPs generally believe that airport terminal workers need better cargo-handling skills. Attention to detail was repeatedly cited as a key skill in air cargo handling, to prevent cargo damage and loss and to reduce processing times.

Several LSPs reported that there is also a high degree of corruption at tally stations, where cargo is measured and weighed by air terminal workers to determine the chargeable weight upon which the freight rate is calculated. One LSP explained that it is common practice for the airport tallyman to make two tallies—one official, the other unofficial. He reduces the chargeable weight on the official tally by 1,000 kilograms, for example, and then solicits 50 percent of savings from certain freight forwarders who are willing to engage in this type of corrupt activity. The transaction takes place only in cash. In the eyes of LSPs, this practice should be discontinued so that ethical airfreight forwarders will no longer be disadvantaged.

Somewhat surprisingly, international integrators observed that, as far as their businesses were concerned, the efficiency of Vietnam's exporting process is virtually at par with global best practice. Cutoff is four hours before wheels up for all freight except heavy freight, which has a 24-hour cutoff. The express facility at TSNA is near the aircraft loading area, which facilitates cargo flow. The airports provide integrators priority cargo handling over regular airfreight shipments.

Supply Chain Impacts to BCOs

While their core competency is, by definition, an ability to adapt to the circumstances and find cost-effective ways to connect shippers and consignees, LSPs in Vietnam are routinely exposed to operational bottlenecks. These stem from (1) transportation infrastructure (e.g., absence of logistics parks, substandard cargo handling facilities, and small airport facilities), (2) challenges arranging for and monitoring the provision of transportation services by LSP partners (e.g., trucking companies, MTOs, and airfreight terminals), (3) manual, cumbersome processes and ambiguous, inconsistently applied regulations of Customs and other government agencies that govern international trade, and (4) a perceived necessity of engaging in payment of facilitation to keep cargo flowing through the system in a reasonably timely manner. The collective negative impact of this landscape on BCOs is substantial. BCOs experience higher-than-necessary transport and logistics costs and increased transit times. BCOs routinely hold additional, redundant safety stock to their supply chains to mitigate the risk of lost sales and customer dissatisfaction. They spend more time monitoring the activities of their LSPs.

Future Freight Flow Impacts

Two issues that undermine freight mobility and the ease of doing business in Vietnam were particularly troublesome to all LSPs:

1. Every LSP interviewed expressed a high degree of concern about corruption among government officials across Vietnam, especially Customs, and how corruption will reduce Vietnam's competitiveness in the future. LSPs believe that if operations were transparent and solicitation of facilitation was curbed,

their costs for activities relating to customs clearance could be reduced by up to 20 percent.

2. The GoV issues decrees, but provincial leaders have to implement them and interpretation of regulations is inconsistent across provinces. Many provincial leaders have trouble understanding decrees in a legal language that is nuanced and subject to interpretation. According to LSPs, regulations seem to be vaguely defined and ever-changing, and it is unclear what the rules are at any given time. LSPs experience a high risk of being noncompliant.

It will be critical for the GoV to address corruption and the uneven implementation and application of regulations to keep Vietnam competitive with its peers.

BCOs generally nominate an LSP to handle cargo in multiple countries or regions. It is the nature of the business for LSPs to offer services in countries where their BCO customers have shifted sourcing or selling. In other words, LSPs follow their customers around the globe. Because Vietnam has proven to be a desirable place for BCOs to purchase and market products, their nominated LSPs have had to locate operations in Vietnam to serve the customers for which they already perform work in other countries. LSPs generally do not have the choice of avoiding or vacating a country that is difficult or unprofitable in which to do business; instead, they remain and develop competencies to provide responsive services to BCOs within the existing system.

Establishing a National Logistics Observatory

A full 80 percent of respondents welcomed the potential establishment of a national logistics observatory that would manage data related to cargo movements for all modes of transport and for import, export, and domestic cargo. This in contrast to the current situation, where they have to rely on sources that either are not considered reliable or do not provide enough relevant information that is up-to-date. In order to be meaningful and useful, however, the observatory should be a neutral-data platform, provide visibility to performance of the transportation and logistics sector as well as costs, and provide an open forum for sharing best practices. Comments from LSPs include the following:

- "Company gets data from different private agencies, chambers of commerce, and embassies, which it uses to cross-check against what is available from the GoV website and other government sources. Government information is generally at an aggregate level and there are gaps in the data, so Company does not use government data to make investment decisions. When making investment decisions, many of the GoV's plans are hard to come by and the timelines on master plans are always inaccurate."
- "The real issue is that an observatory would be unable to capture all the hidden costs of logistics (facilitation payments, corruption, environmental impact, poor productivity, bureaucracy, etc.) since they are either not available or do not translate directly to measurable/traditional logistics costs."

International BCOs

Respondents' Profile

Face-to-face interviews were conducted with 25 international BCOs doing business in Vietnam. Approximately half of these companies (13) can be identified as exporters, three as importers, and the balance both export and import. They are small, medium, and large BCOs. These companies import raw materials, components, and finished goods from a diversified set of origin countries, and export raw materials and finished goods across the globe as well. Four have their main Vietnam offices in the Hanoi area, and the balance are situated around the HCMC region. Production facilities and/or distribution centers are primarily in the Southeast and Northern regions, though several also operate in the Mekong Delta and Central region.

The average value of a loaded 40-foot regular or 40-foot high cube container from all respondents is $96,563 per container. The range is between $10,000 and $300,000 per container, showing that the interviewees import and export low- to high-value raw materials, components, and finished goods.

Figures 3.10 and 3.11 summarize the types of products exported or imported by the BCOs consulted for this report.

The "Other" category includes exports of power products for transformers, general consumer goods, metal products, sports accessories, beverages, diapers, personal care items, and cement and building materials.

The "Other" category includes imports of raw materials for transformer components, automobiles, leather and textile materials, mining/construction machines and tools, raw materials for beverage manufacturing and pharmaceutical products.

Table 3.12 shows the total annual aggregated export volumes for 2011 for all respondents.

Figure 3.10 Type of Products Exported by Respondents

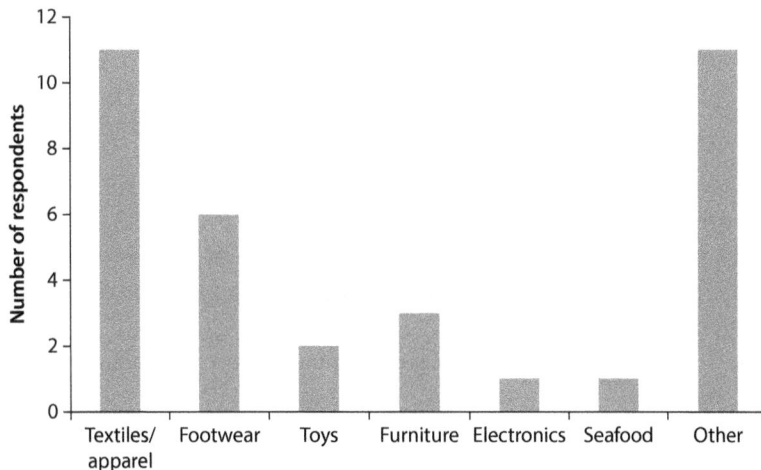

Figure 3.11 Types of Products Imported by Respondents

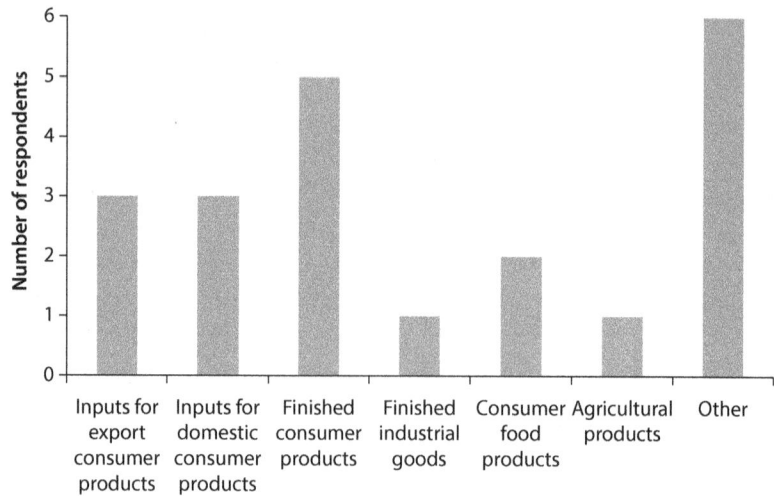

Table 3.12 Total 2011 Annual Export Volumes Reported by Respondents

Total aggregated volume for all respondents	Region of Vietnam		
	South	Central	North
Ocean freight (TEUs)	84,476	1,800	12,408
Air freight (millions of kilograms)	15.2	0.6	1.1

Note: TEU = 20-foot equivalent unit container.

Table 3.13 Total 2011 Annual Import Volumes Reported by Respondents

Total aggregated volume for all respondents	Region of Vietnam		
	South	Central	North
Ocean freight (TEUs)	10,790	0	19,185
Air freight (millions of kilograms)	0.4	0	0.3

Note: TEU = 20-foot equivalent unit container.

Individual responses on freight activity varied substantially. Annual containers exported by region ranged from less than 10 TEU to over 33,000 TEUs, and airfreight volumes ranged from a few thousand kilograms to more than 2.6 million kilograms. The heavy users of airfreight ship, for the most part, high-value or perishable finished goods.

Table 3.13 shows the total aggregated annual import volumes for 2011 for all interviewees.

Containers imported by region ranged from less than 10 TEU to over 17,000 TEUs, and airfreight volumes ranged from a thousand kilograms to more than

250,000 kilograms. It is less common for the BCOs interviewed to import raw materials, components, or finished goods via airfreight.

Use of Maritime Transportation

As reported in figure 3.12, marine terminals at Cat Lai, Haiphong, and Cai Mep-Thi Vai are the most popular with international BCOs; usage of ICDs is also prevalent. Cat Lai is the only terminal in Vietnam handling over one million TEUs per year. It is an efficient operating terminal that is within the HCMC area, close to major manufacturers. Cat Lai BCOs benefit from having closer cutoff times to vessel departures, lower drayage rates, no restricted hours for draying containers to and from the terminal, and preferred customs operations. Cat Lai has the largest number of container feeder services berthing at the terminal.

Supply Chain Impacts Relating to Maritime Transport

The general consensus among international BCOs is that the GoV should focus on developing and modernizing a few key ports, rather than all ports across Vietnam. Several BCOs called for key marine terminals to have electronic track-and-trace systems that would enable them to monitor the status of their containers and track all information related to their shipments (e.g., truck gate-in and exit time), instead of manual tracking. We will discuss the further feedback by region obtained from BCOs below.

Southern Vietnam Marine Terminals

Most BCOs continue to use marine terminals in the HCMC area even though these terminals are served by feeder vessels. Except for one service out of Cai Mep, current feeder services from HCMC terminals connecting with mother

Figure 3.12 Marine Terminals Used by Respondents

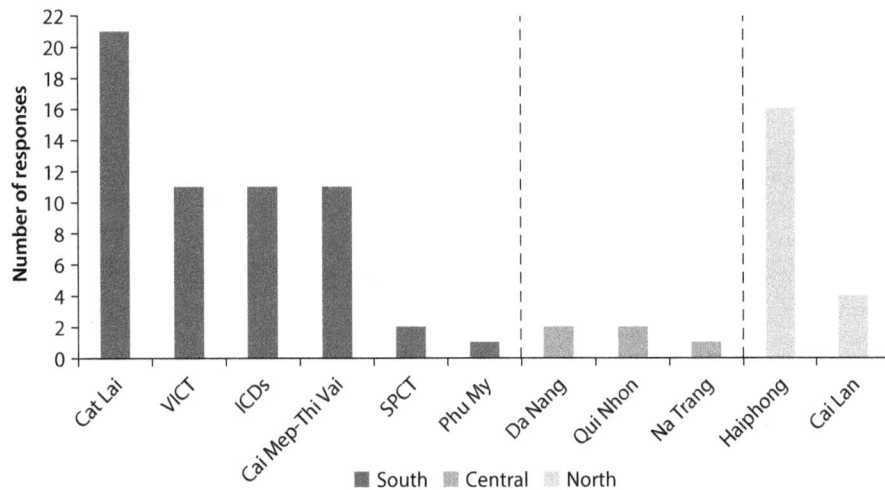

vessels at transshipment hubs in Singapore, Tanjung Pelepas, Hong Kong SAR, China, or Kaohsiung provide the same overall transit time to destinations on the Asia-to-Europe and Mediterranean services and on the Transpacific. Nevertheless, some BCOs, usually shipping time-sensitive, higher-value consumer goods, have switched either all or a portion of their shipments to terminals at Cai Mep-Thi Vai to enable their cargo to be loaded directly on mother vessels, which reduces the chance that the cargo will be delayed during transshipment. For one service from Cai Mep to Los Angeles, California, the transit time is generally three days faster than using feeder service from either Cat Lai or VICT.

Throughout 2012, as they faced continued financial pressure, the aftereffects of the global economic crisis, and continued economic uncertainty in Europe, ocean carriers reduced the number of vessel strings calling Cai Mep-Thi Vai terminals by about half. It is uncertain how soon ocean carriers will add services at these terminals. As a result, several international BCOs noted a current lack of frequency of vessel calls, with the implication that the potential of these terminals is not being fully realized. BCOs felt that scarce foreign direct investment (FDI) and GoV funds were not being put to good use. "Use of Cai Mep-Thi Vai is currently running at just 20 percent of capacity, which is a waste of resources," observed one BCO. Several BCOs were concerned about how the GoV issued operating licenses to foreign operators at Cai Mep-Thi Vai in a way that resulted in numerous small terminals and led to overcapacity. The small footprint of each of the terminals is considered an impediment to smooth operations and quick container turnaround time. "Critical road network projects such as Highway 51, which is targeted to be completed by the second quarter of 2013, need to be completed without delay and with a high degree of quality in order to support the development of deep sea ports," expressed another BCO.

Northern Vietnam Marine Terminals

BCOs reported several connectivity challenges facing Haiphong port in Northern Vietnam. It was noted that (1) dredging is needed to enable larger vessels to berth, (2) container-handling facilities are outdated, and (3) all container services are served by feeder vessels. (Some BCOs assume feeder vessel service is slower than direct mother vessel calls, which has not been the case for all direct mother vessels services from Cai Mep-Thi Vai.) Congestion in surrounding roads and within marine terminals sometimes exists, adding up to an extra three days to transfer goods between the port and distribution centers or factories.

As one BCO pointed out, "Management of Haiphong Port is poor. 80 percent of terminals are operated by SOEs, which are inefficient. Sometimes Company's containers are lost within the terminals because yard management systems do not work well."

Use of Truck Transport

About half of the international BCOs interviewed rely on their ocean carriers and LSPs to arrange truck transportation. A handful of BCOs have their factories deal directly with truck carriers.

Efficient Logistics • http://dx.doi.org/10.1596/978-1-4648-0103-7

A large contrast is seen in trucking cost comparisons between LSPs (figure 3.7), which contract directly with trucking companies on behalf of BCOs, and BCOs' own views on trucking (figure 3.13), who may or may not have direct contracts with trucking companies. Based on the authors' primary research, all-in trucking costs on a per-kilometer basis are higher in Vietnam than in China or Indonesia. LSPs negotiating truck rates know this to be true because of the differences in the price of diesel, inflation rates, facilitation payments, and congestion, among other factors. On the other hand, many of the interviewed BCOs look at the total cost of trucking. As lengths of haul in Vietnam are generally shorter than those in China, for example, total trip costs may seem to BCOs to be less expensive in Vietnam, when on a per-kilometer basis it is just the opposite.

Both LSPs (figure 3.8) and BCOs (figure 3.14) are in general agreement that the service quality of trucking in Vietnam is overall lower than in the other countries they were asked to rate.

Figure 3.13 Trucking Costs in Vietnam Compared with Other Asian Countries

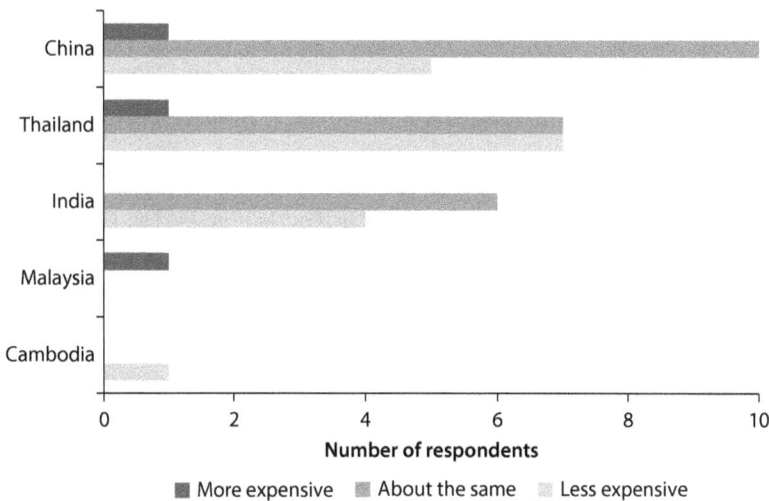

■ More expensive   ■ About the same   ▨ Less expensive

Figure 3.14 Trucking Service Quality in Vietnam Compared with Other Asian Countries

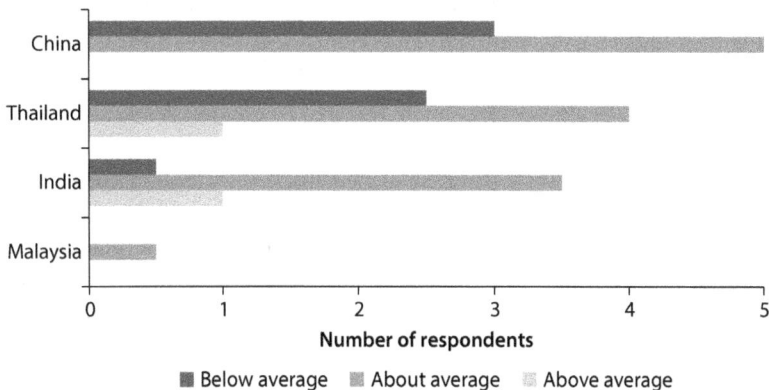

■ Below average   ▨ About average   ▨ Above average

Table 3.14 Trucking Industry Conditions

	Strongly agree	Mostly agree	Disagree	Strongly disagree
There are plenty of trucking companies that provide export container haulage.	2	15	4	
There are plenty of trucking companies that have 10 or more truck heads, chassis, and containers.	4	7	8	2
There are plenty of trucking companies that provide box trucks for haulage to CFS facilities.	1	14	6	
Most of the trucks are old and pollute the environment.	9	10	2	2
I would like to see more trucking companies provide GPS tracking.	15	5	1	1
Cargo security is becoming more of a problem in Vietnam.	9	8	5	1
The cost for cargo insurance coverage is expensive and the coverage provided is not adequate.	5	8	5	

BCOs consider the trucking industry to be fragmented, with many small trucking companies operating in the market—a factor that contributes to the low level of service quality (table 3.14). "Company feels there are only from five to ten quality trucking companies," asserted one BCO. BCOs repeatedly stated that consolidation of trucking companies would be a positive development in the industry.

They also saw direct benefits if the GoV imposed stringent regulations on trucking companies and their drivers and/or strictly enforced those rules through imposition of penalties for noncompliance. A driver licensing system and the need for formal driver training were often brought up in discussions of how to strengthen the trucking industry. "The level of professionalism would improve as a result" was a typical remark.

One BCO advised that it has not found long-term, reliable partners to meet its service standards. "Trucking companies typically do not follow international standards (e.g., contracts, meeting commitments, etc.) and security issues are also a concern. Truck heads are old, of poor quality, and highly polluting." Another BCO reported trucking company workers are "poorly paid and do not have a good work ethic." "No good cold chain for temperature-controlled goods moving via trucks exists. Vehicles are in bad condition and are not maintained well. Company cannot rely on temperature readings," remarked a third BCO.

BCOs noted that trucking subsidiaries operated or contracted by ocean carriers and LSPs, as well as the largest, more professional trucking companies, have good quality trucks, but rates can be up to 40 percent higher than those of local trucking companies typically using old, polluting trucks. In other words, if a BCO desires reliable, quality service, it has to pay higher rates.

The imbalance of trade between the Northern and Southern regions (with more cargo going North than South) also contributes to high truck rates. It is common for trucks to be overloaded (average overloading rates have been estimated at 20–30 percent). This puts BCOs that do not permit their trucking companies to overload trucks at a competitive disadvantage to those that are not concerned about safety. Cargo is often loose-loaded without pallets; this causes cargo to shift, leading to accidents and cargo damage. Cargo security is also viewed as becoming more problematic.

Nearly all BCOs mentioned that undocumented facilitation payments to truck drivers to cover traffic fines inflate the rates they pay for truck transport. Police issue citations to truck drivers for such infractions as speeding, using the wrong lane, turning infractions, overweight loads, worn tires, and carrying the wrong transport documents. Depending upon the offense, a typical traffic ticket costs between $25 and $100. Two LSPs estimated that undocumented facilitation payments are between 50 and 60 percent of the actual ticket price, depending upon the negotiation skills of the truck driver.

It was observed that trucking companies engage in a variety of tactics to minimize delays. For example, it is reportedly common for laden truck drivers to stop at police stations on the main routes on every journey to pay facilitation proactively at each location (typically $7.50–12.50), in order to avoid being stopped by police while en route to their destination (this is not done when transporting empty containers). A BCO said these fees account for "50 percent of the overall trucking fees Company pays to its LSP to transport cargo from Hanoi to Haiphong." Another BCO said, "Some trucking companies pay $10 and $25 to drivers to cover traffic fines for a given trip or time period. Corruption is a major issue in Vietnam and adds to company's business costs."

Use of Highway Infrastructure

Highway congestion is a major concern for international BCOs (figure 3.15). In particular, they view the level of highway congestion in Vietnam as worse than

Figure 3.15 Perceived Level of Highway Congestion in Vietnam Relative to Regional Peers

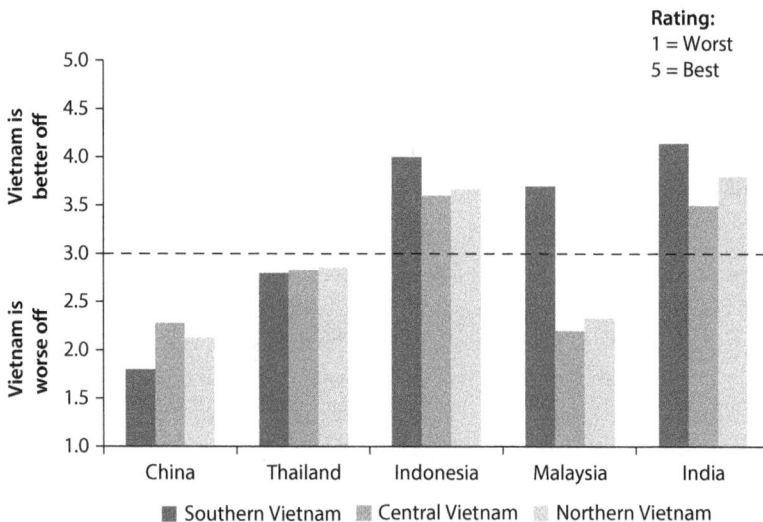

in China, Malaysia, and Thailand, countries that have invested in highway infrastructure, but similar or better than in India and Indonesia, which are known throughout the industry for highway gridlock. India and Indonesia have committed to invest in transportation infrastructure, so they also could surpass Vietnam if Vietnam stands still.

Supply Chain Impacts of Highway Congestion

Interviewees had a great deal to say regarding how highway congestion reduces truck speeds and negatively affects the operations of their supply chains. There was general consensus that highway congestion creates more costs and increases transportation time. This impacts delivery planning and timing, often forcing factories to finish production earlier and rush products to the ports to meet vessel cutoff times. If the cutoff time is missed, the BCO must rebook to a later vessel, which increases administrative work and costs as well as delivery delays at destination. Delivery unreliability causes BCOs to lose the trust of their customers. Similar things happen when raw materials and components are imported and there are delays on highways from the port or airport to the factory. Because of frequent delays, airfreight costs can also increase.

HCMC Highways

Several BCOs noted that the daytime tractor trailer and container truck restrictions in HCMC have a ripple effect. For example, access in and out of Cat Lai at night is constrained because of heavy traffic, which is exacerbated by road infrastructure limitations.

Transit time to one BCO's factory in the HCMC area from Cai Mep is around four hours if the truck travels at night. During daytime travel, it can take seven to eight hours to get to HCMC:

> Road conditions and congestion between Cai Mep and HCMC are terrible, especially at year-end. Three hour delays are common during the peak season. Normal transit time from port to factory is about four hours; during peak season it is over eight hours. Trucking companies charge more as well. Congestion really impacts the Company's operations because the Company tries to have drivers make a round trip of two loads, which sometimes cannot occur due to the production schedule. There is only one lane in each direction with no divider for motorcycles. Construction is underway to expand it to two lanes each way, but it is uncertain when that will be finished

In addition to congestion on NH 51, BCOs encounter congestion on local roads around HCMC and on the Saigon Bridge leading to HCMC marine terminals, especially during peak truck travel times. The access road to the Phu My Bridge is partly made of dirt and partly with poor-quality paving. On Thursdays and Fridays the bridge experiences a high volume of truck traffic because vessels are being loaded at Cat Lai, and congestion is further exacerbated because trucks have to slow down when traveling over the substandard access road. The road infrastructure surrounding TSNA was also called out as being inadequate.

Efficient Logistics • http://dx.doi.org/10.1596/978-1-4648-0103-7

Hanoi-Haiphong Highways

According to one BCO, "There seems to be a disconnect between what the GoV is trying to encourage in terms of production in the Northern region and the volume of cargo that can efficiently be transported on the existing infrastructure." Another BCO reported that, "Transit time from Hanoi to Haiphong averages 4.5 hours because of road congestion compared to two hours without congestion. Trucks must stay in Haiphong half a day to pick up a container (full or empty). There is no separation between motorcycle, cars, and trucks on the Hanoi-Haiphong highway, which is dangerous and slows down the movement of trucks." Another BCO said, "In Haiphong 100 percent of company's containers were delayed from September 2011 to January 2012 due to road congestion."

General Discussion of Highways

One BCO sells its finished goods to customers in the Northern and Central Highlands regions. "The conditions of highways and roads are poor and transit delays are common. Company has to build extra time into the total lead time to account for this, but it is not always possible due to customer delivery requirements."

Many BCOs commented that the general quality of roads is low and repairs must often be made, which causes traffic delays and, according to a BCO, "is a waste of money" in light of the limited funds available for increasing capacity of highways and maintaining existing ones to be of good quality. They are uncertain whether the construction quality is adequate and if the materials will hold up to wear-and-tear, especially because of the common practice of truck overloading.

Use of Airfreight

As demonstrated in tables 3.15 and 3.16, international BCOs generally rate the quality of TSNA and NBA to be adequate relative to their airfreight requirements. However, 14 BCOs indicated it would be helpful to have additional air freighter services at both.

The TCS terminal is considered small and crowded with insufficient storage areas. Trucks have to queue outside, which creates congestion. The general consensus was that service at the TCS terminal is unreliable and SCSC provides better service compared to TCS. A BCO exporting agricultural products stated,

Table 3.15 Quality of Tan Son Nhat Airport

	Strongly agree	Mostly agree	Disagree	Strongly disagree
The airport meets my service needs.		18	1	
Cutoff times to meet uplift are okay for our production.	1	12	4	
I occasionally have damage to cargo due to storage conditions at the airport.	3	5	8	2
I would like to see more freighter aircraft calling the airport.	8	9	1	

Efficient Logistics • http://dx.doi.org/10.1596/978-1-4648-0103-7

Table 3.16 Quality of Noi Bai Airport

	Strongly agree	Mostly agree	Disagree	Strongly disagree
The airport meets my service needs.		9	1	1
Cutoff times to meet uplift are okay for our production.	1	5	2	
I occasionally have damage to cargo due to storage conditions at the airport.	1	5	2	
I would like to see more freighter aircraft calling the airport.	4	6	1	

Figure 3.16 Factors Impacting Airfreight Logistics Costs

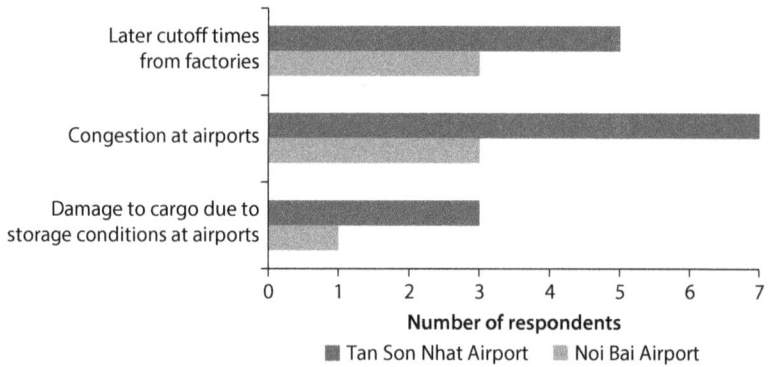

Number of respondents
■ Tan Son Nhat Airport   ▨ Noi Bai Airport

"TSNA has no cold storage warehouse available so company stores product in a HCMC cold storage facility while waiting for the flight departure."

NBA's storage area is small, and infrastructure at NBA needs to be improved to increase capacity. During the peak season, one BCO noted, it "[is difficult] getting cargo onboard flights and there are few alternatives" to rely on. According to another BCO, "timely processing of airfreight shipments in general could become a problem with increased airfreight volume." A third BCO explained: "Improvements needed include new equipment for security checking and weighing cargo. Storage costs are high when Customs delays the clearance process. NBA is able to handle the recent 50 percent growth in imports because a larger warehouse to handle exports was built. Shipments on weekend flights require longer time to clear customs."

Congestion at TSNA is viewed as the most critical factor negatively impacting airfreight-based supply chains (figure 3.16). One BCO reported that "Company's confidence in the security levels at both airports is low and during wet weather cargo damage occurs." Another said it pays higher airfreight costs in Vietnam compared with other Asian countries.

Use of Third-Party Warehouses

International BCOs operating in Southern Vietnam generally consider warehouses there to be satisfactory (see figure 3.17). This is not surprising, considering that over the past decade more third-party warehouse development has taken place in the Southern region than in the Northern region to support the

Figure 3.17 Adequacy of Warehouse Facilities

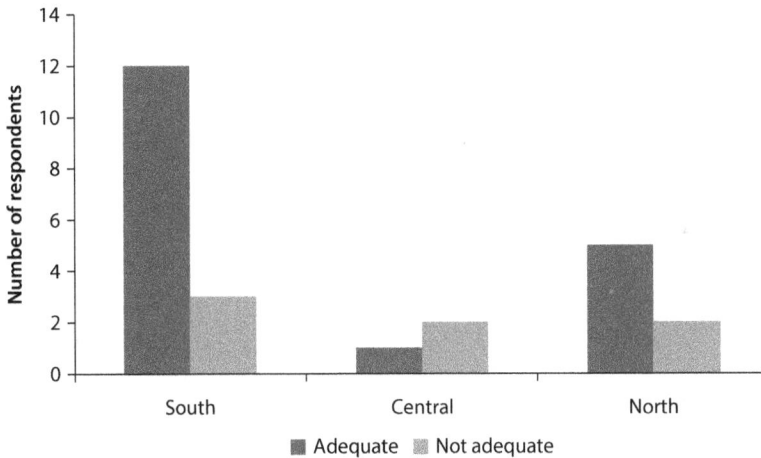

growth in production and evolving requirements of BCOs. Of those interviewed, seven BCOs use warehouses in the Northern region, and five of them consider them to be adequate. Only three BCOs use warehouses in the Central part of Vietnam, and their opinions differ, although a majority of them view available facilities as generally inadequate.

The quality of the warehouse buildings and services often depends upon the types of customers served. One BCO stated the warehouse it uses "is of good quality with very high standards because it handles distribution for a high end consumer products company." However, many small, antiquated cargo-handling facilities are still in use, particularly in the Northern and Central regions. "Company uses three CFS facilities in Hanoi in order to be able to manage its export volume, because there is not enough capacity in just one," noted one BCO.

Another BCO indicated, "Most facilities around Hanoi lack full concrete floors (they are bricks over sand) and have limited ventilation, which impacts product quality if storage is required. These facilities also have substandard cargo and facility security practices. Although a few modern facilities exist, smaller shippers will not benefit from them in the short term because they are full of cargo from large BCOs. Facilities in the Northern region are what facilities were like in the Southern region a decade ago."

This BCO continued: "There is a risk for BCOs in the Northern region because CFS [operations] are less sophisticated than in the Southern region. Facilities have room for improvement to be on par with those in Southern Vietnam. Investment in equipment is necessary to improve the speed of unloading and scanning." Another BCO offered the following view: "The transportation infrastructure and CFS facilities in the Northern region will be inadequate to accommodate the increase in production that is occurring due to government incentives for factories to operate in Northern bonded industrial zones."

More modern warehouses will be required as production increases in Vietnam. Ideally, logistics parks need to be created near production clusters, agricultural

Efficient Logistics • http://dx.doi.org/10.1596/978-1-4648-0103-7

Figure 3.18 Comparison of Warehousing in Vietnam with That of Other Asian Countries

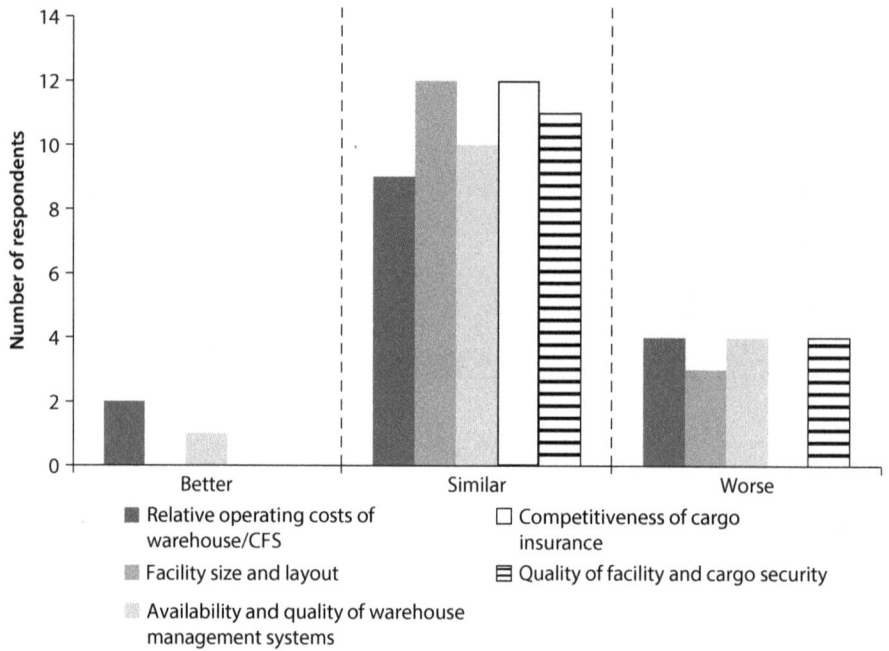

Note: CFS = container freight station.

areas like the Mekong Delta, urban centers, and ports. They should have easy access to highways.

Upgrading warehouse processes such as the use of warehouse management systems and better security controls to be in line with international standards is viewed as a way to reduce the costs charged to BCOs. Time required to unload cargo from containers to warehouses should also be reduced.

One person commented, "The GoV should allow LSPs to consolidate goods from different CFS warehouses into one container, which is not permitted today. There should be clear guidelines and policies for CFS consolidation for Vietnam as a whole. Today Company sees different practices and treatment from Customs in different provinces."

Warehouse facilities, warehouse operations, and costs paid by international BCOs are generally in line with what is found in other Asian countries, as depicted in Figure 3.18. One BCO commented that, "As a whole package, costs for warehousing, transportation, marine terminal operations, customs, systems, etc., in Vietnam are more expensive than in many other Asian countries. But if warehouse costs and facilities are viewed separately, the cost is about average to less expensive."

Customs Clearance Process
International BCOs provided a great deal of insight on their experience with the customs clearance process in Vietnam.[9]

Table 3.17 Characteristics of Customs and the Import/Export Process

	Strongly agree	Mostly agree	Disagree	Strongly disagree
Customs decisions, policies, and/or directions are arbitrary and inconsistent.	6	7	6	1
Customs is bureaucratic, but consistent among the various Customs districts.	5	7	6	1
Customs operations are consistent with other Asian countries.		9	9	1
Customs operations are better than in other Asian countries.		3	10	2
Customs officials work cooperatively with our company to address issues.	1	10	7	1
Customs fees are well publicized and consistently applied.	1	11	2	4

Table 3.17 shows responses from BCOs regarding six questions covering various aspects of customs policies and procedures, operations and fees, and their interactions with Customs officials in importing and exporting products. About half of the respondents said Customs decisions, policies, and directions are arbitrary and inconsistent, while seven disagreed. The general consensus is that application of customs regulations is not consistent across provinces and among Customs officials. Those indicating it is more cumbersome to work with customs administration officials in Vietnam than in other Asian countries and those who say it is about the same were nearly even. About half of the interviewees consider customs operations in Vietnam to be more cumbersome than in other Asian countries, and only three considered it was better. More respondents feel they can work cooperatively with Customs officials than those who say the opposite. Two-thirds of those who answered the question said they understood the published customs fees and consider these fees to be consistently applied across the country.

The majority of BCOs interface with Customs via the Customs web-portal system, which allows customs brokers to (1) electronically complete Customs entry documents on their internal systems and (2) apply for a Customs entry number. Customs brokers print the entry documents referencing the assigned entry number and hand-deliver them to Vietnam Customs for final sign-off. The exception to this procedure is land-border crossings, where Customs has not installed its web-portal system. The benefit of the web-portal is that customs brokers can complete all Customs forms electronically, compared to manually having to fill out the forms. The drawback is that part of the process—presenting hard copy documents—is still manual, which leads to unnecessary administrative effort and time.

The next iteration in customs modernization is to transition to a fully automated system for all BCOs. This is scheduled to be available in 2014 to customs brokers and BCOs that invest in technology enabling them to communicate electronically with Vietnam Customs.

Today, in the eyes of international BCOs, the functional area of clearing customs in Vietnam is only better than Cambodia and Indonesia and is less competitive than in other Asian countries. The application of customs policies needs to be simplified and universally applied, say BCOs. Reducing the number of required certificates and licenses would also streamline the clearance process. According to one BCO,

> Customs follows the World Customs Organization guidelines, but how Customs operates is another story. Customs officers' views vary in their interpretation of regulations and this appears to be more of an issue in the Northern region compared to the HCMC area. This variation between Customs offices and even Customs officials within the same office leads to delays in obtaining proper licenses and correctly completing forms, as there are often inconsistencies between different imports of the same material.

The majority of the challenges BCOs find with Customs are on the import side of the business. Most of the BCOs interviewed for this report manufacture goods for export, and their reliance on imported raw materials and components to produce export products ranges from 50 to 75 percent of their input needs. Therefore, inconsistencies in processing imports through Customs represent a significant competitiveness disadvantage, as judged by the nearly unanimous comments on this issue from all interviewed BCOs.

According to these BCOs, and confirming the testimonies obtained from LSPs, facilitation payments to Customs officials to avoid delays are a common practice when clearing imports and exports through Customs. BCOs noted that gaining and maintaining good relationships with Customs officials is generally perceived to be a necessary cost of doing business by international LSPs. BCOs perceive this as a driver of increased supply chain and logistics costs. When queried during interviews, BCOs were typically unable to estimate the cost of facilitation because it is a hidden, undocumented cost to them. But the general consensus among LSPs and BCOs was that facilitation fees to Customs officials, either as direct payments or in the form of social entertainment, was between 5 percent and 50 percent of customs brokerage fees, with 30 percent being about average. Other instances where facilitation payments are reportedly common are to reduce duty liabilities, settle disputes over tariff classifications and duties, and arrange for the import of restricted items.

Impediments to Streamlined Import and Export Customs Clearance

The generally high import content of Vietnam's manufacturing exports makes the country's trade competitiveness particularly vulnerable to customs clearance delays for import logistics. Imported raw materials, components, and parts account for 50–70 percent of the inputs Vietnamese factories need to manufacture products for export. Despite this, imported goods typically remain at the port for four to five days because of procedural bottlenecks and Custom's operating setup (e.g., Customs does not work weekends or at night). In response, just-in-time (JIT) manufacturers are forced to carry additional inventory. Many LSPs noted that Customs is rarely able to notify them about the potential length of delays, further increasing management complexity and elevating the cost of doing business.

For single import shipments, the BCO must submit its buying contract to obtain an import license upon arrival of the goods at the port or airport in Vietnam, a process that can sometimes take up to 10 days. This is also true for single export shipments and for all high-valued consumer goods. However, for known importers and exporters, buying and selling contracts, respectively, must be to be presented only with the initial import or export application. BCOs importing or exporting hazardous cargo can apply for licenses in advance of importing or exporting such products, but the GoV often changes its requirements, causing delays when those hazardous products actually arrive or depart.

One manufacturer with factories in Malaysia stated: "Less-than-container load cargo can be cleared in Malaysia in three days compared to six days in Vietnam. Full container loads shipments are cleared in one day in Malaysia compared to three to four days in Vietnam."

Inbound shipments arriving by air need to be weighed by Customs, as that becomes the official weight of the shipment. Due to frequent deviations, even those that are insignificant, between the official weight and the weight customs brokers provide from import documents produced at origin, customs brokers are forced to wait until Customs assigns the weight before preparing and submitting import clearance documents. This adds to the document preparation cost since the customs broker cannot take full advantage of the electronic document feed from their origin offices. As a result, the cargo release is delayed.

Streamlining International Trade Processes by Customs
The following actions to improve the customs clearance process were suggested by international BCOs and manufacturers:

- Promote a better understanding of the business requirements of BCOs and work more cooperatively with them to understand their business needs and processes to avoid unnecessary duty costs and cargo delays.
- Enable quicker clearance of imports by fully implementing a preclearance process in which customs brokers can present customs entries in advance of cargo arrival in Vietnam.
- Minimize the frequency of cargo inspections and speed up inspection time.
- Accept English versions of all clearance-related documents.
- Reduce BCOs' origin consolidation costs by allowing unloading or loading of containers at more than one factory and across Customs districts, and in the case of export shipments, perform customs clearance of co-loaded containers at ports.
- Have consistent policies regarding commodity classification, valuation, and duty payments. There is too much variability in the system, as nearly all BCOs reported that Customs officials seem to repeatedly have a different answer regarding these processes.
- Stabilize customs duty rates in the framework of the World Trade Organization (WTO) and existing trade agreements like the Association of Southeast Asian

Nations (ASEAN) Trade in Goods Agreement, ASEAN-China Free Trade Area Agreement, and the Agreement between Japan and the Socialist Republic of Viet Nam for an Economic Partnership. The Trans-Pacific Partnership (TPP) is expected to follow these trade agreements.

• Work with companies to develop an electronic calculation of raw material usage to finished goods material usage in order to avoid duty payments on imported raw materials used exclusively for manufacturing export products. This process would make it easier for Customs to validate imported raw material usage in finished goods.

• Maintain the exemption allowing 275 days for exporting products manufactured with imported raw materials without paying duty and continue to grant extensions as long as manufacturers can document excess raw materials to future purchase orders. In dealing with some major international buyers, manufacturers occasionally need the flexibility to get longer extensions without having purchase order documentation because the buyer has pushed out its need for the material beyond the next season.

• Assure BCOs that Customs can safeguard BCO records filed electronically in order to successfully handle the year-end reconciliation process between imported raw material value and the export value of finished goods, as duties will be imposed on the manufacturer for any discrepancies.

• Provide better training to raise the level of professionalism of Customs officials in the smaller cities and provinces in order to have a more uniform application of customs regulations.

• Increase the number and/or expand the testing capabilities at the three certified product inspection centers in HCMC in order to minimize delays. BCOs need to have timely and predictable turnaround times for better inventory management or shipment planning.

• Expedite customs inspection at Cat Lai's external customs inspection site by acquiring one or more additional scanners, as this is a bottleneck area. Container inspection usually takes a day depending on the truck queue and arrival time of the container at the port, as Customs works only eight hours a day, five days a week.

• Expedite the processing of export licenses, especially for temperature-controlled products because long delays can result in product spoilage, especially for airfreight shipments, because of the lack of affordable cold storage at airports.

• Be more proactive and consistent in handling hazardous material imports, as procedures that are followed to obtain import licenses in advance of the shipment are frequently changed at the time of import. This leads to delays and added cost. New regulations for all types of cargo need to be communicated in advance and all regulations should be uniformly followed by all Customs agents. This is especially important for domestic products so that BCOs are able to build in the cost of import duties and develop strategies for marketing and selling products in Vietnam.

Efficient Logistics • http://dx.doi.org/10.1596/978-1-4648-0103-7

Suggested GoV Actions for Reducing Logistics Costs

Interviewees offered numerous comments and suggested actions that the GoV could take that would lower their logistics costs. Recommendations covered topics of multimodal transport infrastructure planning; the various modes of transport; warehouse facilities and logistics parks; streamlined processes; transparency and consistent application of laws and regulations, particularly relating to import and export customs clearance; and training of government officials.

Six representative ideas and suggestions from international BCOs are listed below:

- "Company is concerned that the GoV will not pay enough attention to the recommendations from this study and that growth will stagnate. If Vietnam's competitiveness stagnates relative to its peers, company will find it difficult to further invest here." Through the interviews, the study team learned that companies are frustrated in their attempts through trade organizations or other means to have their voices heard by government officials or the lack of action by the GoV to address their collective concerns to make doing business in Vietnam easier and more profitable.

- "Transportation infrastructure projects need to come online now here in Vietnam, or other countries such as Indonesia and Myanmar will sooner rather than later take over the current market position of Vietnam. It is crucial for Vietnam to react now to keep the momentum going, because the other countries here within the region do not sleep."

- "Overall, logistics and transportation infrastructure has been improving compared with several years ago; however, further upgrading and expansion is needed to reach the same level as other Asian countries like China in order to improve Vietnam's competitiveness ranking as well as drive positive economic growth. To avoid waste and/or minimize the risk of not achieving the benefits desired, any future port, logistics or transportation project, from a strategic standpoint, should be planned by keeping the entire system in mind (ports, inland waterway system, airports, highways, access roads, warehouses, etc.) instead of the GoV taking a piecemeal approach."

- "The GoV should take a multimodal approach and consider road infrastructure, ports, waterways, ICDs, warehouses, and other elements of transportation infrastructure holistically as a system. At some point, the labor cost component in Vietnam will not be as competitive, and then it will get down to transportation infrastructure and logistics. Vietnam is still relying on low labor costs to attract foreign investment and production."

- "More infrastructure improvements are needed in highways, ports, airports, and logistics parks to improve product flow, as Company is a JIT manufacturer. Company estimates these improvements might reduce its transportation and warehousing-related costs 10–15 percent."

- "Ministries need to work together cooperatively, rather than in silos, in order to create better transportation infrastructure master plans."

Efficient Logistics • http://dx.doi.org/10.1596/978-1-4648-0103-7

National Logistics Observatory

Two-thirds of interviewees thought it would be wise for the GoV to establish a national logistics observatory to provide BCOs, other freight stakeholders, and public policy makers with actual freight-related data that measure multimodal transportation system performance and cost competitiveness. Only 7 percent said this would not be beneficial to them, and 26 percent had no opinion. Currently, relevant data are limited and difficult to obtain from the GoV, LSPs, MTOs, and other sources. As a result, BCOs routinely engage in guesswork when formulating business strategies. They have few good ways to benchmark or validate information. A neutral third party must collect, audit, and maintain the data to ensure objectivity and accuracy.

Domestic BCOs

Respondents' Profile

The two domestic BCOs with operations in Vietnam that were interviewed for this report ship building materials, automobiles, low-value consumer goods, and electronic consumer goods. One of the BCOs manufactures its products in Vietnam for both export and domestic distribution to wholesalers and retail stores. It is noted that many more domestic companies were contacted for interviews for this report but never returned electronic mail or phone calls.

Cities within Vietnam from which the BCOs source their raw materials include Hai Duong, Phu Tho, Hoa Binh, Haiphong, and Bac Gian. China, Italy, and Spain are also sourcing areas. Primary customers are located in major Vietnamese cities, but one domestic BCO also ships to customers in Australia, Japan, Panama, Taiwan, China, and Thailand.

Trucking Industry and Highway System

Motor carrier service is essential to domestic BCOs, and they overwhelmingly rely on domestic trucking companies as part of their supply chains. In the particular case of the domestic BCOs interviewed, they engage in regular business with the following trucking companies, all but one of which (Yusen Logistics) are Vietnamese: Anh Kiet, Diep Hung, Greenlines Logistics, Logitem Vietnam Company, Phu Son Transportation Company, Thong Nhat, VEAM Transportation Company, Viet Anh, and Yusen Logistics.

Some interesting contrasts were found in domestic BCOs' views about the trucking industry compared with those of LSPs (table 3.8) and international BCOs (table 3.14). While the sample size of domestic BCOs is small, suggesting these views should be taken with considerable caution, it is also true that domestic BCO business requirements differ from those of their international counterparts. For example, domestic BCOs use trucks mainly to transport finished goods to distribution facilities and stores, rather than to haul international container shipments to and from major gateways. Perhaps the main area of contrast was the issue of average fleet size. While all but one of the LSPs agree that trucking companies generally lack the capacity to expand, suggesting a preponderance of small firms, domestic BCOs interviewed for this report appear to be dealing with fewer, relatively larger trucking companies. On the other hand, there is strong agreement among all three of these freight stakeholders (LSPs, international BCOs, and domestic BCOs) that most trucking companies lack GPS tracking capabilities, a service feature that all BCOs interviewed (domestic and international) consider to be a business imperative. This is likely due to the fact that all three stakeholders see cargo security as a substantial risk. Moreover, domestic BCOs' perception of cargo insurance as expensive suggests that trucking companies do not have adequate insurance coverage.

The primary truck corridors these domestic BCOs rely on are Hanoi-Haiphong, Hanoi-HCMC, Hanoi-Danang, and Hanoi–neighboring provinces. Congestion in Southern Vietnam is considered to be heavy. Because of the truck operating restrictions in HCMC during the day, one respondent stated the delivery of products can be late, and the other said its operations are constrained, even though air quality is improved. Highways in the central region allow smooth flow of trucks, and congestion in the Northern region is rated as either having little or no congestion.

Domestic BCOs reported that to improve the highway system, two key initiatives could be implemented. First, road infrastructure should be upgraded on key freight corridors to provide more capacity for trucks, which would improve freight velocity. Roadways need to be viewed as a network to provide access and connectivity for goods and services. Second, traffic laws must be stricter and more consistently enforced. Vehicle operators of all types, including motorbikes, must observe traffic rules. This would improve safety and reduce the congestion caused by traffic accidents.

Supply Chain Impacts to Domestic BCOs

Respondents believe the GoV could take the following actions to reduce their logistics costs:

- The GoV should invest in the inland waterway system to major international seaports and other provinces to reduce congestion and traffic on roadways. This would reduce overall transportation costs for BCOs. This respondent uses coastal shipping services and sometimes experiences delays due to inconsistent electrical supplies at marine terminals when the weather is bad.
- The GoV could improve rail system infrastructure and service delivery to increase rail volumes. One BCO uses rail to a certain extent, as rail's current service profile aligns well for its commodity. Daily train service is available. Transit times from HCMC to Hanoi range from seven days using green (service reference) boxcars and up to 10 days using red (service reference) boxcars. The freight visibility offered by the rail network is poor: No advanced arrival notices are available, and BCOs often ignore which specific boxcars contain their products.

- Bridge height limits should be reviewed along key freight corridors to ensure that height restrictions are valid. Low bridge height restrictions enable the police to frequently stop truck drivers to issue tickets, and costs are passed on to one domestic BCO. Despite cargo equipment being 4.7 meters high, height restrictions are set at 4.5 meters.

Trucking Industry

Respondents' Profile

Four trucking companies operating in Vietnam agreed to be interviewed for this study. These firms ranged from fewer than 10 to 500 employees, with the former size being more typical of Vietnamese trucking companies. Because of the large size of one of the trucking companies, which allows it to have a more modern fleet of trucks, information collected on average age of trucks is skewed (56 percent are between 2000 and 2007 models, and the remaining are 1995–2000 model trucks). In a larger sample size, more trucks would be in the 1995–2000 model year range. Besides the tractor heads[10] to pull containers and trailers, trucking companies own straight trucks that haul products between factories and LSPs' CFS facilities. Three out of the four companies either leased or owned their own warehouses, with an average facility size of 35,000 square meters.

Trucking Industry Performance

The truck carriers indicated that road and port congestion has the highest dollar impact on their businesses, followed by port productivity and government regulations (mostly in the form of taxes). In addition, one trucking company noted that it pays police 20–30 percent of truck rates to operate, suggesting that facilitation payments to the police are a major determinant of all-in rates to BCOs and LSPs.[11]

Not surprisingly, all four companies expressed concern with the GoV's decision to increase the vehicle licensing fee on trucks by $70 per month and impose, for the first time, a licensing fee on chassis of $27.50 per month. These fee increases, originally planned to be implemented in June 2012, have been made effective as of January 1, 2013, and are being rolled out on a province-by-province basis. MoT has indicated that 70 percent of the increased fees would finance improvements to national highways, with the balance used to improve provincial- and local-level roads. To temper the fees' negative impact on trucking companies, toll stations have been closed on all but Build-Operate-Transfer (BOT) based highways.

For one trucking company, the increased fees represent more than $350,000 on an annual basis. This would increase its average per-kilometer cost to transport containers in Vietnam by 3–4 percent. This company also stated that the main reason the fees are unpopular is that they would not fully replace the tolls trucking companies currently pay for road maintenance.

But the measure has other potential disadvantages. While, on the one hand, the fees are straightforward to implement as they are based on vehicle registrations, they do not adequately internalize the road degradation caused by truckers as the fees are independent of actual volume and type (e.g., by vehicle class or actual weight carried) of road use. It is also not clear how the burden of the new fees will be effectively distributed across vehicle types within and outside trucking (to include, for example, buses and passenger cars).

The trucking companies generally concurred that there is an adequate supply of truck capacity in the market at present. But they also observed that too many trucking companies rely on old equipment, lack GPS and other IT tools, and have insufficient access to skilled drivers. There was a mixed response to inflation being a major contributor to higher truck rates for their BCO customers compared with other countries, but upon further questions they suggested that government taxes and highway tolls are major contributors to truck rate increases.

These trucking companies—along with ocean carriers, LSPs and international BCOs—were nearly unanimous in stating that the trucking industry should be more and better regulated. Specifically, it was observed that regulation should not focus on rates, but on driver qualifications; model year requirements for trailers and tractor heads; equipment roadability, including straight trucks of various sizes, tractor heads, and chassis; emissions testing; proper licensing of all vehicles; and monitoring truck and container weights to reduce overloading and highway damage.

Notes

1. See Appendix C for a list of the terminals that were consulted for this study.

2. DWT (Deadweight Tons) is a measure of how much weight a ship is carrying or can safely carry. It is the sum of the weights of cargo, fuel, fresh water, ballast water, provisions, passengers and crew.

3. GT (Gross Tonnage) is a function of the molded volume of all enclosed spaces of the ship.

4. LOA (Length Overall) is the maximum length of a vessel's hull measured parallel to the waterline.

5. The Interport Road project will link the Cai Mep terminals with the Thi Vai terminals. Today it requires a detour of about 5 kilometers to move containers and other traffic between the two terminal complexes. Road 965 from NH 51 will connect to this interport road.

6. This information is based on interviews with one domestic (Vinalines, largest Vietnamese shipping company, six container vessels) and four foreign flag containerized ocean carriers (by 2010 Global Ranking: Maersk [no. 1, 2.1 million TEU, 509 vessels], APL [no. 4, 0.6 million TEU, 144 vessels], MOL [no. 11, 0.4 million TEU, 100 vessels], and NYK [no. 14, 0.4 million TEU, 88 vessels]), expert industry knowledge, and trade publications. These four foreign carriers account for approximately 22 percent of the world's cellular containership fleet capacity.

7. Article 8 of the Organisation for Economic Co-operation and Development (OECD) tax convention states: "Profits from the operation of ships or aircraft in international traffic shall be taxable only in the Contracting State in which the place of effective

management of the enterprise is situated". Vietnam is not a member of the OECD, but the double taxation agreement it operates under has similar language.

8. Asian Development Bank, Project Number 40198-02 (September 2008), Proposed Loan to the Socialist Republic of Viet Nam: Ho Chi Minh City–Long Thanh–Dau Giay Expressway Construction Project.

9. High-level charts depicting the import and export Customs clearance processes are shown in appendix E.

10. Tractor heads are the power units that connect to chassis to transport containers.

11. Based on a representative sample of trucking companies nationwide, World Bank (2011) estimates that, on average, Vietnamese intercity trucking firms devote 8.4 percent of total operating costs to informal facilitation payments. While still being a significant portion of operating costs, this is considerably lower than the magnitude of facilitation payments referenced by the one trucking company (out of four interviewed) that was willing to provide details on this subject for this study. However, the 20–30 percent level would be consistent with the magnitude of facilitation payments in Customs clearance reported by a much larger number of BCOs and logistics service providers (LSPs) interviewed for this report. Obtaining a more definitive understanding of the magnitude and nature of facilitation payments in the trucking industry is an area in need of further research.

Reference

World Bank. 2011. *Vietnam Urbanization Review: Technical Assistance Report.* Hanoi: World Bank.

CHAPTER 4

Issues Screening and List of Actionable Recommendations

The report has so far described (1) the current state of Vietnam's economy and logistics system (chapter 2) and (2) the main challenges and opportunities to reducing logistics costs as perceived and identified by key freight stakeholders nationwide (chapter 3). The purpose of this chapter is to integrate these findings into a cohesive analytical framework where they can serve as a basis to produce actionable advice to the Government of Vietnam (GoV). While it is clear that Vietnam's logistics challenges and opportunities are numerous and span virtually all elements of the supply chain, taking action on these issues requires that they be prioritized and properly sequenced. To that end, this chapter synthetizes the issues and assesses them based on multicriteria analysis. This will help determine the most pressing, highest-priority challenges, for which a targeted intervention agenda will be proposed.

Freight Logistics Challenges

The most salient challenges identified in chapters 2 and 3 have been distilled in table 4.1; these are the 23 most significant challenges in Vietnamese logistics identified by this report. The challenges have been grouped into three categories: Infrastructure, Freight Operations, and Policy, as defined below:

- *Infrastructure:* Issues related to the physical assets of ports/marine terminals, inland waterways, highways, roads, and rail.
- *Freight Operations:* Issues related to freight-handling operations at Tan Son Nhat Airport (TSNA) and Noi Bai Airport (NBA), warehouses operated by logistics service providers (LSPs), and trucking company operations.
- *Policy:* Issues that arise from regulations, laws, and circulars issued by the GoV and the application, interpretation, and enforcement of these regulations, laws, and circulars by the General Department of Vietnam Customs (hereafter

Table 4.1 Most Significant Challenges Impacting Freight Logistics Costs in Vietnam

No.	Issue description	Impact for freight stakeholders
Infrastructure issues		
I-1	Transportation infrastructure planning at the central and provincial government levels is not conducted using a macro-approach. Planning is done in modal silos without having a multimodal, integrated, holistic perspective. The multimodal transportation network is not viewed as a total system that is critical to freight stakeholders when moving raw materials and components to production locations and finished goods to point of consumption. There seems to be no clear conviction that an efficient, cost-effective multimodal transportation system is integral to facilitating international trade and economic development. Infrastructure projects are executed in a piecemeal manner without regard to the importance of establishing smooth links between the various modes of transport and addressing bottlenecks along entire strategic freight corridors. Funding is not always allocated to the projects that will deliver the greatest benefit to BCOs and other freight stakeholders.	Unnecessary cost and time is added to BCO supply chains. Vietnam's competitiveness relative to peer countries is diminished. Network bottlenecks remain in place longer than would otherwise be the case. Maintenance expenditures are not properly assessed and balanced relative to capital expenditures. Relatively low economic returns to scarce state budget resources invested in infrastructure projects.
I-2	The master plan for the development of seaports in Vietnam from 2010 to 2020, approved by the prime minister in December 2009, promoted the development of a regional transshipment hub at Van Phong in Central Vietnam despite the limited demand for such a port. After continuous delays to the planned schedule, the GoV formally suspended the Van Phong project in September 2012, even though construction work had already stopped in August 2011 after initial piling works were done by a Korean contractor at a cost of VND 146 billion ($7.3 million). The suspension came at the request of the MoT, because of Vinalines's financial difficulties. Despite this, the GoV continues to emphasize the development of the port at Van Phong, with the MoT directing Vinamarine and local provincial authorities in Khanh Hoa to set up plans to call for domestic and foreign investments in the construction of the port.	Potential expenditure of infrastructure capital would be diverted from more critically needed projects that would better serve higher volume freight corridors.
I-3	The master plan has failed to match market demand to supply, with the excess supply in the greater HCMC area, including Cai Mep-Thi Vai, expected to last through 2020 due to the haphazard granting of new port operation licenses. New port developments continue to be approved in the Cat Lai and Hiep Phuoc areas, despite the current oversupply and the concurrent development of Cai Mep-Thi Vai. Left with small terminal footprints, MTOs are finding it difficult to attract sufficient containerized ocean carrier business to be profitable.	Cai Mep-Thi Vai MTOs' operating costs and return-on-investment have been negatively impacted.
I-4	The existing master plan provides for the ports at Cai Mep-Thi Vai to receive container ships of between 4,000 and 8,000 TEUs (60,000 and 100,000 DWT) although ships of 11,000–14,000 TEUs (130,000–160,000 DWT) have already successfully docked at the port. Foreign-owned ocean carriers are not receiving sufficient incentives to offset the relatively low container move counts at Cai Mep-Thi Vai currently (of 1,000–2,000 TEUs per call), tonnage and pilotage fees form a high percentage of their operating costs on a per TEU basis and are facing obstacles in getting approval to bring in larger ships over 80,000 DWT.	Restrictions on access to Cai Mep-Thi Vai terminals increase ocean carriers' operating costs, which eventually increases transportation costs for importers and exporters.

table continues next page

Table 4.1 Most Significant Challenges Impacting Freight Logistics Costs in Vietnam *(continued)*

No.	Issue description	Impact for freight stakeholders
I-5	The development of the port system at the key gateway ports of HCMC (including Cai Mep-Thi Vai) and Haiphong (including Cai Lan) remains highly fragmented. The country continues to favor the development of new terminals based on outdated berth designs (e.g., of 200–300 meters each when latest generation large containerships are 300–400 meters long) and relatively small terminal facilities compared to international standards.	Economies of scale have been difficult to achieve in the large gateway ports because cargo is dispersed. Ocean carriers select ports to call based on cargo demand. Funding spent on small ports and terminals has yielded little benefit for BCOs.
I-6	The potential for Cai Mep-Thi Vai to act as a transshipment hub for other Vietnamese ports has not been fully exploited. In 2013 foreign carriers will no longer be permitted to carry empty containers and international laden containers between Vietnamese ports on foreign-flagged ships because of cabotage restrictions. Unable to rely upon Vietnamese-flagged carriers to provide suitably reliable feeder services between Vietnamese ports, these international laden containers will be shipped to foreign ports for consolidation.	Cabotage restrictions increase operating costs for ocean carriers, resulting in higher transportation costs for BCOs.
I-7	The development of Lach Huyen Port continues to face delays and could miss the 2016 target for operations to commence. Haiphong could face a potential port congestion problem by 2016, with demand exceeding supply if Lach Huyen Port does not proceed as planned. Planners of the Lach Huyen port could repeat the same mistakes made in the development of Cai Mep-Thi Vai with the competing ports at Cai Lan and the potential development at South Do Son, which could result in the dispersion of cargo volumes and the inability to exploit the benefits of large-scale marine terminal operations.	Delays will result in a shortage of vessel capacity and longer wait times for available vessel space for BCOs.
I-8	Most Vietnamese highways intersect at traffic circles that are especially congested Monday through Saturday. Today there are few overpasses or flyovers that allow traffic from one highway system to merge with another highway system to keep traffic moving. HCMC does have plans to construct overpass bridges at two major traffic circles, Hang Xanh Crossroads and Thu Duc Crossroads, on the main highways to the industrial areas in Binh Thanh and Dong Nai and to NH 51 and the Cai Mep-Thi Vai terminals. Exits to major port terminal areas like Road 965 to Cai Mep-Thi Vai are controlled by signals as opposed to overpasses that allow through traffic to continue to flow. Besides creating congestion issues, poor highway safety is a major challenge. Highways are not constructed to handle truck weights connected with today's larger sized, 45-foot containers and/or heavier smaller containers.	Freight velocity and highway safety are compromised, resulting in increased fuel consumption, more air pollution, and higher personal liability and cargo insurance claims. BCOs need to add more buffer time when planning transportation, which increases inventory carrying costs. Weight restrictions, lower maximum highway speeds, and congestion combine to increase the cost of freight shipments in Vietnam compared to countries like China.

table continues next page

Table 4.1 Most Significant Challenges Impacting Freight Logistics Costs in Vietnam (continued)

No.	Issue description	Impact for freight stakeholders
I-9	The concept of logistics parks (a campus environment where many LSP-managed distribution and warehouse facilities are colocated) is not well-understood in Vietnam. Cargo-handling facilities are usually standalone near factories, ports, or airports. Vietnam lacks adequate logistics parks alongside major highways leading to the Haiphong ports and NH 51 to Cai Mep-Thi Vai. Ideally, logistics parks should be located next to inland waterways, major highways, and rail yards to accommodate multimodal freight options. Highway access to the parks would provide quick easy-on, easy-off access to the main highway or road adjacent to the park. Designating land for logistics parks along new expressways should be a requirement for highway investors. These logistics parks could be developed with FDI funds.	Exporters cannot benefit from later cutoff times because of the absence of logistics parks located along major highways. The absence of appropriately located logistics parks increases overall cargo-handling costs for both importers and exporters. The process for moving finished goods or raw materials and components out of or into Vietnam is not seamless.
I-10	Although some modern buildings exist, the quality of CFS warehouses and other cargo handling facilities is generally poor relative to other Asian countries such as China, Indonesia, Malaysia, and Thailand. Facilities are generally small in size and availability is limited. It is not uncommon to find buildings with floors made of packed dirt, especially in the Northern region, which is not conducive for handling and storing cargo, particularly high-value products. Some international and domestic LSPs have modern warehouse facilities supported with warehouse management systems, but this is not the norm across Vietnam.	It is a challenge for LSPs to locate quality facilities that enable cost-effective and efficient operations. More modern warehouses operated by international LSPs are often too expensive for domestic BCOs to use.

Freight operations

No.	Issue description	Impact for freight stakeholders
F-1	TSNA has two terminal operators, TCS (operates facilities TCS1 and TCS2) and SCSC. TCS is partially owned and operated by Vietnam Airlines, the national flag carrier, which has pressured many air carriers to only serve TCS, even though BCOs and airfreight forwarders generally rate SCSC's service as superior.	Operations at TCS1 and TSC2 are less efficient than SCSC. Capacity at SCSC is underutilized. Airfreight rates are higher than they should be.
F-2	Airfreight forwarders cannot perform cargo consolidation at TSNA and NBA; consolidating cargo on build-up pallets is only done by ground handling agents. Airfreight forwarders are allowed to perform this function in most other Asian countries.	Airfreight rates for BCOs are higher than they might be if cargo consolidation by airfreight forwarders was unrestricted.
F-3	The trucking industry is fragmented, with fewer than 10 large trucking companies and about 100 midsized ones operating in Vietnam. There are no pan-Vietnam trucking companies. BCOs, ocean carriers, and LSPs must contract with numerous trucking companies to take care of demand. This increases operational costs of ocean carriers and LSPs because they have to manage many trucking contracts to be assured of service during peak shipping periods due to the limited number of trucks any one trucking company can commit to the ocean carrier or LSP. Truck tariff rates are low. In order to make a profit, trucking companies frequently overload trucks and avoid tolls roads. To minimize the risk of being stopped by local police, some trucking companies make special payment arrangements with the local police in exchange for "protection" at a particular road segment.	Although BCOs reported that trucking rates are generally lower than in peer countries, most are dissatisfied with the poor quality of service delivered by trucking companies and the lack of visibility of cargo when transiting in trucks. Low truck rates contribute to instability in the industry and delivery of substandard service.

table continues next page

Table 4.1 Most Significant Challenges Impacting Freight Logistics Costs in Vietnam *(continued)*

No.	Issue description	Impact for freight stakeholders
F-4	Because the trucking industry mainly comprises small companies, it is difficult for them to gain economies of scale. Most operators cannot afford to properly maintain their trucks, which contributes to air pollution and unsafe vehicles. Overloading of trucks is common. Regulations governing trucking companies and drivers such as on-duty driver hour limits, use of GPS units in trucks, driver training and safety, cargo load ceilings, vehicle quality, equipment depreciation, and road speed limits are not stringent enough to change how the trucking industry operates.	While BCOs benefit from competitive trucking rates, trucking practices like overloading containers cause highway damage. The lack of driver training leads to accidents, which increases the trucking companies' cost of doing business, reduces road safety, and increases logistics costs to BCOs. Improper truck maintenance increases air pollution.
Policy issues		
P-1	Government-issued regulations, including those made by Vietnam Customs, are often not clear or easy to understand. This uncertainty in new circulars and laws creates a risk exposure for BCOs and LSPs in making business decisions. BCOs also stand the risk of being in violation of laws previously not enforced. Implementation of decrees at the provincial and local levels is not consistent. Interpretation of regulations can be different from province-to-province, official-to-official, and day-to-day. Enforcement of regulations is based on shades of gray, not black and white.	The ambiguity in regulations and the inconsistency in interpreting and enforcing regulations creates unexpected costs to BCOs for unintentional noncompliance; delays in getting imports cleared necessitates that importers carry higher levels of safety stock; missed aircraft and vessel departures for exporters; and higher-than-normal administrative costs to monitor and react to government regulations.
P-2	Bureaucracy throughout the central and provincial governments and requirements for multiple certificates and documents slows the clearance of imports and exports. Multiple ministries can be involved in the import and export process. Import licenses are required on many types of consumer goods, particularly those considered by the GoV to be luxury items. Obtaining import licenses can take from 4 to 10 days, while the cargo sits at the port or airport before customs clearance can be completed.	The number of licenses that are required to do business and the lengthy process that must be followed to obtain licenses bogs down the system; creates delays, unnecessary work and costs for BCOs; and generates additional inventory carrying costs.
P-3	The GoV considers movement via barge between HCMC or Cai Mep and Cambodia to be "transit" rather than "transshipment" because the border is an inland border. Cambodia permits imports of secondhand machinery and autos originating in the United States that are prohibited from being imported into Vietnam, so this type of restricted cargo cannot be transported to Cambodia through Vietnam via barge. This is an arbitrary rule imposed because of GoV concerns about smuggling, but this reduces the pool of cargo that can travel on the barge service (likely via Cai Mep-Thi Vai). Now this cargo goes through Singapore to Sihanoukville and bypasses Vietnam altogether. Currently the trade between Vietnam and Cambodia is imbalanced with more cargo coming out of Cambodia than going in. But if this restriction were lifted, the trade would come into balance and barge operators could be more profitable in this barge trade.	Barge operators in Vietnam and the Vietnam economy lose potential revenue from Cambodia's large secondhand automobile and machinery market as a result of this inland border restriction.

table continues next page

Efficient Logistics • http://dx.doi.org/10.1596/978-1-4648-0103-7

Table 4.1 Most Significant Challenges Impacting Freight Logistics Costs in Vietnam *(continued)*

No.	Issue description	Impact for freight stakeholders
P-4	Corruption in various forms is endemic at all levels of government. Payment of facilitation, as noted by freight stakeholders interviewed, accounts for anywhere between 5 and 50 percent of their customs clearance costs in Vietnam. Companies believe that facilitation payments, which are illegal in Vietnam, are nevertheless necessary to expedite the movement of goods through Customs. Facilitation relates to frequent small payments made by BCOs and other freight stakeholders to government officials to get routine activities accomplished in a timely manner. But it may also refer to outright bribery, such as paying Customs agents to accept wrong data on documents (e.g., inaccurate weights or Harmonized Tariff System numbers) or missing documentation. The system therefore operates on wrong and missing information, which is inefficient. LSPs believe it necessary to engage in constant relationship building to get things done in their cargo-handling facilities, which includes pampering Customs agents, taking them to dinner, providing gifts, etc. Customs has a policy of rotating agents every six months to other facilities, which reportedly forces LSPs to start the relationship building all over again.	Business dealings are not transparent, and the playing field is not level for all participants. Because of facilitation, BCOs, for example, can never be certain how long it will take to clear cargo, or if inspection of cargo will be required, how long the inspection will take, and how much it will cost. Inventory carrying costs are high because of the extra time built into the supply chain. LSPs find it difficult to work efficiently and provide superior service to their customers because government officials are perceived as deliberatively slowing down processes as leverage to exact facilitation payments.
P-5	The application of customs policies is inconsistent and not universally applied. Customs is supposed to adhere to the World Customs Organization guidelines, but how Customs operates is another story. The interpretation of customs regulations varies among different Customs officials and between provinces. In some cases, local Customs officials are not aware of special arrangements granted to certain BCOs.	The lack of transparency of regulations and enforcement oversight increases uncertainty (and therefore costs) in supply chains and leads to undocumented facilitation payments to Customs officials.
P-6	E-Customs has only been partially implemented. Entries are required to be filed with Customs electronically, but hard copy documents must also be presented for signature. Vietnam Customs is planning to implement a single-window, fully automated customs solution called the Vietnam Automated Cargo and Port Consolidated System and the Vietnam Customs Information System (VNACCS/VCIS) by 2014, but it is uncertain if this schedule will be achieved.	Hybrid customs model creates unnecessary administrative work for BCOs and LSPs, higher operating costs, clearance delays, and opportunities to exchange facilitation payments.
P-7	Business licensing requirements are generally vague, and the licensing process is very controlled. For example, obtaining CFS licenses is very difficult due to the lack of straightforward laws, and LSPs cannot easily determine what the rules really are. Often licenses are granted through facilitation payments and relationships, rather than based on clear rules.	LSP operating costs increase.
P-8	The skill level of some government officials who work directly with the movement of cargo is perceived to be poor. Often they get their jobs by having relationships with people in power or through payment of facilitation, not because they are qualified. This is more likely to be the case in rural areas. GoV human resource systems are not merit-based.	Delays in moving cargo occur and operating costs increase for freight stakeholders. Situations arise where facilitation payments may be offered or requested.

table continues next page

Table 4.1 Most Significant Challenges Impacting Freight Logistics Costs in Vietnam *(continued)*

No.	Issue description	Impact for freight stakeholders
P-9	International BCOs and LSPs have difficulty hiring managers experienced in supply chain and logistics. Vietnamese with this experience are expensive to recruit and retain. International LSPs find it more cost-effective to staff senior management level positions with experienced expatriate staff. The GoV has recently required that expatriate work visa requests include a development plan for a Vietnamese employee to assume the expatriate's position when the expatriate departs Vietnam.	Operations costs for international BCOs and LSPs increase. Identifying local staff to assume an expatriate's position so far in advance is difficult.

Note: BCO = beneficial cargo owner; CFS = container freight station; DWT = deadweight tons; FDI = foreign direct investment; GoV = Government of Vietnam; GPS = Global Positioning System; HCMC = Ho Chi Minh City; LSP = logistics service provider; MoT = Ministry of Transport; MTO = marine terminal operator; NBA = Noi Bai Airport; SCSC = Saigon Cargo Service Corporation; TCS = cargo terminal at TSNA; TEU = 20-foot equivalent unit container; TSNA = Tan Son Nhat Airport; Vietnam Customs/Customs = General Department of Vietnam Customs.

"Vietnam Customs" or simply "Customs"), provincial authorities, and other government officials.

The challenges, as listed, are not ranked in order of significance.

Development of a Multicriteria Evaluation Matrix

A multicriteria evaluation matrix was created to prioritize the above list of challenges (table 4.4). The matrix scores each of the major challenges according to key impact variables as defined in table 4.2, along with a timeline indicator showing whether full implementation could be accomplished within the next five years (short-term), 5–10 years (medium-term), or beyond 10 years (long-term).

Prior to evaluating the key challenges, similar issues (e.g., those driven by similar root causes) were grouped together, resulting in 14 major categories (second column of table 4.4). Using a three tier scoring system of Low, Medium, and High (see table 4.3) to reflect expected impact on logistics costs along each of the criteria of table 4.2, categories were given a weighted impact score (second to last column of table 4.4). The five highest-scored categories are the primary challenges this report suggests the GoV should address with the highest level of priority to have (1) the greatest economic and financial impact on logistics costs for freight stakeholders and (2) a more enduring improvement in trade competitiveness.

Five goals were developed for the highest-rated challenges. Table 4.5 indicates how these goals impact the various freight stakeholders using the same scoring system as shown in table 4.4.

For each of the chosen priority challenges/cross-cutting goals of table 4.5, section 4.3 will (1) describe their relevance (e.g., impact on freight stakeholders), (2) recommend solutions and, where appropriate, implementation strategies, (3) identify barriers and obstacles to implementation, and

Table 4.2 Multicriteria Evaluation Impact Variables

Code	Description of key impact variables
GSC	Impacts global BCO supply chains that demand JIT deliveries, visibility of product flow, and high responsiveness.
FSI	Has cost impact to BCOs and other freight stakeholders.
FFF	Impacts future freight flow decisions in Vietnam in five to ten years, given authors' container volume projections.
LAW	Impacts compliance with international laws governing fair trade and anti-corruption practices as demanded by trade agreements like the Trans-Pacific Partnership.
COR	Requires strategic freight corridor investments or policy.
ENV	Provides an opportunity to reduce the environmental carbon footprint of freight shipments.
SOL	Has a reasonable solution that is implementable based on anticipated costs, associated government policy changes, and/or freight stakeholder pushback.

Timeline for full implementation (years)	
ST	0–5
MT	5–10
LT	Longer than 10

Note: BCO = beneficial cargo owner; JIT = just in time.

Table 4.3 Scoring System

Expected impact on logistics costs	Score	Symbol	Description of measure
No or low impact	1	O	No impact; or only has an insignificant positive or negative impact; or is unlikely to be implemented by the GoV, at least during the next 10 years.
Medium impact	3	◕	May create a measureable positive or negative impact on logistics costs, infrastructure planning, fair trade, and/or the environment and would not likely result in reevaluating strategies and business practices; or has a reasonable chance of being implemented by the GoV.
High impact	5	●	Will create a measureable positive or negative impact on logistics costs, infrastructure planning, fair trade, and/or the environment and could result in reevaluating strategies and business practices; or has a good chance of being implemented by the GoV.

Note: GoV = Government of Vietnam.

(4) sketch what a successful implementation timetable could look like, as well as potential funding mechanisms (in selected cases).

Goals Assessment and Recommendations to Improve Performance

Customs Modernization
Why This Is Relevant
The administrative effort associated with the current customs clearance process is time consuming and costly to customs brokers, who pass along their costs to beneficial cargo owners (BCOs). Clearing customs is fraught with

Table 4.4 Significant Challenges: Weighted Average Scores

Task no.	Category description	GSC	FSI	FFF	LAW	COR	ENV	SOL	Impact score	Time line
	Weights =>	4	4	2	3	1	1	2		
P-5 P-6	Cumbersome and inconsistently applied customs policies, procedures, and practices	●	●	●	●	○	○	●	77	ST
P-1/P-2 P-4	Inconsistent implementation, interpretation and enforcement of government regulations; lack of transparency; bureaucracy; and facilitation payments	●	●	◐	●	○	○	○	65	MT
I-1 I-7 I-8	Infrastructure projects: Nonintegrated multimodal transportation infrastructure planning Development of port at Lach Huyen	●	●	●	○	●	◐	◐	67	LT
F-3/F-4	Fragmented trucking industry delivering suboptimal service	●	●	○	○	○	●	●	61	MT
I-4/I-6	Lack of critical mass of Cai-Mep/Thi Vai as transship terminals	◐	●	●	○	●	○	●	61	ST
I-9 I-10	Absence of strategically located logistics parks integrated with ports, airports, highways, and production facilities	◐	◐	◐	○	●	◐	●	51	MT
F-1/F-2	Inefficient terminal ownership structure and operations at TSNA and inability for airfreight forwarders to consolidate cargo	◐	◐	◐	◐	○	○	◐	47	ST
I-3	Imbalanced of supply and demand at marine terminals in Southern Vietnam	○	●	●	○	◐	○	○	43	LT
P-7	Cumbersome business licensing processes for LSP cargo-handling facilities	○	●	◐	◐	○	○	○	43	LT
P-8	Inadequate education and skills of government workers relating to logistics	◐	◐	◐	○	○	○	◐	41	LT
I-5	Small footprint of marine terminals in Southern Vietnam	○	●	◐	○	◐	○	○	39	MT
P-3	Underutilized Cambodia barge service	○	◐	◐	○	◐	○	◐	35	ST
P9	Lack of skilled Vietnamese managers who are knowledgeable in logistics	○	◐	○	○	○	○	●	33	MT
I-2	Van Phong Seaport development	○	○	◐	○	○	○	○	21	LT

Note: LSP = logistics service provider; TSNA = Tan Son Nhat Airport.

Efficient Logistics • http://dx.doi.org/10.1596/978-1-4648-0103-7

Table 4.5 Key Goals and Impact on Freight Stakeholders

Key issue identifier	Cross-cutting goals	Impact on freight stakeholders				
		MTOs	LSPs	Trucking	Ocean carriers	Shippers
P5, P6	Customs modernization	▼	●	●	○	●
P1, P2, P4	Transparent and consistently applied, interpreted, and enforced government regulations and operations; reduced bureaucracy	○	●	●	▼	●
I1, I7, I8	Strategic corridor planning	●	▼	▼	●	▼
F3, F4	More professional trucking industry	○	●	●	▼	▼
I4, I6	Expanded business opportunities at Cai Mep-Thi Vai	●	▼	○	●	▼

facilitation payments to officials as a perceived requirement to "get things done," primarily due to a high level of human involvement and variation in interpretation of customs regulations. It is also a major contributor to extended delays in processing import and export shipments, with the greatest impact on imports.

Customs modernization is a key component of Vietnam's trade liberalization and international integration agenda. For example, it will likely strengthen Vietnam's participation in the TPP multilateral trade agreement, currently under negotiation between Australia, Brunei Darussalam, Canada, Chile, Malaysia, Mexico, New Zealand, Peru, Singapore, the United States, and Vietnam. In meeting this requirement Vietnam stands to gain tremendous growth opportunities in key export products—such as apparel and electronics—through the reduction of duties among trading partners. Both the president and prime minister of Vietnam have expressed commitment to securing Vietnam's position in this trade agreement.

Customs modernization is also required by Vietnam's commitments to the ASEAN Economic Community (AEC). These commitments call for simpler, harmonized customs procedures in line with international standards and best practices. The AEC also calls for smooth customs valuation with origin determination and establishing ASEAN e-Customs.[1]

In all interviews with BCOs and LSPs doing customs brokerage and/or international expedited freight shipments, the prospects of moving to an e-Customs platform in 2014 was seen as a giant leap toward reducing their operating and inventory costs. In particular, it was consistently seen as an effective way to reduce points of what has sometimes been referred to as "system nervousness"—choke points in the supply chain that account for a disproportionate share of delays and itinerary unpredictability (including of cost and time).

Recommended Solutions

Vietnam Customs' primary goal should be to implement a fully automated system by 2014 as planned. This will significantly reduce human intervention and paperwork and will provide a consistent, predictable and transparent clearance process. When customs clearance is aided by a fully electronic exchange of data and documents, products are not only cleared in a timely manner, but all interaction with Customs officials (e.g., to establish tariff classifications, proper licenses, and other customs formalities) is settled in advance of the physical importation and exportation of the BCO's inputs and finished goods. By eliminating the physical handling of documents, no paper documents are printed or compromised. Customs officials are still expected to occasionally inspect shipments to validate the BCO's compliance to what the electronic records report.

In connection with a paperless environment, Vietnam Customs will need to assure BCOs that it can safeguard data in the records filed electronically. The relevance of this stems from the handling of the year-end reconciliation process between imported raw material value and the export value of finished goods. Since this reconciliation determines whether manufacturers can avoid duties imposed for documentation discrepancies, Customs' ability to safeguard the integrity of electronic records would be a critical component of paperless clearance.

Not only does operating in an e-commerce environment with Customs expedite the customs clearance process, it should greatly reduce instances where facilitation payments to Customs officials are offered or requested. It also provides a strong foundation upon which to develop a formal (e.g., well-established, IT-enabled) "trusted shipper" or "green lane" concept that works well in other countries and country groups, notably the United States and the European Union (EU). The physical inspection of documents is a significant revenue stream for Customs and Customs officials. But it contributes greatly to the delay of cargo, especially import cargo where every container is inspected either partially or fully. Under a "trusted shipper" program, inspections would be reduced in number and scope. Scope may range from door inspections of several cartons to full inspection of container contents, where the sample size is defined by accepted (e.g., industry standard) statistical methodologies.

Vietnam Customs should also adopt the World Customs Organization standards for classification, filing practices and common electronic data interchanges (EDI) like File Transfer Protocol (FTP). This would relieve LSPs and BCOs from having to customize their international systems in order to exchange information with Vietnam Customs.

Recommended Strategies

Assuming the e-Customs system is completed in 2014 (as planned), the system should be implemented under a phased deployment over a period of at least 12 months. Beyond an electronic interface, the customs clearance process can be further streamlined by taking some of the following actions:

- Begin implementing a "trusted shipper" program that is based on a to-be-determined compliance level for document and shipment accuracy based on a formula that considers such things as the BCO's length of time doing business, location of BCO's buyers (e.g., the United States or the EU, which have more stringent cargo security requirements), frequency of shipments, type of commodity, and volume of shipments. It is recommended that compliance be less than 100 percent, but more than 95 percent.
- Establish an effective prearrival classification system that allows BCOs to obtain official product classifications and required customs forms for timely product clearance upon cargo arrival.
- Accept small variations in weight for airfreight imports such that customs brokers can be confident in preparing customs documents prior to cargo arrival.
- Simplify documentation requirements for purchase orders and sales contracts on imported items to be consistent with other ASEAN countries.
- Use trucking companies' bills of lading as the only document truck drivers need to possess instead of carrying a complete set of documents.
- Operate Customs inspection and testing stations with sufficient staff and equipment, and adequate cargo storage areas (e.g., with refrigeration for perishable food products), to expedite the cargo inspection process and to maintain shipment integrity.
- Staff Customs offices, inspection sites, and testing stations six days a week to process shipments to and from factories and marine terminals, as the latter operate on that schedule.
- Communicate well in advance any new regulations for all types of cargo, with assurance that they will be uniformly followed by all Customs officials upon cargo arrival.
- Develop an electronic calculation process to measure raw material content in finished goods to prevent redundant duty payments on imported raw materials used exclusively for the manufacturing of export products. Also maintain, as a minimum, the 275 days currently allowed for duty-free imports to be exported in finished goods.
- Stabilize customs duty rates within the framework of existing free trade agreements.
- Raise the level of professionalism of Customs officials through improved training (this can be an area for South-South collaboration) and performance evaluation, especially in the smaller cities and provinces, to promote a more uniform application and interpretation of customs regulations.
- Establish an open "hot line" for communication with Vietnam Customs such that BCOs can report inconsistencies in the way customs rulings are applied by officials.

Barriers and Obstacles

An implementation roadmap and performance benchmark have already been established by the e-Customs "Gold Standard" system developed and operated for one high-profile international BCO in the HCMC area. All the freight stakeholders interviewed were supportive of this paperless system.

Customs officials could be the biggest barrier to full implementation of an electronic customs process that would minimize human touch, since this would redefine their role in the clearance process and potentially take away a major if informal source of income. Another potential obstacle is the definition of customs regulations, which at present are prone to subjective interpretation. To the extent that the application of regulations is significantly streamlined (e.g., made more predictable and consistent) by reducing the need for in-person interaction between officials and BCOs, this risk can be mitigated through the e-Customs system. However, a strong case can be made that, irrespective of the customs clearance process in place, customs regulations should be simplified. Best practice examples from advanced and middle-income countries in the region can be used as an initial benchmark.

Definition of Success

By the end of 2015, the e-Customs system will ideally be available for use by customs brokers for the timely processing of import and export shipments at any of Vietnam's water or land entry points for ocean, truck, and airfreight shipments. Deployment of the new system will be field-tested prior to a phased deployment over a one-year period (in 2015) in order to avoid unnecessary disruption to the flow of commerce.

Transparent, Streamlined Government Regulations and Operations

Why This Is Relevant

Inconsistent implementation and interpretation of government regulations beyond customs is widespread across Vietnam, as reported by every international BCO and LSP interviewed for this report. This stems largely from red tape (e.g., cumbersome procedures), a legal framework whose gaps give de facto discretion and power to officials, and a lack of transparency and accountability. Root causes include (1) gaps in institutional capacity, (2) unnecessarily complex, incomplete and/or ambiguously drafted regulations, and (2) inadequate recruitment and compensation management processes at the various levels of government. Besides having a number of direct impacts on the ease of doing business and the profitability of freight stakeholders, this provides fertile ground for (and is therefore a root cause of) the solicitation and/or offering of undocumented facilitation payments.

BCOs and LSPs incur higher-than-necessary administrative costs to monitor and react to government regulations that are constantly changing. Moreover, this increases the risk of incurring penalties for unintentional noncompliance. For example, BCOs risk being in violation of regulations that were not previously enforced. BCOs and LSPs spend unexpected and unnecessary administrative time to assess how to change their business practices to comply with new or revised regulations.

Bureaucracy and complex procedures increase the time involved in moving inputs and finished goods in and out of Vietnam and make this process unpredictable. Cumbersome and sometimes onerous clearance regulations create bottlenecks in the import and export process. A single import shipment may require dealing with Vietnam Customs, Ministry of Health, Ministry of Information and Technology, Ministry of Agriculture, and Ministry of Culture and Communication, all of which may require myriad documentation. Because Customs does not register the importer using an official number or code, the importer must copy and present its import buying contract with each bill of lading. Obtaining import licenses can take from 4 to 10 days, while the cargo sits at the port or airport before customs clearance can be accomplished. BCOs can rarely be certain how long it will take to clear cargo, if inspection of cargo will be required, how long the inspection will take, and how much it will cost. LSPs stated that these issues undermine their ability to operate efficiently and provide superior service to their customers.[2]

Because of the need to add redundant safety stock to their supply chains to account for clearance delays, BCOs experience higher-than-necessary inventory carrying costs (table 4.6). It takes three days longer to clear[3] imports and two days longer to clear exports in Vietnam compared with Malaysia.[4] It is conservatively estimated that, if Vietnam's clearance times matched Malaysia's, manufacturers and BCOs engaged in nondomestic imports and exports of containerized cargo could have saved $96 million in inventory carrying costs in 2012. Taking into account projected growth in international trade, savings in inventory carrying costs from faster clearance times could reach $182 million in 2020.

With remarkable consistency, interviewees across all freight stakeholder categories stated that situations routinely arise where facilitation payments are exchanged between BCOs/LSPs/truck drivers and government officials (particularly Customs and the police). Most international BCOs were unable to pinpoint the relative magnitude of facilitation payments as a share of logistics costs, since facilitation is typically paid by their LSPs or trucking companies and built into their customs entry, cargo handling, and trucking rates. Some stakeholders, however, estimated that these nontransparent facilitation

Table 4.6 Interest Cost on Extra Inventory Due to Import-Export Clearance Delays
Millions of dollars

Interest cost on extra inventory due to clearance delays:	2012	2015	2020
In import shipments	46.6	58.4	86.7
In export shipments	49.5	62.7	95.1
Total capital cost of carrying inventory	**96.1**	**121.1**	**181.8**

Source: Authors; see table A.3 for details.

costs added as much as 50 percent to these rates. All ocean carriers, LSPs, trucking companies, and BCOs that deal directly with trucking companies and/or customs brokers stated unanimously that the undocumented facilitation payments made to Customs officials and police constitute anywhere between 5 and 50 percent of customs brokerage fees, cargo inspections, and trucking.

The estimated cost of facilitation payments paid to Customs officials and police is $78 per FEU on imports and $76.50 per FEU on exports (table 4.7). These facilitation amounts were calculated assuming that a 30 percent facilitation fee[5] is included in what LSPs identified as "good market rates" for customs brokerage and trucking. As a percentage of total origin costs,[6] facilitation fees are estimated to be 15.1 percent and 13.4 percent of import and export origin costs, respectively, for general merchandise cargo in a 40-foot container.

For illustrative purposes, assuming that all foreign import and export containers were subject to the above estimated facilitation payments, annual facilitation fees associated with clearing customs and transporting containers over the road would be $261 million in 2012 and $493 million in 2020 (table 4.8).

Table 4.7 Import and Export Origin Costs for General Merchandise Cargo in 40-Foot Container (FEU)

Charge types	Cost per FEU (dollars)	Facilitation payments[a] (dollars)	Facilitation payment % total origin cost
Import costs			
Delivery order	35.0	n.a.	n.a.
Terminal handling charge	130.0	n.a.	n.a.
Related ocean charges	70.0	n.a.	n.a.
Origin administration fees	20.0	n.a.	n.a.
Foreign security filing	n.a.	n.a.	n.a.
Customs brokerage and container inspection	75.0	22.5	n.a.
Trucking from port to factory	185.0	55.5	n.a.
Total origin costs	**515.0**	**78.0**	**15.1%**
Export costs			
Bill of lading	35.0	n.a.	n.a.
Terminal handling charge	130.0	n.a.	n.a.
Related ocean charges	15.0	n.a.	n.a.
Origin administration fees	75.0	n.a.	n.a.
Foreign security filing	62.0	n.a.	n.a.
Customs brokerage and container inspection	70.0	21.0	n.a.
Trucking from port to factory	185.0	55.5	
Total origin costs	**572.0**	**76.5**	**13.4%**

Source: Authors; see table A.2 for details.
Note: n.a. = not applicable.
a. Facilitation payments that are included in the customs brokerage, container inspection, and trucking origin costs (cost per FEU column).

Table 4.8 Estimated Cost of Facilitation Payments in Clearing and Transporting Import and Export Containers
Millions of dollars

Annual facilitation payments based on:	2012	2015	2020
Total foreign import volumes	134.6	168.7	250.3
Total foreign export volumes	126.2	159.9	242.4
Total facilitation costs	**260.8**	**328.5**	**492.8**

Source: Authors; see table A.5 for details.

Recommended Solutions

Solutions to promote consistent implementation, interpretation, and enforcement of regulations, and to streamline government processes related to international trade, are generally feasible of short-term implementation. Interventions to minimize the incidence of facilitation payments are medium- to long-term in nature, given the strong behavioral component of such initiatives and the obvious entrenched interests that would oppose reform. Specific recommendations are as follows:

- The GoV should be as clear and transparent as possible when stating policies and issuing decrees and laws related to international trade in order to remove vagueness, ambiguity, and room for individual (and especially idiosyncratic) discretion; there should be no or minimal room for different interpretations by different government officials.
- The GoV should establish an audit system whereby it could set up selected key regulations governing international trade as test cases. By surveying BCOs and LSPs on a set schedule over the course of one to two years, the GoV could review how those regulations were implemented by the various ministries and provincial governments. Identified gaps and issues could then be addressed, and strategies for more consistent application and interpretation of laws could be applied for general rule making and execution.
- Using other ASEAN countries as models, the GoV and Customs should streamline import and export clearance processes by loosening onerous requirements and reducing the number of required documents and certificates.
- The hiring, promotion, salary scale, and salary-adjustment system for government officials should transition to being merit based.
- The GoV could embark on a communications campaign that promotes transparency in supply chain transactions, highlights ongoing public sector efforts on this front, and engages the BCO and LSP community, whose members in many instances assume that facilitation payments are necessary as a matter of course.

Possible Funding Mechanisms

Establishing more easily understandable circulars and decrees in the future should not cost the GoV more than the amount of administrative time expended today. The GoV will incur some cost to study existing laws and regulations relating to the import and export process and determine how they can be made more streamlined and transparent. This should come from the general treasury.

To ensure consistent application, interpretation, and enforcement of regulations, the GoV will need to spend more administrative time auditing the performance of individual Customs officials across provinces. This audit activity could be funded, at least partially, through higher Customs entry filing.

Some amount of effort will need to be applied by the GoV to review the regulations governing international trade in effect in Vietnam today to determine how to simplify them and reduce the number of documents and certificates required to import and export. This activity should be funded from the general treasury.

Eliminating facilitation payments to Customs officials and police will in part require the restructuring of hiring, pay, and benefit programs for these officials. Funding to pay for skills-aligned, merit-based salary increases for Customs officials can come from increasing the published filing fees for import and export clearance, cargo inspections, and other inspections. The expectation is that the new, higher published fees will be less than what LSPs are currently charging BCOs for customs brokerage services.

Funding for police officers should come from the general treasury, as is the case in advanced countries. The role of the police is to serve the general public; the general public should therefore bear the cost of their service.

Roles and Responsibilities

Going forward, the prime minister's office and National Assembly could devote more attention to establishing unambiguous laws and regulations governing international trade activities; assessing how existing laws and regulations can be clarified; implementing a process to routinely audit how individual Customs officials in the provinces apply, interpret, and enforce those laws and regulations; and evaluating how import and export regulations and documentation can be streamlined and simplified to reduce logistics costs for BCOs and LSPs.

Laws will need to be enacted to change the hiring and compensation basis of Customs officials and police officers to coincide with implementation of the e-Customs solution. The Ministry of Finance could have responsibility to administer a new human resources administration program.

Barriers and Obstacles

To simplify laws and regulations, ensure consistency among Customs agents, and streamline customs processes the Prime Minister should make a clear case to government officials and the public of the benefits to be derived from such actions in terms of making Vietnam an easier place for freight stakeholders to conduct business. Changing attitudes and behaviors will take time, and overcoming systemic inertia will be challenging.

Efficient Logistics · http://dx.doi.org/10.1596/978-1-4648-0103-7

As seen throughout this report (and as noted by other studies), facilitation payments are commonplace in Vietnam, and there will likely be significant barriers of resistance to implementing the recommended strategies. It will take a concerted effort by the prime minister's office to recognize the need for this transformation and to steer the necessary legislative and social changes needed to eliminate facilitation payments and increase transparency.

Custom's proposed deployment of an e-Customs system can be the prime driver for making the hiring, promotion, and compensation system for Customs officials more merit based.

Definition of Success

In 2015–16, when surveyed by the GoV, BCOs, and LSPs will report that Vietnam is an easier place to do business and is comparable to other Asian countries such as China and Thailand.

Beginning in 2016, facilitation payments will be significantly reduced, aided by the rollout of higher, documented rates for import and export clearance filings. By the end of 2019, facilitation payments to Customs officials and police will no longer be routinely reported by LSPs and BCOs, and police will be enforcing highway laws with clearly defined citation amounts with documented payments.

Strategic Freight Corridor Planning
Why This Is Relevant

Mode-specific, silo-based planning with limited avenues to foster logistics-informed (e.g., integrated) transport infrastructure has resulted in inadequate connectivity and broad demand-supply mismatches. A lack of complementary land-side infrastructure reduces international competitiveness for Vietnam's ports. The overbuilding of port facilities in Southern Vietnam, which stand underutilized, has translated into financially weak investments for terminal operators. This undermines supply chain stability and increases risks not only to terminal operators themselves but also ultimately to BCOs.

While Southern Vietnam ports are plagued by overcapacity, Northern ports in the Hanoi area are at risk of saturation in the medium term. Demand at the Northern region ports is expected to reach 5.5 million 20-Foot Equivalent Unit Containers (TEUs) by 2020, from about 2.7 million TEUs in 2011. The existing terminals are expected to reach full capacity (4.8 million TEUs) by 2018. Even with additional capacity from two additional terminals planned in Dinh Vu, which would raise total capacity to 5.8 million TEUs, the terminals are still expected to reach full capacity by 2020.

The development of Lach Huyen, a deep-water facility at Haiphong port, is expected to bring about immediate benefits, allowing vessels between 2,000 and 8,000 TEUs to call Northern Vietnam for the first time. Unit costs per TEU for such ships are significantly lower than existing feeder ships, which could result in savings of up to 60 percent for ocean carriers. The expected cost savings from the elimination of feeder and transshipment costs for Haiphong cargo is estimated at an additional $100–200 per TEU, for an annual savings to ocean carriers that could reach over $74 million[7] by 2020, with much of the cost savings expected to be passed to BCOs.

On the land side, manufacturers and BCOs in both the Northern and Southern regions continue to pay higher trucking fees resulting from significant congestion on the main highways leading to ports and on the access roads from those highways to the marine terminals. In 2012 BCOs will have paid approximately $150 million in additional trucking costs, and up to $270 million in 2020, because of highway congestion (see table 4.9).

Recommended Solutions

The MoT would benefit from adopting a holistic, multimodal approach to planning and executing strategic freight infrastructure development. The concept brings relevant public and private sector freight stakeholders together to (1) build consensus in determining the appropriate investments for each strategic freight corridor, (2) agree upon the needed development timelines, (3) review funding options, and (4) transparently communicate and execute the plan.

Corridor Planning: Strategic corridor planning should replace the MoT's current "stove pipe" planning process. This planning process brings together officials from the highways, ports, waterways, rail, and air transport functional departments to produce multimodal design and management structures for chosen (e.g., high-volume) corridors. This process will also need to include input from key freight stakeholders: marine terminal operators (MTOs), ocean carriers, LSPs, trucking companies, and prominent BCOs.

Specifically, in conjunction with the next five-year Master Plan, the MoT should develop a Multimodal Corridor Investment Plan (MCIP) based on inputs from a tactical planning process that reflects the needs of multisectoral central

Table 4.9 Highway Congestion Cost Impact on Trucking Costs
Millions of dollars (unless otherwise specified)

	2012	2015	2020
North			
Haiphong and Lach Huyen terminals	75.4	95.8	144.9
Cai Lan terminals	4.3	5.4	8.0
Total truck savings: North	79.7	101.2	152.9
South			
HCMC terminals	70.9	84.5	113.0
Percentage barge service to CM-TV	95%	90%	90%
Cai Mep-Thi Vai terminals	1.3	4.1	8.2
Total truck cost savings: South	72.3	88.5	121.2
Total truck savings: Vietnam	**151.9**	**189.7**	**274.1**

Source: Authors; see table A.4 for details.

government officials, provincial government freight leaders, and major freight stakeholders. To ensure the plan is fully executed, resources allocated to provincial governments for infrastructure development should include a commitment-based funding mechanism linked to the timely construction of MCIP-targeted infrastructure projects, such as critical port access roads. This will better ensure that the right projects (e.g., those that will deliver the most benefits to freight stakeholders) are identified, funded, and completed within the prescribed timeframes to keep pace with demand.

Lach Huyen Port Development: Haiphong is the only port in the world today handling annual volumes of over 2.5 million TEUs but with draft limits of less than 9 meters. There is a need for a deep-water port in Northern Vietnam to cater to the expected growth in market volumes as well as the global trend toward the use of larger containerships. The Lach Huyen Port project should be given the highest priority among all ports in Northern Vietnam. It will be the only port in the Northern region able to accommodate vessels above 4,000 TEUs, making it both a game changer for the region and compliant with standard BCO requirements.[8] Based on a planned launch of Lach Huyen in 2016, volumes at the port are expected to reach full capacity (of about one million TEUs) within four years. This would require the early planning for the development of Lach Huyen Phase 2 to meet the potential demand after 2020.

Funding for Lach Huyen includes the construction of the Tan Vu Highway, which will be connected to the new, under construction, Hanoi–Haiphong Expressway. Total budget for this project has been currently set at $1.6 billion.

The new Lach Huyen port complex will benefit ocean carriers (and their BCO customers) by allowing them to deploy larger ships with lower slot costs. It will also result in savings of approximately $74 million per year from the elimination of feeder vessels transshipping containers to foreign ports. More broadly, Lach Huyen will enable significant economic growth opportunities in the northern part of the country. In particular, BCOs will have a more cost-efficient and effective transportation system from factories around Hanoi to end-customers in the global economy.

Recommended Strategies

As part of developing the next five-year Master Plan for ports and land-side infrastructure, the MoT should begin the process of creating an MCIP for each of the six strategic freight corridors discussed in chapter 3, with short-term emphasis on the HCMC–Vung Tau, the Hanoi-Haiphong, and the Mekong Delta corridors.

The development of Lach Huyen Port should address its funding constraints and move forward toward construction completion in 2016 using the experience in developing the Cai Mep-Thi Vai terminals. Crucially, every effort should be made to avoid repeating at Lach Huyen the same mistakes now affecting Cai Mep-Thi Vai (see chapter 2).

The following further contextualizes the challenge of operationalizing a more strategic approach to corridor planning and strengthening the development of port capacity at Lach Huyen:

- **Corridor Planning**
  - *Funding mechanism:* Developing MCIPs will require no major funding effort by the MoT since the extra cost to the current infrastructure planning process will be in the form of additional meetings and committee travel to major production and consumption areas (e.g., Hanoi, HCMC, Danang, Mekong Delta) to hold feedback sessions with local freight stakeholders.
  - *Roles and Responsibilities:* MoT will be responsible for organizing MCIPs that will include government representatives from Vinamarine, inland waterways, highways, rail, airports, the Ministries of Planning and Investment and Finance, and appropriate provincial government representatives of major urban cities within their jurisdictions.
  - *Barriers and Obstacles:* Provincial governments currently have independence in how non–National Highway public funding resources are spent in their jurisdictions on access roads to ports as well as land zoning issues.
  - *Definition of Success:* The next five-year MoT Master Plan is developed with a holistic approach toward addressing transportation infrastructure investments using multimodal solutions to provide freight stakeholders with seamless access to/from international gateways and major domestic destinations.

- **Lach Huyen Port**
  - *Funding Mechanism:* The port is currently funded through a combination of Japanese Official Development Assistance ($900 million) and a Public-Private Partnership (PPP)[9] arrangement comprising a Vietnamese state-owned enterprise (SOE) and a Japanese consortium ($321 million). The PPP component is a joint venture between Vinalines and MOLNYKIT (a group led by Itochu Corporation and including ocean carriers MOL and NYK). However, the latter arrangement is far from stable, given Vinalines's financial struggles.[10]
  - *Roles and Responsibilities:* Vinamarine has responsibility for this high-profile project (Vietnam's prime minister has urged for timely project completion, consistent with launching port operations in 2016). The Ministry of Finance has oversight to ensure foreign and state funding sources are available.
  - *Barriers and Obstacles:* The current financing framework, centered on a single state-owned company (Vinalines) with weak management and under significant financial stress, does not appear to be sustainable. Ongoing discussions to replace Vinalines in the developing consortium may lead to significant delays in implementation, with the associated impact this would have on BCOs who would continue to face substandard international connectivity in the economically vital Hanoi region.

- *Phasing and Dependent Projects:* Lach Huyen will be developed in two phases with the first phase, according to existing plans, completed by 2016. Dredging the access channel and quay side channel to a depth of 14 meters is required.
- *Definition of Success:* Phase 1 of Lach Huyen is operational by 2016, including all the connector roads to NH 5.

Promoting a More Professional Trucking Industry
Why This Is Relevant

With fewer than 10 large trucking companies and about 100 small to midsized carriers, the trucking industry is fragmented. Like their counterparts in China,[11] most Vietnam-based trucking companies are single-truck outfits. This reduces service levels as marginal carriers are constantly exposed to shipment disruption.

In an environment of lax regulation of trucking operations and inconsistent enforcement, barriers to entry in the trucking industry are low. This has led to a race to the bottom in rates as a means for low-performing carriers to stay in business. Because rates are not always compensatory, most operators cannot afford to properly maintain their equipment, resulting in unsafe vehicles, frequent accidents, congestion from truck breakdowns on highways, and air pollution.

Although inflation has put pressure on wages and fuel costs continue to escalate, the competitive pricing of truck rates is a major driver of truck overloading. This further degrades the condition of already poor roadbeds and is a contributor to accidents due to the need for longer minimum stopping distance. Indeed, the prevalence of poorly maintained and overloaded trucks on Vietnam's highways is a major root cause of the country's alarmingly high 13 road crash fatalities per 100,000 people.[12] The rate pressure issue also suggests that truckers will avoid toll roads when possible, which contributes to trucks clogging secondary highways that are even less suited to handle overweight or large trucks. There is little incentive for larger trucking companies to add to their capital stock by investing in newer equipment when truck rates are noncompensatory.

The incidence of facilitation payments to the police increases operating costs and hurts service levels beyond disruptions at the shipment level. Because of special arrangements established by trucking companies with the police on certain road sections (a notable example being Binh Nai to Vung Tau), ocean carriers and other LSPs need to contract with many trucking companies to transport freight on behalf of their BCO customers in order to reduce transit delays due to police stops. This increases management complexity, drives up costs, and acts as a disincentive to long-standing relationships with trucking companies that are critical in times when shipment volumes are high.

While international BCOs may make trucking decisions based solely on price, by and large the substandard portion of the trucking market is believed to be driven by domestic shippers. Most large international BCOs, which tend to manage large volumes of high-value, time-sensitive goods (and/or security compliance obligations like C-TPAT) prefer larger trucking companies because of their ability to better dispatch trucks and track the movement of goods with operable GPS systems. Domestic BCOs tend to have much less demanding operational requirements and their lower service expectations generally lead them to seek the lowest-cost truckers.

Mandating and/or better enforcing suitable operator licenses for truck drivers and properly maintained trucks can be an effective way to encourage industry consolidation; it should also lead to fewer accidents, fewer equipment break-downs on highways, and lower congestion levels. While this would almost certainly require driver wage increases and generate higher maintenance expenses for truck carriers, these additional costs would likely be more than offset by increased equipment utilization (due to fewer itinerary disruptions) and a better ability to command compensatory trucking rates from BCOs and LSPs. Since larger companies are already operating at this level, there could be a contraction in the number of trucking companies (e.g., among marginal carriers) and an overall increase in the average fleet size.

One operational area in need of performance improvement is the high incidence of empty backhauls. Trucking companies benefit when they can secure a high percentage of backhaul cargo, thereby increasing equipment utilization and better spreading operational fixed costs. Not only would this increase trucking sector profitability, it would also reduce congestion, as fewer trucks would be needed to move the same amount of freight.

A younger national fleet could contribute to both reducing shipment disruptions and improving the carbon footprint profile of international and domestic supply chains. If the GoV should impose more stringent requirements regulating the engine emission standards (and therefore model year) of trucks on highways (probably involving a subsidy program), the economic costs of trucking could be reduced. From a financial cost standpoint, trucking companies would likely benefit from lower maintenance costs, but would incur higher capital costs in the form of payments for the purchase of new(er) trucks (partially offset by public subsidies, if these were deemed feasible). The impact on BCOs would likely be higher trucking rates, as resulted from the implementation of the Clean Truck Program recently established by the ports of Los Angeles and Long Beach, California (see box 4.1), partially or fully offset by lower inventory carrying costs in their supply chains through more reliable trucking services.

Recommended Solutions

Trucking regulations should be strengthened, and a revamped enforcement program should be introduced. This two-pronged approach would focus on the following:

- Improving active duty driver qualifications
- Requiring proper licensing of all trucks and chassis
- Requiring semiannual vehicle and chassis inspections and
- Eliminating overweight containers and trailers.

Efficient Logistics • http://dx.doi.org/10.1596/978-1-4648-0103-7

Box 4.1 Ports of Los Angeles and Long Beach Clean Truck Program[13]

In 2008, 1,200 trucking companies were in operation in the Southern California San Pedro Bay region. Drivers operated 16,000 port drayage trucks, of which 5,000 were part-time drivers who mostly worked on weekends and made minimal investments in equipment on their old, fully depreciated trucks. In an effort to reduce air pollution, the ports' Clean Truck Program mandated that all trucks not meeting the 2007 Federal Clean Truck Emissions Standards by January 1, 2012, be banned from entering to the ports.

As of year-end 2012, there were 8,000–9,000 registered trucks and 400 trucking companies serving this region. The two ports offered trucking companies grants of $20,000 and $50,000 to help finance new diesel or liquid natural gas (LNG) trucks, respectively. The Southern California Air Quality Management District offered additional grants of $50,000 and $100,000 for new diesel or LNG trucks, respectively. New trucks partially financed by these grants were required to make 350 trips to the ports annually or the trucks were supposed to be used in the Southern California drayage business for seven years.

The cost of a 2007 or newer diesel truck is approximately $150,000 and $200,000 for an LNG truck. The increased cost to BCOs ranged from $35 to $50 per container move, depending on the length of the trip. The incentive for BCOs to support higher truck rates was that new port infrastructure development was suspended until trucking companies complied with the new regulations. Trucking companies were also required to meet established safety scores for driver performance, the equipment was subject to biannual inspections and drug testing became mandatory for all drivers.

The GoV should also (1) evaluate interventions that can help reduce the number of empty backhauls (as this will lead to an overall reduction of trucks on highways), (2) support firm-level expansion plans (where these are assessed financially viable) by asset-based trucking companies as a means to reduce industry fragmentation and promote better service levels, (3) incentivize the development of a vibrant truck brokerage sector, and (4) strengthen the environmental sustainability of the trucking industry in ways that can also improve trucking profitability.

Recommended Strategies

The following specific actions are recommended to implement the solutions outlined above:

- Set up rigorous truck driver license testing based on the driver's ability to pass a stringent driver's exam and eyesight testing. This should be administered at GoV-sanctioned exam centers (actual operation of such centers could be licensed to private parties under PPP arrangements). Irrespective of the chosen operating arrangement, specialized training should be given to management and staff in order to prevent tests from being compromised by facilitation paid to officials.

- Conduct semiannual vehicle and chassis roadability inspections (head and tail lights in working order, appropriate tread on tires, adequate braking system, and good engine performance) and proof of insurance. These inspections could also be conducted by private parties in partnership with the GoV to promote efficiency.

- Monitor container weights at marine terminal in-gates using electronic scanners.[14] These devices are able to photograph truck license plates and container numbers at marine terminal in-gates to match the container to the trucking company. If the weight scale is not at the in-gate, the container will be weighed later as part of the vessel preload planning process. When overweight containers are identified, the container number can be traced back to the trucking company, which is then automatically issued a fine by the system.

- Off-port overloading controls should be extended where available, and established where not, through permanent weigh stations with weigh-in-motion capability—and ideally operated under PPP arrangements. To increase the impact of a weigh station network, random audits at low-traffic sections may be conducted via mobile scales. Whether on highways or at port locations, overloading fees assessed on offenders should strictly reflect the cost to repair roads from overloading-induced damage.

- Provide access to more affordable, longer-term credit to trucking companies, whether fleet-owning carriers or smaller owner-operators, that have a solid business plan, meet (or have a credible plan to meet) revamped regulations, and/or are seeking possible expansion plans through acquisition or internal growth.

- Promote joint-venture investments by foreign trucking companies.
  - As a potential measure to reduce the incidence of empty backhauls, assess the viability of implementing electronic information exchanges where BCOs can post loads on which trucking companies (for this type of setup, typically owner-operators) can bid. Under such a scheme, the lowest-priced, qualified carrier (e.g., based on requirements posted by the BCO) would be awarded the load. China is testing such a system, known as the "Road Ports" program (see box 4.2).

- As a means both to further reduce backhauls and to increase trucking industry performance, support the development of the truck brokerage sector. This can be done through credit access support, increased openness to foreign company participation, and stronger (e.g., accessible, unambiguous, internationally competitive) regulations for this subsector.

- Develop stronger emission control standards for trucks and review current import regulations for new and used trucks that meet such standards.

Box 4.2 Global Logistic Properties Road Ports: China Test

China is developing electronic exchanges where truck drivers can bid on shipments to reduce empty trips. Global Logistic Properties, a $566 million company and one of the largest logistics property developers in China and Japan, is working on a solution it hopes will make Chinese trucking more efficient and less uncertain. The company partnered last year with China's Transfer Road-Port to build a network of logistics centers and "road ports" throughout China under a joint venture company, Zhejiang Transfer Logistics. Such road ports are now hubs where owner-operators can park trucks, have meals, rest, and find freight using a digitized exchange.

Giving drivers the ability to interact with an electronic software system to bid on freight loads saves time, as it grants owner-operators access to a virtual dispatch office. However, the early stages of implementing the new "road ports" concept have shown that it is difficult to change deep-seated habits of using traditional methods to secure backhaul loads rather than relying on an impersonal, automated, electronic bid system.

Source: Cassidy 2012.

- Develop and disseminate tools (e.g., an interactive website, workshops at areas of high trucking activity, free informational material, university courses) to promote a better understanding, on the part of both truckers and shippers, of the tradeoffs involved in logistics management (e.g., transport costs versus inventory carrying costs), of how to strengthen business operations (e.g., in the case of truckers, practical ways to improve fuel efficiency), and of ways to assess and measure logistics value (e.g., savings and responsiveness in the supply chain). This can improve trucking industry performance from both the supply and the demand side.

Possible Funding Mechanisms

Better enforcement of trucking industry safety standards is an area where PPP arrangements can be pioneered (e.g., to operate testing centers, weigh bridges, and inspection yards) as a funding and efficiency enhancing mechanism. Should these activities be kept government run and implemented, requiring all truck drivers to have their licenses revalidated by passing a driving test and having their eyesight checked will likely require increasing the staff at MoT to develop and administer the tests. Additional staff needed for this activity can be paid in part from examination fees collected from drivers. Similarly, MoT-administered truck and chassis inspections for roadability should be conducted throughout the country and paid by trucking companies.

Marine terminals currently weigh containers upon arrival. Ongoing monitoring of weight information will require additional staff positions and equipment provision, which may be implemented on a fully private or public-private basis. A system of these characteristics can be incrementally implemented, starting with a pilot at one or more selected locations. This would allow for the economics of the intervention to be corroborated and for operational issues to be addressed.

As part of developing stronger truck emission control standards, if the GoV decides to limit the number of imported, used model-year trucks in favor of new or more recent imported model-year trucks that have higher emission standards, it may consider providing subsidies to support this (e.g., this was the case for the Port of Long Beach and Port of Los Angeles Clean Truck Program). For illustrative purposes only, if the GoV were to help finance the purchase of 10,000 new tractor heads countrywide, where these are new $150,000 clean diesel trucks with a $70,000 contribution per tractor head, the GoV's cost would be $700 million over a four-year period. The total cost to all trucking companies participating in the program—assuming they pay a 20 percent down payment plus financing costs on a 10-year 10 percent interest loan—would be $1.1 billion (see table 4.10). The return on investment of such a scheme would be mainly determined by fuel and maintenance savings for transport carriers and the impact of lower diesel emissions on health and environmental outcomes. Reducing the public's associated health costs from lower truck pollution is the key driver for funding a clean truck program.[15]

The concept of setting up an electronic exchange service for improving two-way loads will need to be studied to determine its effectiveness within the trucking community. A China study tour by representatives from MoT and the Vietnam Trucking Association could be suggested, to discuss the "Roads Ports" concept and other approaches to improving industry performance.

Table 4.10 Cost of a Notional Truck Replacement Program

Cost per new tractor head	$150,000				
Number of trucks to be replaced	10,000				
GoV funding per tractor head	$70,000				
Rate of replacement per year	25%				
Down payment (20%) amount	$30,000				
Loan amount per tractor head	$50,000				
Financing cost	10%				
Loan term in years	10				
Monthly loan payment per tractor head	$660.75				
	Year 1	Year 2	Year 3	Year 4	Total
Number of tractor heads to be replaced	2,500	2,500	2,500	2,500	10,000
Down payment paid by trucking companies	$75,000,000	$75,000,000	$75,000,000	$75,000,000	$300,000,000
Loan payment per year	19,822,500	19,822,500	19,822,500	19,822,500	
Over 10 year period	198,225,000	198,225,000	198,225,000	198,225,000	792,900,000
Total cost					**1,092,900,000**

Source: Authors; see table A.6 for details.

Barriers and Obstacles

- Behavioral impediments are a likely obstacle, including the entrenched role of facilitation payments in the various licensing and inspection processes.
- Evidence of the economics of investments in new tractor heads (e.g., from pilot programs) would need to quickly materialize in order to elicit broader support by trucking companies and BCOs, since this initiative will likely increase trucking costs and rates.
- As China has found in the early stages of implementing the new "Road Ports" concept, it is difficult to change cultural habits of using traditional methods to secure backhaul loads versus using an electronic bid system.

Definition of Success

By the end of 2014, the GoV can revamp trucking regulations and develop enforcement plans to be implemented in 2015.

By year-end 2015, all truck drivers should have valid, GoV-issued driver's licenses, and trucks and chassis must have passed mandatory roadability testing.

By the end of 2016, scanning equipment will have been installed at major marine terminals in HCMC, Cai Mep-Thi Vai, and Haiphong and connected to the nation-wide software system, where container weights will be linked back to trucking companies. With significant fines sent to trucking companies delivering overweight containers beginning in 2017, there should be at least some evidence of decline in overweight trucks and containers by the end of 2018.

By the end of 2014, the MoT will have concluded whether a "Road Port" system is justified for Vietnam and, if so, begin plans to implement one or more test sites. The implementation horizon for such sites would depend on the choice of financing arrangement (e.g., public funds, PPPs, or official development assistance).

Ideally in parallel with improved enforcement of road safety regulations (e.g., licensing and roadability tests), the hiring and compensation policies for police officers should be modernized in line with those recommended for Customs officials. Traffic citations should be for valid offenses based on published regulations, and fines should be published and consistently applied. Auditing mechanisms should be in place to assess progress.

By 2020 or sooner, depending on economic viability, the GoV will start implementing a pilot "Clean Truck Program" for drayage-only trucks at one or more selected ports. Such a program can then be extended as feasible to wider implementation.

Expanded Business Opportunities for Cai Mep–Thi Vai Marine Terminals
Why This Is Relevant

The economics of calling at Cai Mep–Thi Vai are weak for most international container shipping carriers. For example, carriers are not receiving sufficient incentives to offset the relatively low container move counts at Cai Mep-Thi Vai (currently 1,000–2,000 TEUs per call), tonnage and pilotage fees form a high percentage of operating costs on a per TEU basis, and carriers are facing obstacles in getting approval to bring in larger ships over 80,000 deadweight tons (DWT). Additional discounts are needed for vessels above 90,000 GT (above 8,000 TEUs), which are now the primary vessels used on the Far East–Europe routes. These additional incentives and the lifting of current restrictions on vessels of over 80,000 DWT could potentially increase the number of direct Vietnam to Europe services from one as of September 2012 to four or five weekly service strings. The lower slot costs on these larger vessels could be passed along to BCOs in terms of lower or more stable rates.[16]

Further regulatory restrictions on Cai Mep–Thi Vai volumes are expected. Effective January 1, 2013, foreign-flagged carriers that are currently arranging their own feedering of international containers from domestic ports to Cai Mep–Thi Vai, will no longer be permitted to do so. Cabotage laws will restrict containers transiting between domestic ports to be only carried on Vietnamese-flagged carriers. Foreign-flagged carriers are expected to transship the vast majority of those international containers to a foreign port, at an estimated cost of between $2.1 and $3.0 million per year[17] because they are unable to rely upon Vietnamese-flagged carriers to provide suitably reliable feeder services.

Targeted (and most likely temporary) incentives to container carriers could bring more volumes to Cai Mep–Thi Vai, benefiting not only the carriers themselves but also MTOs and BCOs. For example, if adequate load rates and/or appropriate GoV discounts on tonnage, maritime security, and wharfage fees at Cai Mep–Thi Vai were implemented on a temporary basis, ocean carriers could benefit from lower slot costs on those larger vessels and avoidance of feeder and higher transship costs at foreign ports. These savings can be passed along to BCOs in terms of lower ocean rates.[18]

Recommended Strategies
- Further capacity additions at Cai Mep-Thi Vai, as scheduled, should be reassessed based on updated demand projections. The program to close or relocate inner-city ports at HCMC should also be reassessed by explicitly addressing the institutional bottlenecks that have prevented a more successful implementation of long-held plans to reduce city congestion while improving international connectivity.
- As a temporary measure, volume discounts on operating fees should be extended for vessels calling Cai Mep-Thi Vai, and especially those above 80,000 GT.
- Cabotage rules should be further relaxed to allow foreign-flag carriers to carry international containers from Haiphong, Danang, and Nha Trang to/from Cai Mep-Thi Vai.
- Incentives should also be provided to attract international transshipment volumes (e.g., from Cambodia, Malaysia, the Philippines, and Thailand) to Cai Mep-Thi Vai.

Efficient Logistics • http://dx.doi.org/10.1596/978-1-4648-0103-7

Possible Funding Mechanisms

Financing for the additional discounts to ocean carriers for calling Cai Mep-Thi Vai can come from the general treasury or by increasing the current Terminal Handling Charge (THC) that ocean carriers charge BCOs. The current THC ranges from $114 to $151 with most carriers charging around $130. Table 4.11 lists the 2012 THCs for neighboring countries, demonstrating that there is room for Vietnam to raise its tariff fee and still be competitive with most Asian countries.

Barriers and Obstacles

One barrier will likely emerge from Vinalines and the other Vietnamese-flagged carriers resisting the continuation of foreign-flagged carriers transshipping international containers from domestic ports to Cai Mep-Thi Vai. However, foreign-flagged carriers have said they will transship these containers at foreign ports because Vietnamese-flagged carriers cannot provide the service needed to make transshipping over Cai Mep-Thi Vai work.

Another barrier may come from the MTOs in the HCMC area targeted to be shut down or relocated.

Definition of Success

In the very short term, continued fee-discount support is provided to ocean carriers calling Cai Mep-Thi Vai, until such time as there is sufficient volume to offset the tonnage, maritime security, and pilotage fees. Further, the GoV continues to allow foreign-flagged carriers to transship international containers from domestic terminals to Cai Mep-Thi Vai.

By 2014 ocean carriers will find it more attractive and financially viable to serve Cai Mep-Thi Vai, resulting in additional liner services for BCOs within two years. Capacity at Cai Mep-Thi Vai terminals will be better utilized.

By 2015 fewer marine terminals will be operating in the HCMC area, bringing supply and demand into closer alignment.

By 2016 Cai Mep-Thi Vai terminals succeed in attracting additional volume and this port complex becomes a viable transshipment hub.

Table 4.11 Terminal Handling Charges for Vietnam and Neighboring Countries, 2012

U.S. dollars

Country	Terminal handling charge
China	$301 (includes new 6% VAT)
Singapore	$219
Thailand	$156
Indonesia	$145
Vietnam	**$130**
Philippines	$120
Cambodia	$115

Source: Authors.

Institutional Mechanisms to Support Logistics Policy Making

Achieving more effective logistics policy making requires Vietnam to adopt a more integrated approach, resembling the integrated (e.g., multimodal) nature of the underlying measures that should be pursued. A critical feature of most of the recommendations proposed in chapter 4 is that their conceptualization, planning, approval, and execution is best conducted through multi-agency (in many cases, multiministry) collaboration and in consultation with a broad base of freight and competitiveness stakeholders—including BCOs, LSPs, trade associations, academia, and the donor community. It should also be informed by verifiable data rather than anecdotal evidence or narrow views of market trends and requirements.

International experience has shown that inclusive institutional arrangements can facilitate multidisciplinary decision making in logistics—and that without it projects tend to continue to be managed in silos. Such arrangements have included in practice logistics councils and committees made up of senior representatives of a wide array of public sector entities, such as modal administrations; Ministries of Planning, Industry and Trade, Economy, Agriculture, and Finance; Customs administrators; police and law enforcement; and governance and anticorruption agencies; and chaired by the country's highest executive authority, such as the president or prime minister. Typically set up at the national level, logistics councils may also be established at the subnational level and be complemented by mechanisms to systematically promote and facilitate public-private avenues of engagement, consultation, and collaboration, such as logistics fora. In East Asia, examples of countries that have implemented dedicated institutional arrangements of this kind include Australia (Australian Logistics Council, state-level Freight Logistics Councils, Transport and Logistics Centre, and the Integrated Logistics Network), Japan (Japan Institute of Logistics Systems), Malaysia (Malaysian Logistics Council), and Thailand (National Logistics Committee).[19] Logistics councils and committees can be particularly effective at (1) coordinating interministerial priorities within budgetary, technical, legal and other constraints—something that can be done, for example, through the crafting of a National Logistics Strategy; (2) monitoring the timely and cost-effective implementation of such priorities; (3) assessing systemwide performance improvements by tracking selected key performance indicators; and (4) informing public policy by evidence-based research and consultations with concerned (public and private) parties. Since some of the latter activities are data intensive, logistics committees are best supported by the establishment of a data-gathering body—for example, in association with one or more academic institution—such as a Logistics Observatory.

However, it should be noted that multistakeholder institutional arrangements are not necessarily a "silver bullet" and should be strictly seen as a means to an end. For example, despite its several years in operation, Malaysia's Logistics Council continues to work toward truly delivering on its promise of coordinating strategies, policies, and regulations across the logistics sector. In Vietnam itself, the donor community has called for the GoV to establish interagency coordination mechanisms and institutions in the context of logistics policy making since at least 2006,[20] to little avail. This reflects the complexity of setting up such institutions in practice.

It is recommended that Vietnam continue to pursue the establishment of inter- and intraministerial coordinating bodies, such as a National Logistics Committee, as well as a Logistics Observatory; it is also recommended for the GoV to develop, adopt, and monitor the implementation of a long-term National Logistics Strategy. Ideally, this should be done in parallel to the implementation of the short- and medium-term recommendations offered by this report, as well as those being generated by academia, the private sector, the broader donor community, and other actors relevant to national and international supply chains.

Notes

1. ASEAN Economic Community Blueprint, http://www.aseansec.org/5187-10.pdf.
2. Frequent and lengthy product inspection and delays in import clearance can cause production schedule complications, missed delivery dates to customers, diminished customer satisfaction and future lost sales. Delays in export clearance can result in spoilage of perishable products because of the length of time it takes to test products and obtain export licenses. The export shipment may miss the intended aircraft or vessel and have to wait for the next available slot.
3. Including not only customs but also technical (e.g., security, legal, etc.) clearance.
4. Customs clearance information was obtained from one beneficial cargo owner (BCO) that manufactures in Vietnam and Malaysia. Data are largely consistent with findings from the World Bank's *Doing Business in 2013* database.
5. With facilitation fees reported at between 5 and 50 percent, 30 percent was used as the approximate median of the reported percentages.
6. Origin costs for imports include import declaration, delivery order preparation, Terminal Handling Charge (THC), Container Imbalance Charge, container inspection as charged by the LSP, and trucking fees for a 100-kilometer drayage haul. Origin costs for exports include bill of lading fee, THC, export declaration, Container Yard Administration Fee, security fillings (for the U.S. and European Union), container inspection, and Load-on/Load-off.
7. Ocean carriers report saving of between $100 and $200 per TEU by not having to transship containers (e.g., at Hong Kong SAR, China). Assuming 1.1 million TEUs will be handled at Lach Huyen by 2020, and 45 percent of that volume will be exports, the total savings to ocean carriers using mother vessels will be 1.1 million × 45% × $150 = $74 million.
8. The existing draft limit at Cai Lan Port is insufficient to permit the deployment of ships over 4,000 TEUs, which are commonly utilized in linehaul routes.
9. See appendix F for a brief discussion of PPPs in Vietnam and the key components to successful implementation of PPP projects.
10. As of January 2013, there were discussions by the MoT to replace Vinalines as Lach Huyen developer with Saigon New Port Corporation, another state-owned enterprise and the largest terminal operator in the country.

11. Cassidy (2012).

12. Status Paper on Road Safety (For the Calendar year 2010), available at http://www .unescap.org/ttdw/common/Meetings/TIS/EGM-Roadsafety-2011/Status/Countries /VietNam-2010-Status.pdf.

13. Based on Cambridge Systematics research with several Southern California–based trucking companies.

14. Based on Cambridge Systematics Prior Project Work; see appendix B for more details. Additional information is available at http://www.htsol.com/Files/TOCAsia2003.pdf.

15. Estimating the return on a clean truck program investment of this type for Vietnam was beyond the scope of this report and is offered as a main avenue for future research.

16. As of September 2012, low rates have resulted in ocean carriers in the Asia-to-Europe trade operating in the red; being able to use larger vessels today will only help to defray those losses.

17. Transshipment cost estimates are based on an estimated weekly volume of transship containers for three of the largest ocean carriers of 600–850 TEUs per week at a cost of $68 per TEU.

18. Same note as note 16, except that rates in the Asia-to-U.S. trade are more compensatory to the ocean carriers than in the Asia-to-Europe trade.

19. For a more detailed discussion of the institutional arrangements of the Australian logistics sector in particular and of institutional approaches to logistics policy making see World Bank (2012).

20. Specifically, Meyrick and Associates *et al.* (2006), a World Bank–sponsored report, called for the establishment of an Inter-ministerial Logistics Committee and a National Logistics Forum. Further efforts in this respect are being supported by the World Bank–financed Mekong Delta Transport Infrastructure Development Project (2007–present).

References

Cassidy, William B. 2012. "China Hits the Road." *Journal of Commerce* 13 (34): 15–15.

Meyrick and Associates, Transport Development and Strategy Institute (TDSI), and Carl Bro. 2006. *Vietnam: Multimodal Transport Regulatory Review*. Washington, DC: World Bank.

World Bank. 2012. *How to Decrease Freight Logistics Costs in Brazil*. Transport Papers Series (TP-39). Washington, DC.

Supporting Calculations

Table A.1 Forecast Import and Export Container Volumes

TEUs

Total volumes	2011	2012	2013	2014	2015	2016	2017	2018	2019	2020
Haiphong	1,611,500	1,708,190	1,810,681	1,919,322	2,034,482	2,156,551	2,285,944	2,423,100	2,568,486	2,722,595
Dinh Vu	907,124	1,015,989	1,137,896	1,274,444	1,427,377	1,598,662	1,790,502	2,005,362	2,246,006	2,515,526
Cai Lan	143,981	155,499	167,939	181,375	195,885	211,555	228,480	246,758	266,499	287,819
Total Northern Vietnam	2,664,616	2,881,690	3,118,529	3,377,155	3,659,759	3,968,784	4,306,943	4,677,238	5,083,010	5,527,960
HCMC ports	3,862,653	4,094,412	4,340,077	4,600,482	4,876,510	5,169,101	5,479,247	5,808,002	6,156,482	6,525,871
Cai Mep-Thi Vai	839,684	965,637	1,110,482	1,277,054	1,468,613	1,688,904	1,942,240	2,233,576	2,568,613	2,953,904
Total Southern Vietnam	4,702,337	5,060,049	5,450,559	5,877,536	6,345,123	6,858,005	7,421,487	8,041,578	8,725,095	9,479,775
Combined total	7,366,953	7,941,739	8,569,088	9,254,691	10,004,882	10,826,789	11,728,430	12,718,816	13,808,105	15,007,735
Percentage growth		7.8%	7.9%	8.0%	8.1%	8.2%	8.3%	8.4%	8.6%	8.7%
Total volumes by imports/exports										
Imports										
Northern Vietnam	1,465,873	1,585,378	1,715,763	1,858,141	2,013,718	2,183,838	2,369,994	2,573,839	2,797,210	3,042,145
Southern Vietnam	2,305,827	2,474,405	2,657,632	2,857,067	3,074,465	3,311,803	3,571,312	3,855,511	4,167,251	4,509,756
Total	3,771,699	4,059,783	4,373,395	4,715,209	5,088,183	5,495,641	5,941,306	6,429,350	6,964,461	7,551,901
Exports										
Northern Vietnam	1,198,743	1,296,312	1,402,766	1,519,014	1,646,041	1,784,946	1,936,949	2,103,399	2,285,800	2,485,815
Southern Vietnam	2,396,510	2,585,644	2,792,927	3,020,469	3,270,658	3,546,202	3,850,175	4,186,067	4,557,844	4,970,019
Total	3,595,254	3,881,956	4,195,693	4,539,482	4,916,699	5,331,148	5,787,124	6,289,466	6,843,644	7,455,834

table continues next page

Table A.1 Forecast Import and Export Container Volumes *(continued)*
TEUs

Foreign-only volumes	2011	2012	2013	2014	2015	2016	2017	2018	2019	2020
Imports and Exports Adjusted for Domestic Moves										
Imports										
Northern Vietnam	1,245,992	1,347,571	1,458,399	1,579,420	1,711,660	1,856,262	2,014,495	2,187,763	2,377,629	2,585,823
Southern Vietnam	1,959,953	2,103,244	2,258,987	2,428,507	2,613,296	2,815,033	3,035,615	3,277,185	3,542,163	3,833,292
Total	3,205,944	3,450,815	3,717,386	4,007,927	4,324,956	4,671,295	5,050,110	5,464,948	5,919,792	6,419,116
Exports										
Northern Vietnam	1,018,932	1,101,865	1,192,351	1,291,162	1,399,135	1,517,204	1,646,407	1,787,890	1,942,930	2,112,943
Southern Vietnam	2,037,034	2,197,797	2,373,988	2,567,398	2,780,059	3,014,272	3,272,649	3,558,157	3,874,167	4,224,516
Total	3,055,966	3,299,663	3,566,339	3,858,560	4,179,194	4,531,476	4,919,055	5,346,046	5,817,097	6,337,459
Combined total	6,261,910	6,750,478	7,283,725	7,866,487	8,504,150	9,202,771	9,969,166	10,810,994	11,736,889	12,756,575

table continues next page

Table A.1 Forecast Import and Export Container Volumes *(continued)*

Network-wide assumptions

	Import percentage[a]	Domestic percentage
Haiphong	55%	15%
Cat Lai	56	15
HCMC	51	15
Cai Mep-Thi Vai	40	15

a. Based on 2011 data supplied by Gemadept.

Key Cai Mep–Thi Vai assumptions

	2013	2014	2015	2016	2017	2018	2019	2020
Year-over-year volume growth	15%	15%	15%	15%	15%	15%	15%	15%
Container volume (TEU)	1,110,482	1,277,054	1,468,613	1,688,904	1,942,240	2,233,576	2,568,613	2,953,904
Barge service (in % of total port volumes)	95%	90%	90%	90%	90%	90%	90%	90%
Containers moved by truck	55,524	127,705	146,861	168,890	194,224	223,358	256,861	295,390
Cost of road congestion	$1,536,213	$3,533,289	$4,063,285	$4,672,775	$5,373,693	$6,179,746	$7,106,710	$8,172,714

Source: Authors based on input from Vietnam Port Association, interviews with port operators, and Liner Research Services.
Note: TEU = 20-foot equivalent unit.

Table A.2 Vietnam, China, and Indonesia Landed Cost Comparisons
All cost amounts in U.S. dollars

Export cost comparison of CY 40-foot container shipped to Los Angeles, California, in 2012 from China, Indonesia, and Vietnam			
Description	North America export	Asian import	Base for rate
Yantian, China export costs for CY FEU [a]			
Automated Manifest Service—U.S. Customs (AMS)	35.00		
International Security Filing (ISF)	32.00		
Consolidation fee	125.00	125.00	
Document administration fee	56.00	56.00	
Port construction fee	20.00	20.00	
Port security fee	5.00	5.00	
Terminal handling charge (THC)	301.00	301.00	Market price (a)
Subtotal	574.00	507.00	
Origin trucking	200.00	200.00	Estimated 2012 rate (b)
Total origin costs	774.00	707.00	
Ocean freight with bunker	1,850.00	300.00	Estimated 2012 rate (c)
Total landed cost without duty	2,624.00	1,007.00	

table continues next page

Table A.2 Vietnam, China, and Indonesia Landed Cost Comparisons *(continued)*

Description	NA export	Asian import	Base for rate
Jakarta, Indonesia, Export Costs for CY FEU[a]			
AMS	35.00		
ISF	32.00		
Consolidation fee	145.00	145.00	
Document administration fee	40.00	40.00	
Document verification	40.00	40.00	
Terminal handling charge (THC) lift on/lift off (LO/LO) charge	25.00	25.00	
Terminal handling charge (THC)	145.00	145.00	Market price (a)
Subtotal	462.00	395.00	
Origin trucking	175.00	200.00	Estimated 2012 rate(b)
Total origin costs	637.00	595.00	
Ocean freight with bunker	2,100.00	700.00	Estimated 2012 rate (c)
Total landed cost without duty	2,737.00	1,295.00	
Vietnam export costs for CY FEU[a]			
AMS	30.00		
ISF	32.00		
Bill of lading	35.00		
Delivery order		35.00	
Container imbalance charge (CIC)		70.00	
Seal	4.00		
Consolidation fee	75.00		
Document administration fee	70.00	20.00	
Customs and inspections		75.00	
Lift on/lift off (LO/LO) charge	11.00		
Terminal handling charge (THC)	130.00	130.00	Market price (a)
Subtotal	387.00	330.00	
Origin trucking	185.00	185.00	Estimated 2012 rate (b)
Total origin costs	572.00	515.00	
Ocean freight with bunker	1,960.00	500.00	Estimated 2012 rate (c)
Total landed cost without duty	2,532.00	1,015.00	

Export: estimated landed cost per FEU in Los Angeles, California

Country	Origin cost	Ocean freight	Total	Over/under Vietnam's landed cost per FEU
Vietnam	572.00	1,960.00	2,532.00	
China	774.00	1,850.00	2,624.00	92.00
Indonesia	637.00	2,100.00	2,737.00	205.00

Base for rates for CY FEU[a]

Code	Description
a	Market tariff rates: larger BCOs negotiate lower rates
b	Truck rate: based on best 2012 rate information
c	Ocean rate: average 2012 rate for large BCOs

table continues next page

Table A.2 Vietnam, China, and Indonesia Landed Cost Comparisons *(continued)*

Import: estimated landed cost per FEU at origin

Country	Origin cost	Ocean freight	Total	Over/under Vietnam's landed cost per FEU
Vietnam	515.00	500.00	1,015.00	
China	707.00	300.00	1,007.00	(8.00)
Indonesia	595.00	700.00	1,295.00	280.00

Source: Authors.

a. CY FEU refers to a factory-loaded, 40-foot container drayed to ocean port.

Table A.3 Inventory Carrying Costs from Import-Export Clearance Delays

Key variables		Notes
Additional inventory carrying cost due to delays in clearing import cargo		
Average export container value (FEU)	$90,000	As reported by interviewed shippers
Import value as % of export value	60%	As reported by interviewed shippers
Average import shipment container value (FEU)	$54,000	= Average FEU value times 60%
Average number of days to clear nonagriculture or food imports	6	As reported by interviewed shippers
Acceptable standard import clearance time (days)	3	As reported by interviewed shippers
Additional import clearance time in Vietnam (days)	3	As reported by interviewed shippers
Total value of imports in delayed pipeline	$162,000	= Average import value × additional clearing time
Average interest rate to finance inventory	6%	Estimate
Carrying cost per container (a)	$27.00	FEU volumes
Total no. foreign imported containers 2012 (b)	$46,586,008	1,725,408
Total no. foreign imported containers 2015 (c)	$58,386,904	2,162,478
Total no. foreign imported containers 2020 (d)	$86,658,064	3,209,558

Explanations for both import and export cargo calculations

Code	Explanation
A	Value of imports in delayed pipeline times (6%/360 days)
b, c, d	FEU volumes (shown) times carrying cost per container

Additional inventory carrying cost due to delays in clearing export cargo		
Average export container value (FEU)	$90,000	As reported by interviewed shippers
Average number of days to clear nonagriculture or food exports	3	As reported by interviewed shippers
Acceptable standard export clearance time (days)	1	As reported by interviewed shippers
Additional export clearance time in Vietnam (days)	2	As reported by interviewed shippers
Total value of imports in delayed pipeline	$180,000	= Average FEU value × additional clearing time
Average interest rate to finance inventory	6%	Estimate
Carrying cost per container (a)	$30.00	FEU volumes
Total no. foreign imported containers 2012 (b)	$49,494,941	1,649,831
Total no. foreign imported containers 2015 (c)	$62,687,908	2,089,597
Total no. foreign imported containers 2020 (d)	$95,061,884	3,168,729

table continues next page

Table A.3 Inventory Carrying Costs from Import-Export Clearance Delays *(continued)*

Combined import and export carrying costs

	Additional cost	Total volumes
Total no. foreign imported containers 2012	$96,080,949	3,375,239
Total no. foreign imported containers 2015	$121,074,812	4,252,075
Total no. foreign imported containers 2020	$181,719,947	6,378,287

Interest cost on extra inventory due to clearance delays	Amount (million $)		
	2012	2015	2020
Imports	$46.6	$58.4	$86.7
Exports	$49.5	$62.7	$95.1
Total inventory carrying cost	$96.1	$121.1	$181.8

Source: Authors.
Note: FEU = 40-foot equivalent unit. All monetary amounts in U.S. dollars.

Table A.4 Trucking Cost of Congestion

Additional trucking costs due to congestion		
Average trucking rate for distances less than 55 km (a)	$2.47/km	
Average trucking rate for distances greater than 55 km (b)	$2.17/km	Actual rates obtained from trucking contract negotiated with Vietnamese trucking company as of July 1, 2012
Percent reduction in truck rates if normal travel time (c)	30%	
Fuel as percent of freight rate (d)	30%	
Reduction in diesel fuel usage if normal travel time (e)	15%	
Average no. of kilometers per container truck trip in HCMC (f)	55 km	
Average no. of kilometers per container truck trip in Hanoi (g)	100 km	

	Rate savings without congestion ($)	Rate with congestion ($)	Rate savings (%)
Cost savings per container trip in HCMC area (a)	**34.64**	135.85	25.5
Cost savings per container trip in Hanoi area and Cai Mep-Thi Vai (b)	**55.34**	217.00	25.5

The 25.5 percent savings per km is assessed as conservative given the following testimony from one truck carrier interviewed for this report:

"Reduced congestion results in better utilization of equipment; diesel savings with higher speed limit, less idling time; less stop and go with proper intersection signaling or by-pass; [and an ability to] accommodate heavier trucks. In Busan, Korea, terminal time to pick up or drop off a container is 30 minutes, whereas in Haiphong one hour is normal, but 50 percent of the time it is longer. Hanoi to Haiphong is 100 kilometers, and the normal transit time for truck is 4 hours. For example, if the cost to operate a truck in Vietnam is $1.00 per km, that same truck could operate in China for $0.65 per kilometer."

table continues next page

Table A.4 Trucking Cost of Congestion *(continued)*

Annual savings through less congestion ($)			*Calculation code*	*Projected container volumes in TEU*		
2012	*2015*	*2020*		*2012*	*2015*	*2020*
Northern Vietnam						
Haiphong and Lach Huyen terminals	$75,371,222	$95,780,984	$144,925,713	(c)	2,724,179	3,461,859	5,238,121
Cai Lan terminals	$4,302,269	$5,419,648	$7,963,232	(d)	155,499	195,885	287,819
Total truck savings: North	$79,673,491	$101,200,632	$152,888,945		2,879,678	3,657,744	5,525,940
Southern Vietnam						
HCMC terminals	$70,918,798	$84,465,420	$113,033,796	(e)	4,094,412	4,876,510	6,525,871
Percentage barge service to CM-TV	95%	90%	90%				
Cai Mep-Thi Vai terminals	$1,335,838	$4,063,285	$8,172,714	(f)	965,637	1,468,613	2,953,904
Total truck cost savings: South	$72,254,637	$88,528,705	$121,206,510		5,060,049	6,345,123	9,479,775
Total congestion-related truck costs: Vietnam	$151,928,128	$189,729,337	$274,095,455		7,939,727	10,002,867	15,005,715
Cai Mep-Thi Vai terminals: truck volume						
Total container volume (TEU)	965,637	1,468,613	2,953,904	(g)			
Percentage barge service to CM-TV	95%	90%	90%				
Total containers trucked (FEU)	24,141	73,431	147,695	(h)			
Daily truck trips	80	245	492	(i)			

Calculation explanations	
Code	Explanation
a	Cost savings per trip = ((A×(1−C)) ×D+(A×D×E))*F
b	Cost savings per trip = ((B× (1−C)) ×D+(B×D×E)) ×G
c	= Total container throughput for Haiphong and Lach Huyen times (b) × 0.5 (convert TEUs to FEUs)
d	= Total container throughput for Cai Lan times (b) × 0.5
e	= Total container throughput for HCMC times (a) × 0.5
f	= Total container throughput for Cai Mep-Thi Vai × (1−Barge %) × (b) × 0.5
g	= Total container throughput for Cai Mep-Thi Vai in TEUs
h	= Total container throughput for Cai Mep-Thi Vai × (1−Barge %) × 0.5 (convert to FEUs)
i	= (h)/300 working days per year

table continues next page

Table A.4 Trucking Cost of Congestion *(continued)*

	Amounts (millions)		
	2012	*2015*	*2020*
Northern Vietnam			
Haiphong and Lach Huyen terminals	$75.4	$95.8	$144.9
Cai Lan terminals	4.3	5.4	8.0
Total congestion-related truck costs: North	$79.7	$101.2	$152.9
Southern Vietnam			
HCMC terminals	$70.9	$84.5	$113.0
Percentage barge service to Cai Mep-Thi Vai	95%	90%	90%
Cai Mep-Thi Vai terminals	$1.3	$4.1	$8.2
Total congestion-related truck cost: South	$72.3	$88.5	$121.2
Total congestion-related truck costs: Vietnam	$151.9	$189.7	$274.1
Northern Vietnam			
Haiphong and Lach Huyen terminals	$75.4	$95.8	$144.9
Cai Lan terminals	4.3	5.4	8.0
Total truck savings: North	$79.7	$101.2	$152.9
Southern Vietnam			
HCMC terminals	$70.9	$84.5	$113.0
Percentage barge service to Cai Mep-Thi Vai	95%	90%	90%
Cai Mep-Thi Vai terminals	$1.3	$4.1	$8.2
Total truck cost savings: South	$72.3	$88.5	$121.2

Source: Authors.
Note: FEU = 40-foot equivalent unit; TEU = 20-foot equivalent unit. All monetary amounts in U.S. dollars.

Table A.5 Estimation of Facilitation Costs

	40-foot container with 58 cbms		
Charge types	1 FEU ($)	Estimate facilitation payment[a] ($)	Facilitation payment % total Origin cost
Sea port: imports			
Delivery order (DO)	35.00		
Full containerload terminal handling charge (THC) (average)	130.00		
Document handling fee	20.00		
Container imbalance charge (CIC)	70.00		
Subtotal market-based rates	**255.00**		
Average custom brokerage costs (not duty)	50.00	15.00	
Average container inspection fees (average)	25.00	7.50	
Trucking from port to factory	185.00	55.50	
Subtotal origin rates subject to "tea payments"	**260.00**	**78.00**	**15.1%**
Total origin costs	**515.00**		

table continues next page

Table A.5 Estimation of Facilitation Costs *(continued)*

Charge types	1 FEU ($)	Estimate facilitation payment[a] ($)	Facilitation payment % total Origin cost
		40-foot container with 58 cbms	
Sea port: exports			
Bill of lading fee	35.00		
Full containerload terminal handling charge (THC) (average)	130.00		
SEAL fee (FCL)	4.00		
CY administrative fee	75.00		
Automated Manifest Service—U.S. Customs (AMS)	30.00		
International Security Filing (ISF)	32.00		
Load on/load off	11.00		
Subtotal market-based rates	**317.00**		
Custom brokerage costs	70.00	21.00	
Container inspection fees			
Trucking from factory to port	185.00	55.50	
Subtotal origin rates subject to "tea payments"	**255.00**	**76.50**	**13.4%**
Total origin cost	**572.00**		

	2012	2015	2020	Calculation explanations
Annual foreign volumes (FEUs)				
Foreign import volume	1,725,408	2,162,478	3,209,558	
Foreign export volume	1,649,831	2,089,597	3,168,729	
Total volumes	3,375,239	4,252,075	6,378,287	

	Amount (million $)			
	2012	2015	2020	
Annual facilitation fees based on				
Total foreign import volumes	134.6	168.7	250.3	Respective annual foreign import Volumes times average "tea money" for imports and exports
Total foreign export volumes	126.2	159.9	242.4	
Total facilitation costs	260.8	328.5	492.8	
Annual cost of facilitation payments in truck rates based on:				
Total foreign import volumes	95.8	120.0	178.1	Respective annual foreign import volumes times average "tea money" for trucking
Total foreign export volumes	91.6	116.0	175.9	
Total facilitation costs	187.3	236.0	353.9	
Annual facilitation fees involved in clearing customs based on:				
Total foreign import volumes	38.8	48.7	72.2	Subtracting lower truck rates from annual facilitation costs
Total foreign export volumes	34.6	43.9	66.5	
Total facilitation costs	73.5	92.5	138.8	

Source: Authors.

Note: FEU = 40-foot equivalent container. All monetary amounts in U.S. dollars.

a. Estimated facilitation payment = 30% of cost, based on study survey.

Table A.6 Cost to Finance New Clean Diesel Trucks

Cost per new tractor head	$150,000				
No. of trucks to be replaced	10,000				
Government subsidy per tractor head	$70,000				
Rate of replacement per year	25%				
Downpayment (20%) amount	$30,000				
Loan amount per tractor head	$50,000				
Financing cost	10%				
Loan term (years)	10				
Monthly loan payment	$660.75				

	Year 1	Year 2	Year 3	Year 4	Total
No. of tractor heads to be replaced	2,500	2,500	2,500	2,500	10,000
Downpayment paid by trucking companies	$75,000,000	$75,000,000	$75,000,000	$75,000,000	$300,000,000
Loan payment per year	$19,822,500	$19,822,500	$19,822,500	$19,822,500	
Over 10-year period	$198,225,000	$198,225,000	$198,225,000	$198,225,000	$792,900,000
Total cost by trucking companies					$1,092,900,000

Calculation explanation

Downpayment: 20% paid by trucking company

Loan payment: based on mortgage rate calculator

Source: Authors. All monetary amounts in U.S. dollars.

Overweight Container Audit Process

Miniature Concept of Operations for Automated Weight Auditing and Fine Assessment

The automated weight audit and fine assessment concept can be designed by repurposing technologies utilized in countries such as the United States.[1] The auditing process can be done using primarily roadside equipment:

- *License Plate Readers (LPRs), which are mounted at the side of the gate.* Commonly available LPR devices can manage identification for five to seven jurisdictions (e.g., different plate designs) in real time along with reading the container identification number.
- *Static weight scales, to measure the weight of the vehicle at a full stop.* If the container and truck are not weighed at the marine terminal in-gate, the export container will be weighed prior to loading on board the vessel. If the container is weighed after the truck has departed, the software system can match the overweight container information with the trucking company based on the electronic information (truck license number and container number) captured at the in-gate.
- *A centralized system to tabulate weight information* from each of the gates and check against national or provincial vehicle registration data.

By using the static weight scale to measure the actual gross vehicle weight, the LPR to identify the vehicle, and the centralized system to identify registered weight, a violation audit can be created and demographic information can be tabulated for each violation.

Once an audit trail is constructed, an optional step would be to implement a centralized fine assessment module. Depending on the arrangement carriers may have with national and provincial governments regarding vehicle registration, as well as the processes around vehicle registration renewal and tax payments, various options are possible. Examples include the following:

- Directly invoicing carriers for fines on a weekly or monthly basis
- Attaching accumulated fines to the costs of vehicle registration and
- Attaching accumulated fines to the taxes to be paid.

The estimated costs for the concept would be as follows:

- Auditing Component:
  - Per site costs of should be less than $500 for the LPR and static scale and
  - A single cost of $150,000–$300,000 for the auditing system, depending on the needed interfaces with the national or provincial registration system.
- Overweight Fine Collection Component: $350,000–500,000 depending on the system interfaces required and the process for documenting received fines.

Note

1. This appendix is based on Cambridge Systematics research and advisory work.

Entities Interviewed

International and Domestic Beneficial Cargo Owners: 27

ABB Ltd (power and automation technology), Adidas Sourcing Ltd (footwear, apparel), Audi Vietnam (Automotive Asia Ltd), Columbia Sportswear (footwear, apparel), Esquel Garment Manufacturing (VN) Co., Ltd (apparel), Global Silver Ltd Co. (consumer goods), Ha Noi–Vung Tau Beer JS Company (beverages), HP (computers and electronics), Hung Vuong Corp (seafood), IKEA Trading Hong Kong Ltd (furniture, housewares), Intel Products Vietnam Ltd Co (semiconductors), Kimberly-Clark Vietnam (diapers), MAST Industries (apparel), Metro Cash & Carry (general department store merchandise), Minh Phu (seafood), Nestlé Vietnam Ltd (coffee), Nike (footwear, apparel), Novartis Pharma Services AG (pharmaceuticals), Openasia Heavy Equipment (CFAO Group) (heavy machinery), Penflex Viet Nam (corrugated metal hoses), Phu Thai Group (retail and distribution), Target (general department store merchandise), Thach Ban JSC (construction materials), Toyota Motor Vietnam Co Ltd (autos), Unilever (home, personal care products), Vissai Group (cement, building materials), and ZC International Ltd (precision steel parts).

Factories: 4

Nike (footwear, 2 factories), Nike (apparel, 2 factories).

Logistics Service Providers: 11

APL Logistics, CEVA Freight (Thailand) Ltd, DHL Global Forwarding, DHL Express, Damco, Gemadept, Kuehne + Nagel, Schenker Vietnam Co Ltd, Trimax/OIA Global Logistics, UPS Vietnam Joint Stock Company, and an anonymous global LSP.

Ocean Carriers: 5

APL, Maersk, Mitsui OSK, NYK, Vinalines.

Marine Terminal Operators: 15

Cai Mep-Thi Vi and Cat Lai terminals: SITV, SP-PSA, TCIT, CMIT, SSIT, Saigon New Port, Gemadept, VICT, and SPCT; Cai Lan terminals (2); and Haiphong terminals (4).

Trucking Companies: 4

Ban Mai, Cong Thanh, Dan Thinh, and MACs.

Trade Associations: 4

American Chamber of Commerce (AMCHAM), European Chamber of Commerce (EUROCHAM), US-ASEAN Business Council, and Vietnam Competitiveness Institute.

Government Entities: 4

Ministry of Planning and Investment, Ministry of Transport, Vinamarine, and Vinalines (state-owned enterprise).

Methodology for Calculating the Cost of Congestion on the Vietnamese Economy

Table D.1 shows the cost of congestion as a percentage of gross domestic product (GDP) for Jakarta, Sydney, and a selection of major cities in the United States with significant transportation and logistics activity. The data for both Jakarta and Sydney show the total costs of congestion including passenger and truck delay, as well as vehicle operating costs. The data for U.S. cities parse out the value of truck commodity value and truck delay, a specific component of overall congestion costs relevant for this study. These data range from 0.16 percent of GDP to 0.47 percent of GDP costs to congestion from truck delays. This is likely a conservative estimate of the costs of congestion in cities in Vietnam, as U.S. road networks and infrastructure are more mature. With regard to total costs of congestion from annual hours of delay for commuters and trucks, excess fuel consumed, vehicle operating costs, and commuter stress, the values in the United States range from 0.76 percent of GDP to 1.65 percent of GDP.

Using the upper range of congestion factors based on table D.1, one can apply a GDP factor to various cities and/or regions in Vietnam. This provides an estimate of the cost of congestion for various cities.

For Vietnam as a whole it is conservatively estimated that truck delays cause approximately $487 million of cost to the Vietnamese economy annually, as shown in table D.2. Table D.3 shows total costs of congestion, estimated at $1.7 billion, including additional factors such as annual hours of delay for commuters and trucks, excess fuel consumed, vehicle operating costs, and commuter stress.

Table D.1 Estimates for Costs of Congestion in Various Sample Cities

Urban area	Costs included	Cost (million $)	Population	Cost/capita ($)	% of GDP[d]
Jakarta (2010)[a]	Fuel, other VOC, delay	5,200	9,594,000	542	5.70
Sydney (2005)[b]	Fuel, other VOC, delay, reliability, CO_2, other emissions	3,500	4,599,000	761	1.60
Chicago area (2010)[c,d]	Truck commodity value and truck delay, 2010	2,317	8,583,000	270	0.47
Chicago area (2010)[c,d]	Total congestion costs, 2010	8,206	8,583,000	956	1.65
Los Angeles–Long Beach–Santa Ana (2010)[c,d]	Truck commodity value and truck delay, 2010	2,254	13,124,000	172	0.31
Los Angeles–Long Beach–Santa Ana (2010)[c,d]	Total congestion costs, 2010	10,999	13,124,000	838	1.49
New York–Newark NY-NJ-CT (2010)[c,d]	Truck commodity value and truck delay, 2010	2,218	18,852,000	118	0.17
New York-Newark NY-NJ-CT (2010)[c,d]	Total congestion costs, 2010	9,794	18,852,000	520	0.76
Houston, TX (2010)[c,d]	Truck commodity value and truck delay, 2010	689	4,056,000	170	0.18
Houston, TX (2010)[c,d]	Total congestion costs, 2010	3,203	4,056,000	790	0.83
Washington, DC-VA-MD[c,d]	Truck commodity value and truck delay, 2010	683	4,536,000	151	0.16
Washington, DC-VA-MD[c,d]	Total congestion costs, 2010	3,849	4,536,000	849	0.91
Seattle, WA[c,d]	Truck commodity value and truck delay, 2010	467	3,237,000	144	0.20
Seattle, WA[c,d]	Total congestion costs, 2010	1,913	3,237,000	591	0.83

Source: Authors' compilation from selected sources as follows:
Note: VOC = vehicle operating costs.
a. Arditya 2011.
b. Australian Bureau of Transport and Regional Economics 2005.
c. Schrank, Lomax, and Eisele 2011.
d. Bureau of Economic Analysis 2011.

Table D.2 Estimates for Truck Delay Costs of Congestion in Vietnamese Cities and Regions, 2010

Urban area	Population	GDP (million VND)[a]	GDP (million $)	% of GDP factor	Cost of congestion (million $)[b]	Congestion costs (% of total country)
Whole country	**87,840,000**	**2,963,499,700**	**148,175**	**0.47**	**487**	**100.0**
Red River Delta	19,999,300	474,576,709	24,814	Calculated based on regional size and GDP	121	24.9
Of which: Hanoi	6,699,600	159,933,872	8,362		97	19.9
Northern midlands and mountain areas	11,290,500	57,243,307	2,993		8	1.6
North-central area and central coastal area	19,046,500	185,165,779	9,682		19	4.0
Central highlands	5,282,000	15,202,338	795		2	0.4
Southeast	14,890,800	1,049,645,827	54,882		268	55.1
Of which: Ho Chi Minh City	7,521,100	398,546,234	20,839		215	44.1
Mekong River Delta	17,330,900	199,080,039	10,409		68	14.0

a. General Statistics Office of Vietnam, authors' estimates.
b. Cost of congestion is derived from applying the GDP factor from comparable U.S. cities and applying it to Vietnam. The GDP factor accounts for truck commodity value and truck delays and in the United States ranges from 0.16 percent of GDP to 0.47 percent of GDP.

Table D.3 Estimates for Total Costs of Congestion in Vietnamese Cities and Regions, 2010

Urban area	Population	GDP (million VND)[a]	GDP (million $)	% of GDP factor	Cost of congestion (million $)[b]	Congestion costs (% of total country)
Entire country	**87,840,000**	**2,963,499,700**	**148,175**	**1.65**	**1,709**	**100.0**
Red River Delta	19,999,300	474,576,709	24,814	Calculated based on regional size and GDP	426	24.9
Of which: Hanoi	6,699,600	159,933,872	8,362		341	19.9
Northern midlands and mountain areas	11,290,500	57,243,307	2,993		27	1.6
North-central area and central coastal area	19,046,500	185,165,779	9,682		68	4.0
Central highlands	5,282,000	15,202,338	795		7	0.4
Southeast	14,890,800	1,049,645,827	54,882		942	55.1
Of which: Ho Chi Minh City	7,521,100	398,546,234	20,839		753	44.1
Mekong River Delta	17,330,900	199,080,039	10,409		239	14.0

a. General Statistics Office of Vietnam, authors' estimates.
b. Cost of congestion is derived from applying the GDP factor from comparable U.S. cities to Vietnam. The GDP factor accounts for the value of truck commodities and truck delays, as well as for additional factors such as annual hours of delay for commuters, excess fuel consumed, vehicle operating costs, and commuter stress. The values for cities in the United States range from 0.76 percent of GDP to 1.65 percent of GDP.

References

Arditya, Andreas D. 2011. "Congestion Costs Jakarta Rp 46 trillion." The Jakarta Post. http://www.thejakartapost.com/news/2011/03/16/congestion-costs-jakarta-rp -46-trillion.html.

Australian Bureau of Transport and Regional Economics. 2005. Estimating Urban Traffic and Congestion Cost Trends for Australian Cities. Working Paper 71. Canberra: Department of Transport and Regional Services.

Bureau of Economic Analysis. 2011. News Release: GDP by Metropolitan Area, Advance 2011, and Revised 2001–2010. http://www.bea.gov/newsreleases/regional/gdp _metro/gdp_metro_newsrelease.htm.

Schrank, David, Tim Lomax and Bill Eisele. 2011. 2011 Urban Mobility Report. College Station, Texas: Texas Transportation Institute.

Customs Flow Charts

Figures E.1 and E.2 depict Vietnam's customs clearance process for import and export transactions. In light of the fact that manufactured exports tend to incorporate significant levels of imported components, it is pertinent to outline a few key observations about the customs clearance process for imports based on electronic declarations. Managing this process effectively has become critical to the efficient functioning of export supply chains in Vietnam:

- Electronic customs declaration (e-Declaration) for major importers has been in place since 2011.
- In comparison with previous (manual) customs declaration, e-Declaration has some benefits, such as shorter declaration time and fewer required documents.
- Importer of record is required to have an account in the customs system with a user name and password.
- The customs broker can help the importer of record apply for the account at the Provincial Customs Department free of charge.

Standard required documents for import customs clearance include the following:

- House bill of lading or house airway bill
- Original commercial invoice
- Original packing list
- Copy sales contract/purchase order
- Original master list approved by the Provincial Customs Department for duty exemption
- Product catalog/technical data sheet and
- Relevant import license, investment license, and any other relevant license depending on commodity and transaction type.

Figure E.1 Import Customs Clearance: e-Declaration Process Flow

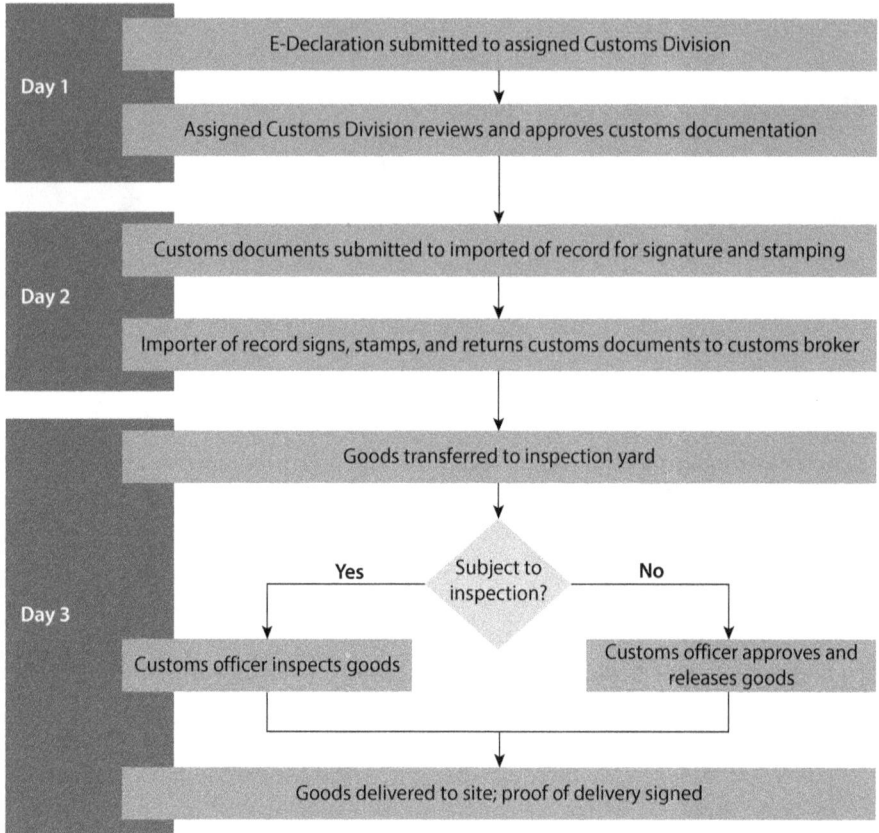

Day 1
- E-Declaration submitted to assigned Customs Division
- Assigned Customs Division reviews and approves customs documentation

Day 2
- Customs documents submitted to imported of record for signature and stamping
- Importer of record signs, stamps, and returns customs documents to customs broker

Day 3
- Goods transferred to inspection yard
- Subject to inspection?
  - Yes → Customs officer inspects goods
  - No → Customs officer approves and releases goods
- Goods delivered to site; proof of delivery signed

Source: Authors.

Figure E.2 Export Customs Clearance Process

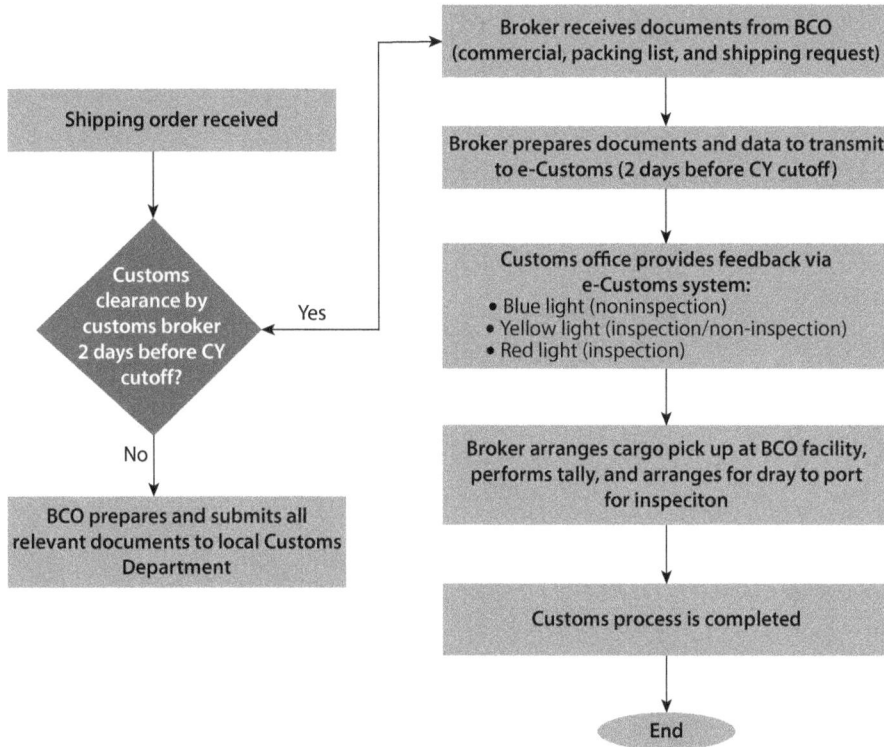

```
                                    ┌─────────────────────────────────────────┐
                                    │ Broker receives documents from BCO        │
                                    │ (commercial, packing list, and shipping   │
                                    │ request)                                   │
                                    └─────────────────────────────────────────┘
                                                      │
┌──────────────────────────┐                          ▼
│ Shipping order received   │       ┌─────────────────────────────────────────┐
└──────────────────────────┘       │ Broker prepares documents and data to     │
            │                        │ transmit to e-Customs (2 days before CY   │
            ▼                        │ cutoff)                                    │
        ◇ Customs                    └─────────────────────────────────────────┘
     clearance by      Yes                          │
     customs broker  ──────►         ┌─────────────────────────────────────────┐
     2 days before CY                 │ Customs office provides feedback via      │
       cutoff?                        │ e-Customs system:                          │
            │ No                      │ • Blue light (noninspection)               │
            ▼                         │ • Yellow light (inspection/non-inspection) │
┌──────────────────────────┐        │ • Red light (inspection)                   │
│ BCO prepares and submits  │        └─────────────────────────────────────────┘
│ all relevant documents to │                       │
│ local Customs Department  │        ┌─────────────────────────────────────────┐
└──────────────────────────┘        │ Broker arranges cargo pick up at BCO      │
                                     │ facility, performs tally, and arranges     │
                                     │ for dray to port for inspeciton            │
                                     └─────────────────────────────────────────┘
                                                      │
                                     ┌─────────────────────────────────────────┐
                                     │ Customs process is completed               │
                                     └─────────────────────────────────────────┘
                                                      │
                                                  ( End )
```

Source: Authors.
Note: BCO = beneficial cargo owner.

Components of Successful Public-Private Partnerships

Freight infrastructure projects in Vietnam have generally been funded by state budget resources, Official Development Assistance (ODA) or through public-private partnerships (PPPs), where the latter mobilize private capital with or without partial government co-funding. All of the new port terminals at Cai Mep-Thi Vai, as well as Cai Lan's new Cai Lan International Container Terminal (CICT) terminal, have used PPP arrangements. Lach Huyen's first phase terminal development will also utilize a PPP modality, complemented by Japanese ODA.

When the new HCMC–Vung Tau Expressway is eventually constructed, the Government of Vietnam (GoV) may consider a PPP approach, whereby it may provide a subsidy (sometimes referred to as viability gap financing) and seek private investors to mobilize the balance of the investment. An alternative is to use a Build-Operate-Transfer (BOT) arrangement, similar to that used by the State of Florida Department of Transportation in selecting a single company to design, build, finance, operate, and maintain Interstate 595 (I-595) for 35 years (see box F.1).

As pointed out by the U.S. Asian Business Council and the Vietnam Competitive Institute in interviews conducted for this report, Vietnam does not have an established record of structuring and managing PPPs and has had difficulty putting in place a comprehensive legal and regulatory framework for them. The country also lacks a supportive ecosystem for PPPs, such as long-term commercial financing options and large, sophisticated, privately held construction and engineering firms. This has discouraged some foreign companies to participate in PPPs. One freight-related example of a mismanaged PPP is the investment made by foreign marine terminal operators (MTOs) in some of the Cai Mep-Thi Vai terminals. Government promises to close some of the HCMC inner-city terminals have not been kept. This is one reason why the utilization rate of the Cai Mep-Thi Vai terminals, as of year-end 2012, is a small fraction of their combined capacity. As a result, those PPP investments are operating at a loss for the MTOs.

Box F.2 summarizes the viewpoints provided by the U.S. ASEAN Business Council, the Vietnam Competitiveness Institute, and others on what Vietnam could do to strengthen the way it manages and structures PPPs.

Box F.1 Florida State Department of Transportation PPP for I-595

After considering several PPP alternatives, the Florida Department of Transportation chose to move forward with improvements to I-595 with a single concessionaire responsible for the design, building, financing, operation, and maintenance (DBFOM) of the highway asset over a 35-year period. Under a DBFOM, the public agency owns the facility, but the concessionaire is given the exclusive right to operate the facility from the start of construction through the end of the agreement. At the end of the term, the concessionaire transfers the facility back to the public agency in compliance with the hand-back standards described in the Concession Agreement. This arrangement encourages high-quality construction at the outset and ensures that the facility will be carefully maintained.

Sources: Authors; http://www.dot.state.fl.us/financialplanning/finance/P3%20Summary.pdf.

Box F.2 Structuring Successful Public Private Partnerships

Discussions conducted for this report with the U.S. ASEAN Business Council and Vietnam Competitiveness Institute revealed that there are concerns among investors as to whether Vietnam's business climate can support a critical mass of PPP projects in the freight sector. The following are actions that the GoV could take to structure successful PPP projects:

1. A strong transportation infrastructure master plan must be developed, and the GoV must not be influenced by SOEs or private parties to amend the plan for their own benefit.
2. The GoV must manage a truly competitive bid process and not be inclined to award the project to SOEs or favored private companies, since that will only add unnecessary costs to the project.
3. A "go to" person(s) in the GoV must be assigned authority and responsibility for making decisions and facilitating the timely issuance of licenses necessary for the successful completion of the project on time and within budget.
4. Since tolls are not likely to provide sufficient revenue for the PPP contracting company to build, say, a highway, any land adjacent to the highway given to the contractor for developing logistics-related facilities must be used for that exclusive purpose.
5. To minimize the risk to both private and public sector parties, the GoV needs to safeguard their contractual rights against arbitrary decisions made by government agencies and/or

box continues next page

Box F.2 Structuring Successful Public Private Partnerships *(continued)*

by provincial governments that are contrary to MoT and Ministry of Planning and Investment directives. Corruption is major concern of international companies.

6. The GoV must ensure loan negotiations can stand the test of public scrutiny.

7. Only contractors with proven track records in managing large scale projects that are delivered on time and within budget should be hired. Competitive bidding can make a critical difference towards meeting this goal.

The following are additional points and suggestions related to freight sector PPP projects in the United States that can serve as lessons learned for Vietnam:

1. When tolling as a revenue source and PPPs as a project delivery mechanism are pursued at the same time, toll rate setting control appears to move from the public sector, where elected officials are accountable, to private companies that are motivated by rates of return. When toll rate setting is taken away from politically motivated officials, the asset value of the project increases, as the revenue source is sufficient to keep the highway properly maintained.

2. PPPs are not a source of public revenue; in fact, to be financially feasible, they require a stable revenue source. However, they can be used to free up existing public revenue, increase the certainty of project lifecycle costs, and protect general revenue from revenue shortfalls.

3. Most PPPs in the United States have not been exclusively privately financed. Most PPPs have required public sector financial support in the form of up-front capital contributions or credit assistance to attract private investment.

4. PPPs are not a panacea to the transportation funding shortage. PPPs are not a source of free money, so their pricing includes a healthy, market-appropriate profit.

5. PPPs are not "privatization." While the private sector plays a larger role in delivering PPPs, the public sector retains ownership and directs what the private partner can and cannot do through statute and contract.

6. Availability payments, where the public sector partner retains demand risk, represent one way in which public agencies have structured PPP contracts to attract more bids that are competitive and keep financing costs down.

Sources: Authors based on interviews with U.S. ASEAN Business Council and Vietnam Competitiveness Institute; Buxbaum and Ortiz 2009.
Note: GoV = government of Vietnam; PPP = public-private partnership; SOE = state-owned enterprise.

Reference

Buxbaum, Jeffrey N. and Iris N. Ortiz, Consultants. 2009. *Public Sector Decision-Making for Public-Private Partnerships*, National Cooperative Highway Research Program Synthesis 391. Washington, DC: Transport Research Board.

Organizational Structure of the Ministry of Transport of Vietnam

Figure G.1 MoT Organization: 2012

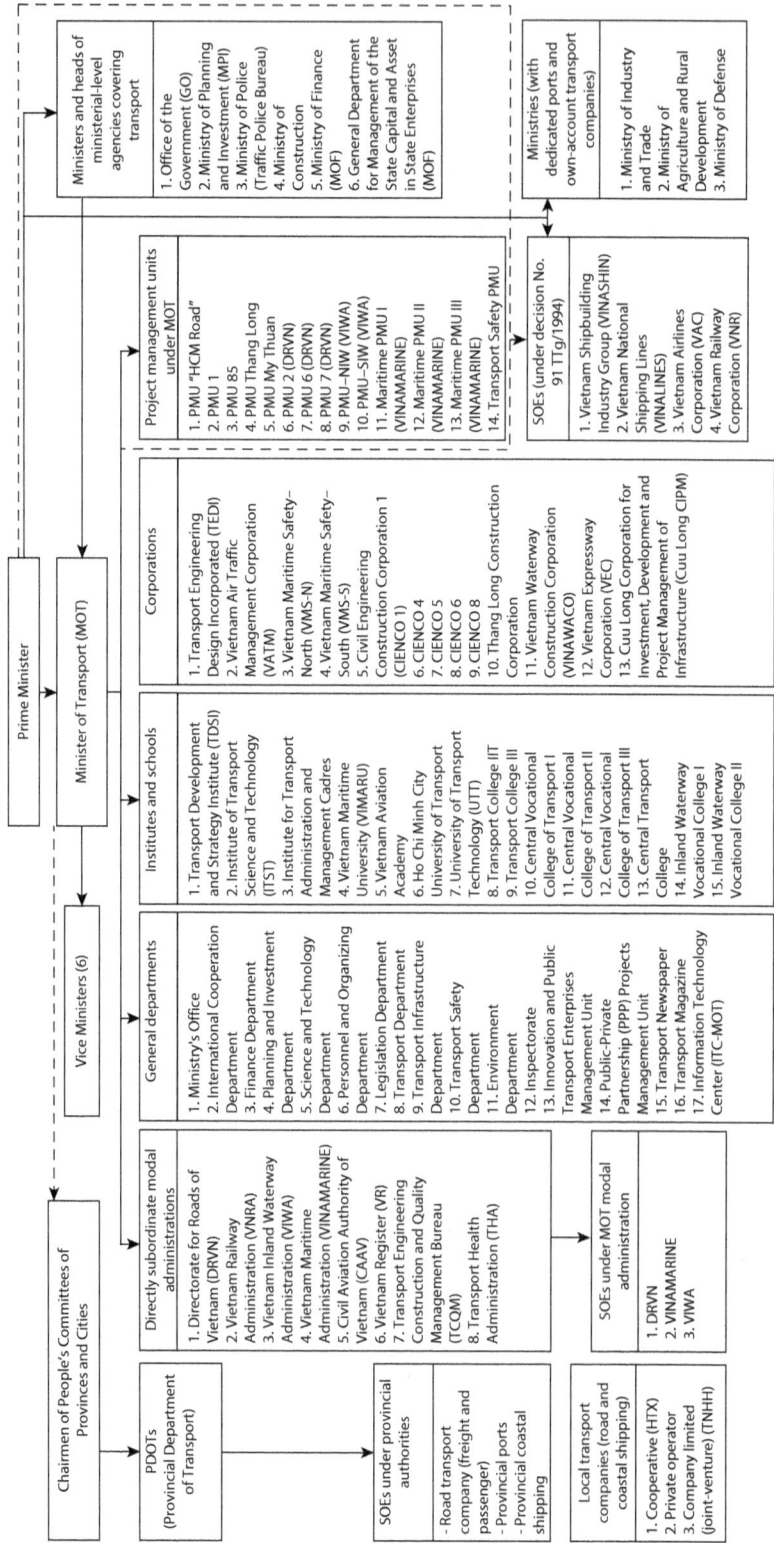

Prime Minister

Chairmen of People's Committees of Provinces and Cities

Minister of Transport (MOT)

Vice Ministers (6)

Ministers and heads of ministerial-level agencies covering transport
1. Office of the Government (GO)
2. Ministry of Planning and Investment (MPI)
3. Ministry of Police (Traffic Police Bureau)
4. Ministry of Construction
5. Ministry of Finance (MOF)
6. General Department for Management of the State Capital and Asset in State Enterprises (MOF)

Ministries (with dedicated ports and own-account transport companies)
1. Ministry of Industry and Trade
2. Ministry of Agriculture and Rural Development
3. Ministry of Defense

Project management units under MOT
1. PMU "HCM Road"
2. PMU 1
3. PMU 85
4. PMU Thang Long
5. PMU My Thuan
6. PMU 2 (DRVN)
7. PMU 6 (DRVN)
8. PMU 7 (DRVN)
9. PMU–NIW (VIWA)
10. PMU–SIW (VIWA)
11. Maritime PMU I (VINAMARINE)
12. Maritime PMU II (VINAMARINE)
13. Maritime PMU III (VINAMARINE)
14. Transport Safety PMU

SOEs (under decision No. 91 TTg/1994)
1. Vietnam Shipbuilding Industry Group (VINASHIN)
2. Vietnam National Shipping Lines (VINALINES)
3. Vietnam Airlines Corporation (VAC)
4. Vietnam Railway Corporation (VNR)

Corporations
1. Transport Engineering Design Incorporated (TEDI)
2. Vietnam Air Traffic Management Corporation (VATM)
3. Vietnam Maritime Safety–North (VMS-N)
4. Vietnam Maritime Safety–South (VMS-S)
5. Civil Engineering Construction Corporation 1 (CIENCO 1)
6. CIENCO 4
7. CIENCO 5
8. CIENCO 6
9. CIENCO 8
10. Thang Long Construction Corporation
11. Vietnam Waterway Construction Corporation (VINAWACO)
12. Vietnam Expressway Corporation (VEC)
13. Cuu Long Corporation for Investment, Development and Project Management of Infrastructure (Cuu Long CIPM)

Institutes and schools
1. Transport Development and Strategy Institute (TDSI)
2. Institute of Transport Science and Technology (ITST)
3. Institute for Transport Administration and Management Cadres
4. Vietnam Maritime University (VIMARU)
5. Vietnam Aviation Academy
6. Ho Chi Minh City University of Transport
7. University of Transport Technology (UTT)
8. Transport College III
9. Transport College III
10. Central Vocational College of Transport I
11. Central Vocational College of Transport II
12. Central Vocational College of Transport III
13. Central Transport College
14. Inland Waterway Vocational College I
15. Inland Waterway Vocational College II

General departments
1. Ministry's Office
2. International Cooperation Department
3. Finance Department
4. Planning and Investment Department
5. Science and Technology Department
6. Personnel and Organizing Department
7. Legislation Department
8. Transport Department
9. Transport Infrastructure Department
10. Transport Safety Department
11. Environment Department
12. Inspectorate
13. Innovation and Public Transport Enterprises Management Unit
14. Public-Private Partnership (PPP) Projects Management Unit
15. Transport Newspaper
16. Transport Magazine
17. Information Technology Center (ITC-MOT)

Directly subordinate modal administrations
1. Directorate for Roads of Vietnam (DRVN)
2. Vietnam Railway Administration (VNRA)
3. Vietnam Inland Waterway Administration (VIWA)
4. Vietnam Maritime Administration (VINAMARINE)
5. Civil Aviation Authority of Vietnam (CAAV)
6. Vietnam Register (VR)
7. Transport Engineering Construction and Quality Management Bureau (TCQM)
8. Transport Health Administration (THA)

PDOTs (Provincial Department of Transport)

SOEs under provincial authorities
- Road transport company (freight and passenger)
- Provincial ports
- Provincial coastal shipping

Local transport companies (road and coastal shipping)
1. Cooperative (HTX)
2. Private operator
3. Company limited (joint-venture) (TNHH)

SOEs under MOT modal administration
1. DRVN
2. VINAMARINE
3. VIWA

Figure G.1 MoT Organization: 2012 *(continued)*

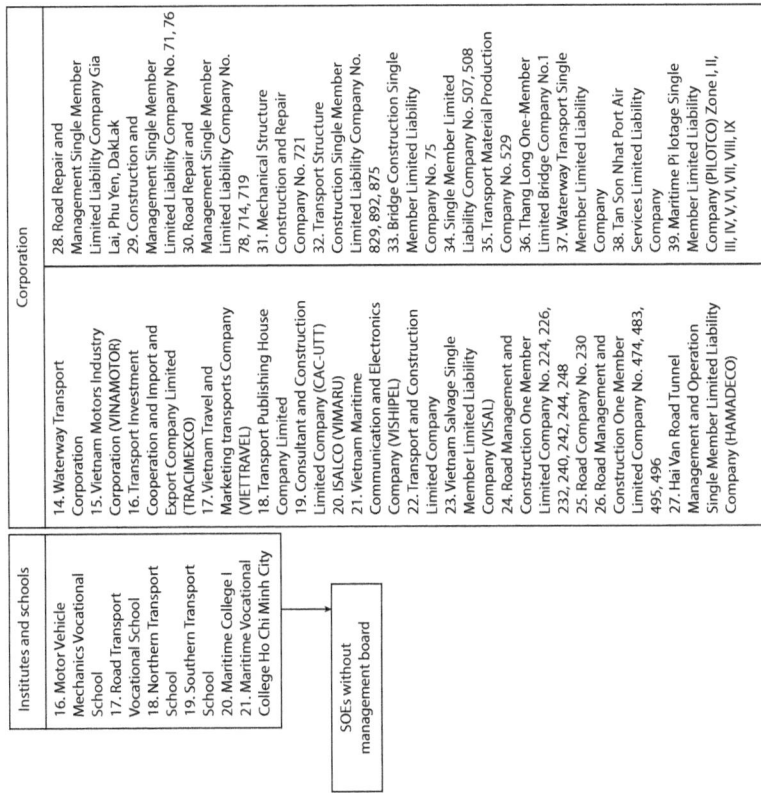

Institutes and schools	Corporation	
16. Motor Vehicle Mechanics Vocational School 17. Road Transport Vocational School 18. Northern Transport School 19. Southern Transport School 20. Maritime College I 21. Maritime Vocational College Ho Chi Minh City	14. Waterway Transport Corporation 15. Vietnam Motors Industry Corporation (VINAMOTOR) 16. Transport Investment Cooperation and Import and Export Company Limited (TRACIMEXCO) 17. Vietnam Travel and Marketing transports Company (VIETTRAVEL) 18. Transport Publishing House Company Limited 19. Consultant and Construction Limited Company (CAC-UTT) 20. ISALCO (VIMARU) 21. Vietnam Maritime Communication and Electronics Company (VISHIPEL) 22. Transport and Construction Limited Company 23. Vietnam Salvage Single Member Limited Liability Company (VISAL) 24. Road Management and Construction One Member Limited Company No. 224, 226, 232, 240, 242, 244, 248 25. Road Company No. 230 26. Road Management and Construction One Member Limited Company No. 474, 483, 495, 496 27. Hai Van Road Tunnel Management and Operation Single Member Limited Liability Company (HAMADECO)	28. Road Repair and Management Single Member Limited Liability Company Gia Lai, Phu Yen, DakLak 29. Construction and Management Single Member Limited Liability Company No. 71, 76 30. Road Repair and Management Single Member Limited Liability Company No. 78, 714, 719 31. Mechanical Structure Construction and Repair Company No. 721 32. Transport Structure Construction Single Member Limited Liability Company No. 829, 892, 875 33. Bridge Construction Single Member Limited Liability Company No. 75 34. Single Member Limited Liability Company No. 507, 508 35. Transport Material Production Company No. 529 36. Thang Long One-Member Limited Bridge Company No.1 37. Waterway Transport Single Member Limited Liability Company 38. Tan Son Nhat Port Air Services Limited Liability Company 39. Maritime Pi lotage Single Member Limited Liability Company (PILOTCO) Zone I, II, III, IV, V, VI, VII, VIII, IX

SOEs without management board

Source: Ministry of Transport of Vietnam.

Glossary

BCO: Beneficial Cargo Owner. This is the entity owning the product; it may refer to a manufacturer, a shipper/seller, or a consignee/buyer.

Vietnam Customs/Customs: General Department of Vietnam Customs. It is the agency of the Government of Vietnam, under the Ministry of Finance, responsible for customs administration. Local Customs Departments under the control of the General Department of Vietnam Customs manage customs procedures and implement regulations at the provincial level.

CFS: Container Freight Station. A cargo-handling facility owned or leased and operated by a third-party logistics service provider.

CIC: Container Imbalance Charge, assessed by ocean carriers on importing shippers for having to reposition empty containers. Vietnam tends to have large amounts of TEU containers from imports that cannot be used for the majority of export commodities, as well as a shortage of FEU containers for export cargo.

C-TPAT: Customs-Trade Partnership Against Terrorism, is program administered by the United States Customs and Border Protection certifying that member BCOs, ocean carriers, and other freight stakeholders have taken measures to better secure their supply chains against potential acts of terrorism.

CY: Container Yard. A facility where empty and loaded containers are stored. It is typically managed by an ocean carrier.

EDI: Electronic Data Interchange. EDI refers to the electronic transmission of data between parties to reduce or eliminate manual processes and paper.

FEU: 40-Foot Equivalent Unit Container. An FEU is a standard container size used in ocean transportation.

FTP: File Transfer Protocol. A network protocol used to transfer files electronically over the internet.

ICD: Inland Container Depot. Ocean carriers and LSPs establish ICDs near ports or in inland locations as facilities and bases where empty and loaded containers can easily be picked up or dropped off.

JIT: Just-In-Time. Usually referred to in manufacturing settings, JIT implies the use of controlled and efficient processes in tight timelines by which inputs are delivered to the factory and production occurs to reduce redundant safety stock, costs, and time within supply chains.

Landed Cost: This includes the cost of the products being shipped, all export and import documentation costs, all related transportation costs to ship the products from the designated free-on-board point to final destination listed on the bill of lading, and duty payments at the destination country. Notably, for the purposes of this report, landed cost does not include inventory carrying costs.

LSP: Logistics Service Provider. A third party that furnishes ocean freight forwarding, airfreight forwarding, warehousing and distribution, and/or customs brokerage services to BCOs.

MCIP: Multimodal Corridor Investment Plan. This is a transportation infrastructure plan prepared by a government agency that incorporates the perspective that beneficial cargo owner supply chains are multimodal and connections between modes should be as seamless as possible to facilitate efficient and cost-effective supply chains.

MoT: Ministry of Transport of Vietnam. This is the ministry responsible for transportation planning and infrastructure development.

NH No.: This refers to a National Highway in Vietnam under the Ministry of Transport's responsibility for planning, constructing, and maintaining.

PPP: Public-Private Partnership. As referred to in transportation infrastructure projects, PPP is a funding mechanism in which one or multiple private entities team with a public agency to develop and/or manage a transportation infrastructure project or asset, such as a highway. The private partner usually recoups its investment through tolling the asset over a period of time.

SOE: State-Owned Enterprise. An SOE is a company established by the government sector to produce goods and services or manage infrastructure assets.

TEU: 20-Foot Equivalent Unit Container. A TEU is a standard container size used in ocean transportation.

THC: Terminal Handling Charge. The THC is the fee BCOs or factories pay to the marine terminal operator to lift the container on or off the vessel.

TPP: Trans-Pacific Partnership. The TPP is a multilateral trade agreement under negotiation at the time of writing. Potential participating countries include Australia, Brunei Darussalam, Canada, Chile, Malaysia, Mexico, New Zealand, Peru, Singapore, Vietnam, and the United States.

VPA: Vietnam Port Association. VPA is a transport association comprising 40 member ports in Vietnam, representing over 80 percent of the country's total annual port throughput. The association strives to create business opportunities for its member ports and fosters collaboration both among ports and between ports and the broader shipping community.

WTO: World Trade Organization. The WTO is a multilateral entity that engages in the global rules of trade between nations. As of August 2012, the WTO comprised 157 member countries.

Efficient Logistics • http://dx.doi.org/10.1596/978-1-4648-0103-7

Environmental Benefits Statement

The World Bank Group is committed to reducing its environmental footprint. In support of this commitment, the Publishing and Knowledge Division leverages electronic publishing options and print-on-demand technology, which is located in regional hubs worldwide. Together, these initiatives enable print runs to be lowered and shipping distances decreased, resulting in reduced paper consumption, chemical use, greenhouse gas emissions, and waste.

The Publishing and Knowledge Division follows the recommended standards for paper use set by the Green Press Initiative. Whenever possible, books are printed on 50 percent to 100 percent postconsumer recycled paper, and at least 50 percent of the fiber in our book paper is either unbleached or bleached using Totally Chlorine Free (TCF), Processed Chlorine Free (PCF), or Enhanced Elemental Chlorine Free (EECF) processes.

More information about the Bank's environmental philosophy can be found at http://crinfo.worldbank.org/wbcrinfo/node/4.

green press
INITIATIVE

www.ingramcontent.com/pod-product-compliance
Lightning Source LLC
Chambersburg PA
CBHW080612270326
41928CB00016B/3016